PRO/CON VOLUME 5

SCIENCE

Published 2002 by Grolier Educational
Sherman Turnpike
Danbury, Connecticut 06816

© 2002 Brown Partworks Limited

Library of Congress Cataloging-in-Publication Data

Pro/con
  p. cm
Includes bibliographical references and index.
Contents: v. 1. The individual and society – v. 2. Government – v. 3. Economics – v.
4. Environment – v. 5. Science – v. 6. Media.
 ISBN 0-7172-5638-3 (set : alk. paper) – ISBN 0-7172-5639-1 (vol. 1 : alk. paper) –
ISBN 0-7172-5640-5 (vol. 2 : alk. paper) – ISBN 0-7172-5641-3 (vol. 3 : alk. paper) –
ISBN 0-7172-5642-1 (vol. 4 : alk. paper) – ISBN 0-7172-5643-X (vol. 5 : alk. paper) –
ISBN 0-7172-5644-8 (vol. 6 : alk. paper)
 1. Social problems. I. Grolier Educational (Firm)

HN17.5 P756 2002
361.1–dc21

                                                                    2001053234
Printed and bound in Singapore

SET ISBN 0-7172-5638-3
VOLUME ISBN 0-7172-5643-X

for Brown Partworks Limited
Project Editors: Aruna Vasudevan, Fiona Plowman
Editors: Sally McFall, Dawn Titmus, Matt Turner,
Ben Way, Ben Hoare, Dennis Cove
Consultant Editors: Clive Carpenter and Robert Field, Associate Professor
of Health Policy, University of the Sciences in Philadelphia
Designer: Sarah Williams
Picture Researcher: Clare Newman
Set Index: Kay Ollerenshaw

Managing Editor: Tim Cooke
Design Manager: Lynne Ross
Production Manager: Matt Weyland

GENERAL PREFACE

"All that is necessary for evil to triumph is for good men to do nothing."
—Edmund Burke, 18th-century British political philosopher

Decisions

Life is full of choices and decisions. Some are more important than others. Some affect only your daily life—the route you take to school, for example, or what you prefer to eat for supper—while others are more abstract and concern questions of right and wrong rather than practicality. That does not mean that your choice of presidential candidate or your views on abortion are necessarily more important than your answers to purely personal questions. But it is likely that those wider questions are more complex and subtle and that, you therefore will need to know more information about the subject before you can try to answer them. They are also likely to be questions about which you might have to justify your views to other people. In order to do that, you need to be able to make informed decisions, be able to analyze every fact at your disposal, and evaluate them in an unbiased manner.

What is *Pro/Con*?

Pro/Con is a collection of debates that presents conflicting views on some of the more complex and general issues facing Americans today. By bringing together extracts from a wide range of sources—mainstream newspapers and magazines, books, famous speeches, legal judgments, religious tracts, government surveys—the set reflects current informed attitudes toward dilemmas that range from the best way to feed the world's growing population to gay rights, and from the connection between political freedom and capitalism to the fate of Napster.

The people whose arguments make up the set are all acknowledged experts in their fields, and that makes the vast differences in their points of view even more remarkable. The arguments are presented in the form of debates for and against various propositions, such as "Does Global Warming Threaten Humankind?" or "Should the Media Be Subject to Censorship?" This question format reflects the way in which ideas often occur in daily life: in the classroom, on TV shows, in business meetings, or even in state or federal politics.

The contents

The subjects of the six volumes of the set—*Individual and Society, Government, Economics, Environment, Science*, and *Media*—are issues on which it is preferable that people's opinions are based on information rather than simply on personal bias.

Special boxes throughout *Pro/Con* comment on the debates as you are reading them, pointing out facts or analyzing arguments to help you think about what is being said.

Introductions and summaries also provide background information that might help you reach your own conclusions. There are also comments and tips about how to structure an argument that you can apply on an every day basis to any debate or conversation, learning how to present your point of view as effectively and persuasively as possible.

3

VOLUME PREFACE
Science

The importance of science

In 1786 Thomas Jefferson wrote in a letter to a friend that knowledge was the only foundation on which freedom and happiness could be preserved. Jefferson believed that information and education would allow U.S. citizens to understand the world in which they lived and make educated decisions on important matters.

An understanding of science and the ethical and moral issues associated with the great advances in scientific knowledge that have occurred in the last 200 years is essential for living in the world today. Scientific discoveries have affected every aspect of our lives from the cars we drive to the appliances in our kitchens. Scientific advances have helped eradicate virulent diseases, aided people who previously were considered infertile to have children, allowed the genetic modification of genes and crops, and led to the development of atomic weaponry.

However, while science has undeniably helped civilizations advance and prosper and has enabled people to live longer and healthier lives, it has also had negative results. Scientific advances can lead to ethical dilemmas for researchers and citizens alike since every scientific discovery brings new and sometimes troubling questions to light. When individuals decide that scientific knowledge has been misused, issues of responsibility and accountability are raised—as in the case of the atomic bombing of Hiroshima and Nagasaki—and society must decide whether the benefits of a particular discovery outweigh the disadvantages.

Each individual has his or her opinion on such matters, and it is often influenced by factors such as family, education, and religion. But sometimes it is difficult to know the right decision to make—for example, how do you know when a scientific advance is worth the set of risks it brings? In order to make a clear, informed judgment, it is important to have all the facts before you; only then can you make an educated decision.

Pro/Con

Science is a vast subject that covers a variety of issues—and it would be impossible to cover every major topic or debate here. This volume focuses on genetics, medicine and health, and science in the future. The issues covered emphasize the importance of science and how much it shapes the world in which we live. The format of *Pro/Con* allows important ethical and topical questions to be discussed fairly. It gives you access to both sides of the argument, providing you with pointers on how to construct or deconstruct any one opinion—to see its advantages and its faults, where the author has been successful in putting his or her point across, and where he or she has failed—useful skills in any walk of life.

HOW TO USE THIS BOOK

Each volume of *Pro/Con* is divided into sections, each of which has an introduction that examines its theme. Within each section are a series of debates that present arguments for and against a proposition, such as whether or not the death penalty should be abolished. An introduction to each debate puts it into its wider context, and a summary and key map (see below) highlight the main points of the debate clearly and concisely. Each debate has marginal boxes that focus on particular points, give tips on how to present an argument, or help question the writer's case. The summaries to the debates have supplementary material to help you do further research.

Boxes and other materials provide additional background information. There are also special materials on how to improve your debating and writing skills. At the end of each book is a glossary that provides brief explanations of key words in the volume. The index covers all six books, so it will help you trace topics throughout the set.

background information
Frequent text boxes provide background information on important concepts and key individuals or events.

summary boxes
Summary boxes are useful reminders of both sides of the argument.

further information
Further Reading lists for each debate direct you to related books, articles, and websites so you can do your own research.

other articles in the *Pro/Con* series,
See Also boxes list related debates throughout the *Pro/Con* series.

marginal boxes
Margin boxes highlight key points in the argument, give extra information, or help you question the author's meaning.

key map
Key maps provide a graphic representation of the central points of the debate.

CONTENTS

PART 1
GENETICS

INTRODUCTION

Genetics is the name given to the general study of heredity, which is the transmission of characteristics from an ancestor to a descendant; more particularly, it is also used to describe the study of genes, the biological units that pass on characteristics in plants and animals. Those characteristics range from height, skin type, eye color, and intelligence to genetic disorders, such as color blindness or Down's Syndrome. The science of genetics has been used to diagnose, prevent, and treat hereditary diseases, breed plants and animals, and develop industrial processes that use microorganisms.

The legacy of Mendel

Although the importance of heredity has long been recognized in cases such as breeding high-yield crops, genetics is a relatively modern science. It began with the work of the Austrian monk Gregor Mendel (1822–1884). In 1856 Mendel conducted a series of experiments with plants. By studying well-defined pairs of characteristics— tall and short plants, red and white flowers—through three generations, he formulated theories that now form the basis of the laws of inheritance. Mendel's work, however, went largely unnoticed until 1900, when it was rediscovered. Since then genetic research has developed quickly.

In 1902 U.S. scientist Walter Sutton proposed that "chromosomes" were the site of Mendel's hereditary factors or genes. In 1910 the U.S. geneticist Thomas Hunt Morgan confirmed that genes occur on chromosomes. In 1944 Oswald T. Avery showed that deoxyribonucleic acid (DNA) was the chromosome compound that carried genetic information, but it was not until 1953 that James Watson and Francis Crick worked out the molecular structure of DNA (see page 14), and Jacques Monod discovered the process by which DNA directs protein synthesis in a bacterial "code." Such developments opened the way to genetic engineering, or the manipulation of DNA to change hereditary factors or produce biological products, such as plants that are resistant to disease, drugs like human insulin, or bacteria designed to break down industrial waste products.

A sensitive issue?

Today the benefits and costs of genetic research are the cause of great controversy. While scientists work to eradicate hereditary conditions, people protest around the world against genetically modified produce. Many people worry about the potential misuse of genetic research, which they see as interfering with nature or "playing God." Supporters point to the benefits of genetically increasing crop yields or eradicating fatal diseases and hereditary conditions.

Patenting genes

The debate about genetics is further complicated by the interest of big business. In 2001 scientists announced that they had decoded the human genome—the catalog of around 30,000 genes that determine every human characteristic. The possibilities for genetic research seemed limitless. But the discovery also led people to ask who actually owned the genome and whether or not genes should be possibility when the Roslin Institute in Scotland genetically replicated or cloned Dolly the Sheep from the nucleus of an egg cell (see page 22). Dolly's birth highlighted the ethics of cloning, as debated in *Topic 2 Should It Be Legal to Clone Humans?*

Linked to the same fundamental issues is gene manipulation and whether it is ethically wrong. Topic 3 asks *Is Gene Manipulation Wrong?* Both articles consider the possibility of

---

"We can now pick and choose individual genes from one organism to introduce into a totally different and unrelated organism, crossing all biological boundaries in combinations that nature never could and never would bring together."

—JONATHON PORRITT, FORMER DIRECTOR OF FRIENDS OF THE EARTH AND AUTHOR OF *PLAYING SAFE*

---

patented by researchers. This issue is examined further in *Topic 1 Should Genes be Patented?*, which looks at the implications of the commercialization of genetic research.

Cloning and gene manipulation

Writers from Mary Shelley to Aldous Huxley have imagined genetically altering human beings, sometimes with nightmarish results. In July 1996 the cloning of mammals, and thus potentially of humans, became a creating perfect people with no hereditary weaknesses, but wonder if such a development is desirable.

Cloning human beings remains in the future. Other applications of genetics are very much part of modern life. *Topic 4 Should U.S. Privacy Laws Include Genetic Testing?* considers one of them. It looks at whether insurance companies should be allowed to know people's genetic profiles, which might lead them to discriminate against people with hereditary conditions.

Topic 1
SHOULD GENES BE PATENTED?

YES
"SUMMARY"
HOUSE COMMITTEE ON THE JUDICIARY, SUBCOMMITTEE ON COURTS AND
INTELLECTUAL PROPERTY, JULY 13, 2000
JAMES A. SEVERSON

NO
"PATENTING LIFE—STIFLING HEALTHCARE"
GENEWATCH UK
SUE MAYER AND RICARDA STEINBRECHER

INTRODUCTION

Humanity seems to be on the brink of understanding its genetic inheritance. The knowledge has taken many years to gather and involved countless researchers. Funding has come from both government agencies and private organizations around the world. But who does the knowledge belong to? If a corporation's research successfully decodes a gene, can that company patent it? Or is knowledge of the human genome a common heritage to be shared by all humanity? At the heart of the debate is the conflict between the public's right to free access to research data on the one hand, and the need of businesses to make a profit on the other.

In 2001 scientists announced that they had decoded the human genome. The genome comprises about 30,000 genes that determine every inherited human characteristic, and its decoding is one of the world's most outstanding scientific achievements. But just as the discovery culminated a century

of genetic investigation, it also raised a number of new questions. Of these, one of the most important was the issue of who, if anyone, effectively owned the human genome.

Genes are the linear sections of DNA molecules. Each gene carries all the information—the code—to determine the structure of a particular protein or ribonucleic acid (RNA) molecule. Each gene also carries one human characteristic. The sum of all the material carried by the genes is known as the genome. In a human being about 30,000 genes—many fewer than originally suspected—make up the entire genome.

Scientists in many countries began to discuss the possibility of decoding the human genome in the 1980s. The result was the Human Genome Project (HGP), an international research program that aimed to construct detailed genetic maps of the human genome. The target was a map of the complete nucleotide sequence—the inherited genetic "instructions"—of human DNA. (The HGP will also try to decode the complete nucleotide sequence of several other organisms, starting with the mouse genome.)

In 2001 new technologies enabled scientists to achieve their breakthrough. The detailed knowledge of the human genome will be used by scientists, doctors, and others in research and in biomedics, and the implications are enormous. New fields of medical research will open, and new drugs and treatments may become available. However, there are a number of controversial issues that surround the discovery, and many believe that the genome project is open to exploitation.

> *"The goal was to understand life better and when you understand life better you understand disease better."*
>
> —DR. JAMES WATSON, ON THE HUMAN GENOME PROJECT

James A. Severson—the Pro author—concentrates on the academic world, arguing that genes should be patented. He states that this allows research results to reach the commercial marketplace for public benefit, and that it is an important way for universities, hospitals, and research institutes to demonstrate the relevance of their research programs. He goes on to stress that patenting introduces innovation into the commercial sector that ultimately enriches people's lives.

A key point in Severson's argument is that patenting is a practical way to induce a company to assume the risks of time and investment in early-stage inventions, and that patent protection on genes is essential to finance the necessary research and development.

Critics have suggested that the time and effort involved in obtaining a patent can delay and obstruct the creation of new drugs or medical treatments. However, Severson claims that the need for a patent only rarely delays the publication of results. In addition, he does not see an incompatibility between obtaining a patent and sharing information and know-how. Severson also points out that patenting generates billions of dollars for the U.S. economy each year.

Sue Mayer and Ricarda Steinbrecher—the Con authors—reject Severson's argument. They believe that working out a gene sequence and its function is a process of discovery, not invention, and therefore should not be patented. Furthermore, they state that the process of trying to obtain a patent prevents or hinders development of new or improved medicines and treatments, and limits access to healthcare by increasing the cost of diagnostics and treatment for certain diseases.

The Con authors back up their argument by examining three different companies, respectively involved in breast cancer diagnostics, kidney failure and dialysis treatment, and treatment for combating AIDS. In each instance the company aggressively patents its findings, blocking further research and inflating the cost of treatment. The authors use these examples to show that it is the companies that benefit from gene patents, and not the public, and they therefore call for an end to the practice.

... ON COURTS AND INTELLECTUAL PROPERTY
James A. Severson

YES

Technology transfer, the transfer of research results to the commercial marketplace for public benefit, is an important way for universities, teaching hospitals, and research institutions to demonstrate the relevance of their research programs, introduce innovation to the commercial sector, and enrich the lives of citizens. It has been estimated that in fiscal year 1998 the patent and licensing activities of U.S. universities resulted in $33.5 billion in economic activity, supported 280,000 jobs in the economy, and resulted in $7 billion in federal and state tax revenues.

Patents to genetic discoveries made during university research can be pursued without disrupting the core values of publication and sharing of information, research results, materials, and know-how. Universities pursue patents to gene discoveries in the context of the Bayh-Dole Act, the pioneering, enabling legislation that enabled universities to take title to inventions made with the use of federal research support. Within the concepts embodied in the Bayh-Dole Act, universities carefully consider and balance the needs for publication of research results, the sharing of materials with other researchers, and the desire for commercial development of discoveries in the public interest. Often, the technology transfer manager and the researcher work collaboratively to protect an invention within the deadlines that the researcher has for publication. Universities can, and do, protect inventions to genetic information for commercial development, and effectively disseminate research results and materials. This activity supports economic growth, allows universities to attract, retain, and reward talented faculty, and promotes closer ties with industry that often result in additional research support.

... I understand that this subcommittee is interested in learning how patents for genes affect openness and sharing of information among academic institutions. This issue is complex and impinges upon the publication and dissemination of research results, and the sharing of research tools.

Find out more about the Bayh-Dole Act at www.tmc.tulane. edu/departments/ techdev/Bayh.html.

Most universities are not engaged in gene sequencing to the same extent as companies, and universities have not engaged in the broad scale patenting of genetic information. For the most part, invention disclosures made for gene sequences are considered for patenting on a case-by-case basis and in the context of the requirements of Bayh-Dole. Specifically, the question that universities ask is: "What is the best means to protect and disseminate this information for the public good?" Many inventions made at universities are at a very early stage of development and require extensive follow-on research, including proof of principal, before any company will invest in its commercial development. In many cases, innovations never reach the threshold for commercial development.

Should patenting go forward, one issue that is considered is the effect on the publication of the results of the research. Publication of research results is a core value for universities, and in my experience the ability of university researchers to publish is carefully protected by university administration, grant and contract officers, and technology transfer managers. In practice, the pursuit of a patent rarely delays the publication of results. Technology transfer practitioners at universities work to protect an invention within the deadlines that researchers have to publish a manuscript or present data at scientific conferences. Often the parties must balance collaboratively the need to publish against the desire to protect valuable intellectual property. Accordingly, much of the gene sequence information that is developed at universities is placed into the public domain by publication in scientific literature, or by listing the gene sequence in publicly available databases for broad access by the scientific community.

If a university pursues a patent, licensing on a nonexclusive basis (that is, making it available to a number of companies) is often the best means for technology transfer to benefit the public, especially if the gene is useful as a tool, or if the gene is a potential target for drugs. This practice makes the invention widely available and derives the broadest benefit from the invention. I would like to give you an example from our program at Cornell. In 1989, Professor Ray Wu of the Department of Molecular Biology and Genetics disclosed to the Cornell Research Foundation a gene that he isolated and sequenced from rice for a protein called actin and its associated promoter. The discovery was striking because of the strength with which the promoter affected the transcription of the gene. Feeling that the strong promoter might have value, the case manager at the Cornell Research

Find out more about gene sequencing at http://genomics.ucdavis.edu/what.html.

Do universities have an obligation to serve the "public good"? If so, why?

Cornell Research Foundation online can be found at www.crf.cornell.edu.

13

COMMENTARY: Discoverers of DNA's structure

The U.S. geneticist James Watson and his English colleague Francis Crick were two of the most celebrated scientists of the 20th century. Their discovery of the structure of DNA—a double helix—was a major step in unlocking the mystery of life. In their work the two more famous scientists were aided by a New Zealander, Maurice Wilkins. All three received the Nobel Prize in 1962 for their vital research on the molecular model of DNA.

There is a fourth name in the story, that of Englishwoman Rosalind Franklin. For decades Franklin's role in the discovery of DNA was often overlooked, but recently she has begun to receive more credit. An x-ray crystallographer, Franklin made discoveries about DNA's structure that the others used as crucial scientific evidence for their double-helix model. And when Crick and Watson published their monumental paper in 1953, Franklin was at work on a paper that drew similar conclusions. It is thought by many that she may have deduced the nature of the backbone of the helix before Crick and Watson.

Nine years after their famous paper Crick and Watson, along with Wilkins, were honored by the Nobel Prize committee. Franklin was not there. She had died of cancer in 1958.

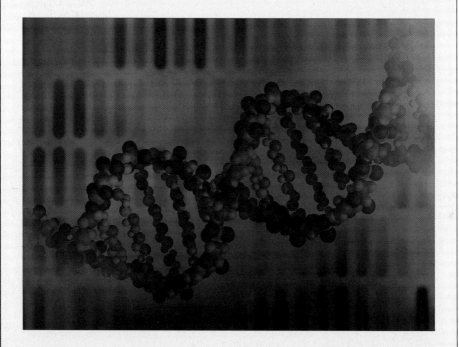

Closeup of a strand of DNA showing the double-helix structure that was discovered by James Watson, Francis Crick, Maurice Wilkins—and Rosalind Franklin.

Foundation initiated a patent application on the discovery. In addition to pursuing a patent for the discovery, Dr. Wu and Cornell made the invention widely available to other researchers through biological materials transfer agreements, a common mechanism for researchers to exchange research materials. As a result of this wide distribution, the promoter was available to numerous research programs, and, subsequently, it was discovered that this promoter is the best available in helping make plants tolerant to certain herbicides. At this point, Cornell Research Foundation has nonexclusive licenses with 12 companies that are developing crop plants with herbicide tolerance.

I make this example to illustrate two points. The first is that even if a patent has been pursued, there is still the opportunity for the university to share the gene itself, and associated information and biological materials, with other researchers for further discovery and potential development. The second point is that discoveries made at universities are an early stage and may take a significant time to make their way into products. Professor Wu made his discovery in 1989, but products that make use of his discovery are still in development.

In other instances, exclusive licensing may be preferred, and may offer the only practical way to induce a company to assume the risks of time and investment in early-stage inventions. ...

In summary, technology transfer, the transfer of research results to the commercial marketplace for public benefit, is an important way for universities, hospitals, and research institutes to demonstrate the relevance of their research programs, introduce innovation into the commercial sector, and enrich the lives of citizens. These discoveries can be pursued without disrupting the core values of publication and sharing of information, research results, materials, and know-how.

Do you think it is right to interfere with nature in this way, even if it is for our benefit?

Find out more about Professor Wu's work on the rice genome at http://rgp.dna. affrc.go.jp/rgp/ ricegenome newslet/nl1.html

Severson's conclusion repeats phrases from his introduction for added emphasis.

PATENTING LIFE—STIFLING HEALTHCARE
Sue Mayer and Ricarda Steinbrecher

NO

Every day, new patents are filed for discoveries about genetic material—including gene sequences and gene fragments. Whilst the biotechnology industry claims that patent protection on genes is essential to finance research and development, evidence is emerging which shows that patents are already:

- preventing or hindering development of new or improved medicines and treatments;
- limiting access to healthcare by increasing the cost of diagnostics and treatment for certain diseases;
- inhibiting the free exchange of information between researchers;
- involving unsuspecting parties in … costly legal battles.

Read more objections to gene patenting at www.access excellence.com/ WN/SUA01/ rifkin.htm.

If genetic research is to be of benefit to the public, it is essential that scientists and citizens join forces to bring an end to the practice of patenting genetic material….

Background

Since 1980 patents have been increasingly extended to include living organisms, their organs or body parts, and their genes. Some countries—particularly those in the developing world—are resisting such moves but, citing free trade rules, the United States and industry are pushing for all countries to allow patents to be granted on genes and living organisms. However, the trend towards patenting genes is opposed by many scientists, including many who are involved in the Human Genome Project itself, because working out a gene sequence and its function is a process of discovery, not invention.

The authors have made a strong point here—do you agree with them?

Breast cancer diagnostics and therapeutics

Approximately 5–10 percent of breast cancer cases are associated with a genetic defect. The case of Myriad Genetics and breast cancer susceptibility genes shows how determined a company can be to enforce its monopoly control through patents and how this can force up costs and hinder research. By the end of 2000, Myriad Genetics had

Find out more about Myriad Genetics and their work at www.myriad.com/.

been awarded a total of nine U.S. patents on the breast/ovarian cancer susceptibility genes, BRCA1 and BRCA2, and two on another tumour suppresser gene (p15) as well as patents covering antibodies to the BRCA and p15 genes. Similar patents have been granted in Canada and Japan and filed in the UK and Europe.

Find out more about the genetic causes of breast cancer at http://pubs.acs.org/hotartcl/mdd/00/jan/mortbox1.html.

Cashing in on medical treatments

The BRCA1 and BRCA2 patents provide Myriad with exclusive rights to commercialize laboratory testing services, diagnostic test kits, and therapeutic products that use the BRCA1/2 DNA sequences. For diseases like breast cancer, which are common and may have an inherited component, the economic potential for testing is great. ...

However, ...the discovery of the first gene for a predisposition to breast cancer (BRCA1) was based on international collaboration and the open exchange of information between groups around the world. Women carrying the gene helped by providing material and by investigating their family histories to provide clues. But as research got closer to isolating the gene, Myriad Genetics moved in and finally claimed a patent on the basis of being the first to complete the identification of the gene.

Similarly, much of the work on the second gene (BRCA2) took place in Britain at the Sanger Centre in Cambridge and the Institute of Cancer Research (ICR). Myriad filed its patent application literally hours before the ICR published its discovery of BRCA2 in the journal Nature and the ICR still insists it discovered the gene first. This is recognized in the UK where, at least for now, the ICR holds a patent for which it does not charge a license fee.

Nature magazine online has a dedicated genome website. It can be found at www.nature.com/genomics/.

Monopolizing research?

In the United States Myriad has threatened or taken legal action against anyone who markets or performs genetic breast cancer tests and, as a result, Myriad Genetics now has exclusive rights to OncorMed's patents (current and pending) for BRCA1 and BRCA2 genetic testing. U.S. cancer researchers and laboratories have accused Myriad Genetics of using its patents to stifle genetic breast cancer research and restrict women's access to DNA testing.

The cost of screening

Myriad's monopoly means screening for a particular mutation known to occur in a patient's family will cost between £179 ($250) and £357 ($500). Full sequencing of both BRCA genes to check for any mutation that could occur in either gene will cost about £1,714 ($2,400).

Anaemia treatment

Erythropoietin (EPO) stimulates red blood cell production and is normally produced in the kidney and liver. Because failing kidneys do not produce enough EPO—leading to chronic anaemia—an artificial version of EPO has a huge potential market among a growing number of dialysis patients, estimated to be 220,000 in the United States alone. Amgen's patent on the EPO gene has given them a monopoly on its production by exploiting earlier public sector research and clever maneuvering has allowed them to extend the patent lifetime to 30 years.

The EPO protein was first identified at the University of Chicago by molecular biologist Eugene Goldwasser in 1977 after two decades of government-funded research. However, Amgen won the race for the gene patent in the mid 1980s although it had to go through protracted litigation to win exclusive rights to manufacture its recombinant version of EPO—called Epogen—which is now the most expensive drug in the U.S. Federal Government's Medicare programme.

… Patents are generally granted for 17 years yet, having spaced their five patents on EPO conveniently—the first of Amgen's EPO patents was issued in 1987 while the last will expire in 2015.… As a result, the prices are rising for patients and stifling competition.

Amgen funded the National Kidney Foundation—a patient advocacy group—to conduct a medical literature research project to provide guidelines aimed at reducing the death rate among U.S. dialysis patients. In 1997 the Foundation recommended raising hematocrit (a measure of red blood cell levels) into the 33 to 36 percent range, thus necessitating higher dosages of Epogen. Once Amgen had spread the word, doctors started prescribing levels even above 36.

In 1999, total U.S. Epogen sales were approximately $1.8 billion, making it one of the top-selling pharmaceutical products worldwide.

Human Genome Sciences and the AIDS virus

When [Human Genome Sciences] HGS isolated the HDGNR10 gene—later to be known as the CCR5 gene—it concluded that it had found a gene belonging to the family of cell receptors. It filed a patent on the gene believing it to be a receptor for chemokines, which play a role in inflammatory diseases such as arthritis. HGS had no idea that the receptor

Find out more about Epogen at http://wwwext. amgen.com/product /epogenHome.html.

The authors concentrate on the financial effects of patenting. Is this more or less effective than discussing the ethics of who can "own" genes?

COMMENTARY: Chain reaction

Scientists need large quantities of DNA for use in experiments. In order to obtain copies of a piece of DNA quickly, they use a technique called polymerase chain reaction, which is more often known by its initials, PCR.

The PCR technique was developed by the U.S. biochemist Kary B. Mullis, who won the Nobel Prize for Chemistry in 1993 for his work. The technique relies on the natural way in which cells replicate DNA strands.

How PCR works

The DNA that contains the strand that is to be replicated is known as the template. Two small strands of nucleotides (subunits of DNA), known as primers, bind to the template. These primers are the starting point and finishing point for the stretch to be copied. Free nucleotides form the "building material" to make the new DNA strand between the primers. And an enzyme, a DNA polymerase, accomplishes the building by adding one free nucleotide to another. The process is rapid and happens in repeated cycles. The PCR technique has many scientific applications, from analyzing tissue to tracing viruses and diagnosing diseases.

was one of the entry points for the HIV virus into human cells. This was discovered by scientists from several academies, who, after painstaking work, found and isolated a protein that the AIDS virus requires to infect cells—the CCR5 receptor. They eventually isolated the gene, knowing that any drug which can block the protein could be used in the fight against AIDS.

However, the gene had already been claimed by HGS and, when the patent was granted, the company announced that: "HGS receives patent on AIDS virus entry point," causing its stock price to soar…. AIDS researchers globally have expressed their disbelief and even outrage over this patent, saying that wherever the patent is valid, "research would be immediately taxed if it was ever fruitful."

Conclusion

[P]atents on genes and gene fragments seriously threaten the future of medical research. They can stifle research and increase prices through patent monopolies, neither of which serve the public interest. A review of gene patents is long overdue.

…The simplest solution is for genes and gene fragments to be made unpatentable—political action is needed now before the companies clean up on gene patents and society is left counting the cost.

Genewatch is dedicated to reviewing the risks of genetic engineering. Find out more at www.genewatch.org.

Summary

The authors fundamentally disagree about a key point: The Pro author, James A. Severson, has not—in his experience—seen the publication of research results delayed by the need to obtain a patent. The Con authors—Sue Mayer and Ricarda Steinbrecher—disagree, arguing that patenting prevents and hinders the development of new or improved medicines and treatments. They also add that patents inhibit the free exchange of information between researchers, a point that is contested by Severson.

The Con authors go on to state that patenting is wrong because working out a gene sequence and its function is a process of discovery, not invention. Again, the Pro author counters this by arguing that patenting is necessary because research institutes and universities need to protect genetic information so that it can become a commercial development. In response the Con authors maintain that the commercialization of research benefits business and not the public: Companies are able to monopolize their research findings to exclusively develop drugs and treatments at inflated prices. They illustrate this assertion with three "real world" examples of gene-patenting companies.

This is a complicated argument with valid points made by both sides of the debate. The information below will help you increase your knowledge on the subject, and the key map opposite sums up the main points.

FURTHER INFORMATION:

Books:

Keller, Evelyn Fox, *The Century of the Gene*. Cambridge, MA: Harvard University Press, 2000.

Morange, Michel, *The Misunderstood Gene*. Cambridge, MA: Harvard University Press, 2001.

Ridley, Matt, *Genome: The Autobiography of a Species in 23 Chapters*. New York: HarperCollins, 2000.

Useful websites:

ci.mond.org/9520/952021.html
See article "The Great Gene Patent Race" by Thomas Caskey.

rarediseases.about.com/health/rarediseases/library/weekly/aa011201a.htm
Mary Kugler, "Gene Patent: For Mankind's Good, or For Profit?"

www.er.doe.gov/production/ober/hug_top.html
Comprehensive overview of the aims and applications of the Human Genome Project.

www.immunet.org/immunet/atn.nsf/page/a-223-04
John S. James, "Religious Coalition Opposes Gene Patents."

www.theage.com.au/news/20000319/A17591-2000Mar18.html
Penny Fannin, "Patent critics try to stop human-gene slave trade."

The following debates in the Pro/Con series may also be of interest:

In this volume:

Topic 2 Should it be legal to clone human beings?

Topic 3 Is gene manipulation wrong?

Topic 4 Should U.S. privacy laws include genetic testing?

SHOULD GENES BE PATENTED?

YES: Patenting ensures that research leads to the development of drugs and treatments, which ultimately benefits the public

YES: We all have the right to share in the benefits of research

BENEFITS
Does gene patenting benefit the general public?

OWNERSHIP
Because human genes are part of what makes up all human beings, should they not belong to the public at large and be exempt from patenting?

NO: The pursuit of patents is primarily a commercial venture that benefits business, not people

NO: Companies do not own genes merely by having a patent—they merely have research rights to clearly defined applications

SHOULD GENES BE PATENTED? KEY POINTS

YES: Without the protection of a patent companies would not risk research in the first place, since other companies would be able to make undeserved profits from the original research

YES: Corporations deserve to earn a return on their investment in research

COMMERCE
Should patents be awarded to promote the profits of a company?

NO: The restrictions imposed by a patent might result in important research being slowed down or limited, since it would prevent any research being done by rival companies

NO: Such commercial emphasis in medical research benefits private companies but not the public institutions that funded a large part of the research

Topic 2
SHOULD IT BE LEGAL TO CLONE HUMAN BEINGS?

YES
"GENETIC ENCORES: THE ETHICS OF HUMAN CLONING"
INSTITUTE FOR PHILOSOPHY AND PUBLIC POLICY
ROBERT WACHBROIT

NO
"THE WISDOM OF REPUGNANCE"
THE NEW REPUBLIC, JUNE 2, 1997
LEON R. KASS

INTRODUCTION

Few creatures have received as much publicity as Dolly the sheep. Her birth in July 1996 galvanized public opinion since Dolly was unique in that she was a clone, produced from the adult cell of another sheep at the Roslin Institute, Edinburgh, Scotland. Dolly was quickly a well-recognized face, gracing the pages of international papers. Although she was a cause for celebration for some scientists, for a significant group of people Dolly raised an uncomfortable vision of a future dominated by Frankenstein-like clones and heralded the possible interference in reproduction to engineer potentially grotesque or "perfect" forms of life.

The Roslin achievement (see *Environment* volume, page 178) crowned more than a decade of research into cloning. Early research centered on a technique called nuclear transfer, in which scientists removed the nucleus of an egg cell. The nucleus was replaced in the egg cell with a cell

nucleus from another organism. The adult that developed from the altered egg was a clone—an exact genetic replication—of the organism from which the DNA had been introduced.

This technique would not work with cells from adult animals, however. Only when the nucleus was taken from an embryo in the early stages of development could a clone be created. So the clone itself was an embryo, and the success rate was low.

By 1996 Ian Wilmut of the Roslin Institute had refined this procedure to use adult cells. Cells were isolated to be stored in a medium that was nutrient-deficient. "Starving" the cell slowed its normal growth rate, effectively putting it into hibernation. "Sleeping" adult cells of this nature seem to be accepted by eggs, and in a number of cases clones were successfully produced later.

It had been thought that to create a clone with adult cells would be impossible. Many scientists argued that mature cells changed in character in order to perform specific roles in the body. It was suggested that these alterations were irreversible, which would explain why only embryo cells could be used to transmit genetic material. Dolly's arrival demonstrated that the DNA in an adult cell—in Dolly's case a cell from the udder of a six-year-old sheep—could produce clones. How these mature cells are compatible is still a mystery; but, in a way not understood, adult DNA seems able to reprogram itself.

"At present it would be inhuman to carry this [process] out with a human being."
—DR. IAN WILMUT, THE ROSLIN INSTITUTE

The initial success with Dolly raised many new questions. The procedure has already been used to clone other species. It was inevitable that sooner or later someone would ask: "Can a human being be cloned?" Many scientists believe it is probable that the technology that created Dolly will be able to clone a human being. And this raises further questions and comments on the ethics and morality of cloning human beings. Yes, society may have the relevant technology, but is it right?

The cloning process has been popular. By 2000 alone there were more than 5,000 clones, all of which appear to be healthy. But question

marks remain over Dolly's aging process. Her cells are six years older than her biological age. Does this mean that she was born with a six-year reduction in life expectancy? How would adult cells in a human clone affect the aging process? It is uncertain whether a human clone could be genetically programmed to have a shorter life than that of a "normal" person.

The potential practice of cloning human beings has been condemned by most of the world's major religions. Neither of the authors of the two articles that follow have adopted a religious standpoint, but even from a secular point of view there are grave issues about the morality of creating an identical copy of a person. Would a human clone be able to be an independent individual, with his or her own mind or character—or even soul?

Here two writers focus on some of the issues surrounding the ethics of human cloning. In the first article, "Genetic Encores," Robert Wachbroit argues that a clone is not, in fact, an identical copy, but more like a delayed identical twin: A clone is a separate person in every way. Wachbroit also describes various scenarios in which human cloning could be used. And he commends the likelihood that, one day, medical science may clone human beings in order to save lives.

In the second article the celebrated biologist Leon R. Kass argues against the use of human cloning. Kass's article "The Wisdom of Repugnance" is widely quoted as one of the cornerstones of the nonreligious argument against the cloning of human beings. Kass sees human cloning as an exercise in control that would alter the whole meaning of having children.

GENETIC ENCORES: THE ETHICS OF HUMAN CLONING
Robert Wachbroit

YES

The writer dismisses a prime objection to the cloning of human beings by using an analogy with twins.

☑ As many scientists have pointed out, a clone would not in fact be an identical copy, but more like a delayed identical twin. And just as identical twins are two separate people—biologically, psychologically, morally and legally, though not genetically—so, too, a clone would be a separate person from her non-contemporaneous twin. To think otherwise is to embrace a belief in genetic determinism—the view that genes determine everything about us, and that environmental factors or the random events in human development are insignificant.

Genetic determinism

Wachbroit uses the nature v. nurture debate to suggest that genes are significantly affected by environment.

The overwhelming scientific consensus is that genetic determinism is false. In coming to understand the ways in which genes operate, biologists have also become aware of the myriad ways in which the environment affects their "expression." The genetic contribution to the simplest physical traits, such as height and hair color, is significantly mediated by environmental factors (and possibly by stochastic [random] events as well). And the genetic contribution to the traits we value most deeply, from intelligence to compassion, is conceded by even the most enthusiastic genetic researchers to be limited and indirect.

Does the dismissal of the opposing argument as "science fiction" strengthen the writer's case?

It is difficult to gauge the extent to which "repugnance" toward cloning generally rests on a belief in genetic determinism. Hoping to account for the fact that people "instinctively recoil" from the prospect of cloning, James Q. Wilson wrote, "There is a natural sentiment that is offended by the mental picture of identical babies being produced in some biological factory." Which raises the question: Once people learn that this picture is mere science fiction, does the offense that cloning presents to "natural sentiment" attenuate, or even disappear? Jean Bethke Elshtain cited the nightmare scenarios of "the man and woman on the street," who imagine a future populated by "a veritable army of Hitlers, ruthless and remorseless bigots who kept reproducing themselves until they had finished what the historic Hitler failed to do: Annihilate us." What happens, though, to the "pity and terror" evoked by the topic of cloning when such scenarios are deprived (as they deserve to be) of all credibility?

Richard Lewontin has argued that the critics' fears—or at least, those fears that merit consideration in formulating public policy—dissolve once genetic determinism is refuted. He [cites] excessive deference to opponents of human cloning, and calls for greater public education on the scientific issue.... Yet even if a public education campaign succeeded in eliminating the most egregious misconceptions about genetic influence, that wouldn't settle the matter. People might continue to express concerns about the interests and rights of human clones, about the social and moral consequences of the cloning process, and about the possible motivations for creating children in this way....

Do you think the American public is well informed about the genetic debate? See www.newscientist. com/hotsubjects/ cloning.

Why clone?

If human cloning technology were safe and widely available, what use would people make of it? What reasons would they have to engage in cloning?

Using rhetorical questions is a useful way to introduce a new part of the argument.

In its report to the President, the (National Bioethics Advisory) Commission (NBAC) imagined a few situations in which people might avail themselves of cloning. In one scenario, a husband and wife who wish to have children are both carriers of a lethal recessive gene.

Rather than risk the one in four chance of conceiving a child who will suffer a short and painful existence, the couple considers the alternatives: To forgo rearing children; to adopt; to use prenatal diagnosis and selective abortion; to use donor gametes free of the recessive trait; or to use the cells of one of the adults and attempt to clone a child. To avoid donor gametes and selective abortion, while maintaining a genetic tie to their child, they opt for cloning.

In another scenario, the parents of a terminally ill child are told that only a bone marrow transplant can save the child's life. "With no other donor available, the parents attempt to clone a human being from the cells of the dying child. If successful, the new child will be a perfect match for bone marrow transplant, and can be used as a donor without significant risk or discomfort. The net result: Two healthy children, loved by their parents, who happen [sic] to be identical twins of different ages."

Wachbroit uses case scenarios that are deliberately emotive. How does this strengthen his argument?

The Commission was particularly impressed by the second example. That scenario, said the NBAC report, "makes what is probably the strongest possible case for cloning a human

A calf (bottom) cloned from the body cells of a cow (top) stands at a farm in Hwasong County, south of Seoul, Korea. The calf is the world's fifth cloned animal.

being, as it demonstrates how this technology could be used for lifesaving purposes." Indeed, the report suggests that it would be a "tragedy" to allow "the sick child to die because of a moral or political objection to such cloning." Nevertheless, we should note that many people would be morally uneasy about the use of a minor as a donor, regardless of whether the child were a result of cloning. Even if this unease is justifiably overridden by other concerns, the "transplant scenario" may not present a more compelling case for cloning than that of the infertile couple desperately seeking a biological child.

Most critics, in fact, decline to engage the specifics of such tragic (and presumably rare) situations. Instead, they bolster their case by imagining very different scenarios. Potential users of the technology, they suggest, are narcissists or control freaks—people who will regard their children not as free, original selves but as products intended to meet more or less rigid specifications. Even if such people are not genetic determinists, their recourse to cloning will indicate a desire to exert all possible influence over the "kind" of child they produce.

> *The writer lists scenarios that critics of human cloning might cite. Which is the more powerful or convincing?*

Human rights

It can be argued, however, that the critics have simply misunderstood the social meaning of a policy that would permit people to clone themselves even in the absence of the heartrending exigencies described in the NBAC report. This country has developed a strong commitment to reproductive autonomy. (This commitment emerged in response to the dismal history of eugenics—the very history that is sometimes invoked to support restrictions on cloning.) With the exception of practices that risk coercion and exploitation—notably baby-selling and commercial surrogacy—we do not interfere with people's freedom to create and acquire children by almost any means, for almost any reason. This policy does not reflect a dogmatic libertarianism. Rather, it recognizes the extraordinary personal importance and private character of reproductive decisions, even those with significant social repercussions.

> *"Eugenics" is the science of trying to improve a race or breed in ways such as by selective breeding. It was widely discredited by Nazi attempts to establish racial superiority for the Germans in the mid–20th century. See box, page 44.*

THE WISDOM OF REPUGNANCE
Leon R. Kass

X Any attempt to clone a human being would constitute an unethical experiment upon the resulting child-to-be. As ... animal experiments (frog and sheep) indicate, there are grave risks of mishaps and deformities. Moreover, because of what cloning means, one cannot presume a future cloned child's consent to be a clone, even a healthy one. Thus, ethically speaking, we cannot even get to know whether or not human cloning is feasible.

> *Kass begins by considering the rights of any human clone.*

Philosophical problems

I understand, of course, the philosophical difficulty of trying to compare a life with defects against nonexistence. Several bioethicists, proud of their philosophical cleverness, use this conundrum to embarrass claims that one can injure a child in its conception, precisely because it is only thanks to that complained-of conception that the child is alive to complain. But common sense tells us that we have no reason to fear such philosophisms.

> *Kass sets out a powerful contrast between common sense on one hand and "philosophisms" on the other.*

For we surely know that people can harm and even maim children in the very act of conceiving them, say, by paternal transmission of the AIDS virus, maternal transmission of heroin dependence or, arguably, even by bringing them into being as bastards or with no capacity or willingness to look after them properly. And we believe that to do this intentionally, or even negligently, is inexcusable and clearly unethical.

Nature v. nurture

The objection about the impossibility of presuming consent may even go beyond the obvious and sufficient point that a clonant, were he subsequently to be asked, could rightly resent having been made a clone. At issue are not just benefits and harms, but doubts about the very independence needed to give proper consent, that is, not just the capacity to choose but the disposition and ability to choose freely and well. It is not at all clear to what extent a clone will truly be a moral agent. For, as we shall see, in the very fact of cloning, and of rearing him as a clone, his makers subvert the cloned child's independence, beginning with that aspect that comes

> *Do you think it matters what circumstances children are conceived or created in?*

from knowing that one was an unbidden surprise, a gift, to the world, rather than the designed result of someone's artful project.

Identity v. individuality

Cloning creates serious issues of identity and individuality. The cloned person may experience concerns about his distinctive identity not only because he will be in genotype and appearance identical to another human being, but, in this case, because he may also be twin to the person who is his "father" or "mother"—if one can still call them that. What would be the psychic burdens of being the "child" or "parent" of your twin? The cloned individual, moreover, will be saddled with a genotype that has already lived. He will not be fully a surprise to the world. People are likely always to compare his performances in life with that of his alter ego. True, his nurture and his circumstance in life will be different; genotype is not exactly destiny. Still, one must also expect parental and other efforts to shape this new life after the original—or at least to view the child with the original version always firmly in mind. Why else did they clone from the star basketball player, mathematician, and beauty queen—or even dear old dad—in the first place?

Since the birth of Dolly, there has been a fair amount of doublespeak on this matter of genetic identity. Experts have rushed in to reassure the public that the clone would in no way be the same person, or have any confusions about his or her identity: As previously noted, they are pleased to point out that the clone of Mel Gibson would not be Mel Gibson. Fair enough. But one is shortchanging the truth by emphasizing the additional importance of the intrauterine environment, rearing and social setting: Genotype obviously matters plenty. That, after all, is the only reason to clone, whether human beings or sheep. The odds that clones of Wilt Chamberlain will play in the NBA are, I submit, infinitely greater than they are for clones of Robert Reich.

Curiously, this conclusion is supported, inadvertently, by the one ethical sticking point insisted on by friends of cloning: No cloning without the donor's consent. Though an orthodox liberal objection, it is in fact quite puzzling when it comes from people (such as Ruth Macklin) who also insist that genotype is not identity or individuality, and who deny that a child could reasonably complain about being made a genetic copy. If the clone of Mel Gibson would not be Mel Gibson, why should Mel Gibson have grounds to object that someone had been made his clone? We already allow

How likely are the scenarios painted by the author?

Kass stretches the logic of his opponents and uses it to reinforce his own point.

researchers to use blood and tissue samples for research purposes of no benefit to their sources: My falling hair, my expectorations, my urine, and even my biopsied tissues are "not me" and not mine. Courts have held that the profit gained from uses to which scientists put my discarded tissues do not legally belong to me. Why, then, no cloning without consent—including, I assume, no cloning from the body of someone who just died? What harm is done the donor, if the

COMMENTARY: Identical twins

A human clone has been described as a "delayed twin." Identical twins might look like carbon copies (below), but each is a complete individual. So-called fraternal twins occur when more than one egg is fertilized, but identical twins—always of the same sex—occur where one egg is fertilized and later divides into two cells. Each cell grows into a separate embryo. The resulting babies may be genetic doubles, but neither is deficient as a whole person. And because identical twins normally share both nature and nurture, they usually share tastes in clothes, friends, and music, and are alike in behavior and mannerisms. Identical twins may buy similar objects, say similar things, and share emotions even if they are brought up apart. Yet that does not make them anything less than independent individuals: Neither is diminished by having a genetic double.

genotype is "not me?" Truth to tell, the only powerful justification for objecting is that genotype really does have something to do with identity, and everybody knows it. If not, on what basis could Michael Jordan object that someone cloned "him," say, from cells taken from a "lost" scraped-off piece of his skin? The insistence on donor consent unwittingly reveals the problem of identity in all cloning.

Genetic distinctiveness

Genetic distinctiveness not only symbolizes the uniqueness of each human life and the independence of its parents that each human child rightfully attains. It can also be an important support for living a worthy and dignified life. Such arguments apply with great force to any large-scale replication of human individuals. But they are sufficient to rebut even the first attempts to clone a human being.

Kass argues that human clones would disrupt established family relationships. Do you think that is an important consideration?

Troubled psychic identity (distinctiveness), based on all-too-evident genetic identity (sameness), will be made much worse by the utter confusion of social identity and kinship ties. For, as already noted, cloning radically confounds lineage and social relations, for "offspring" as for "parents." As bioethicist James Nelson has pointed out, a female child cloned from her "mother" might develop a desire for a relationship to her "father," and might understandably seek out the father of her "mother," who is after all also her biological twin sister. Would "grandpa," who thought his paternal duties concluded, be pleased to discover that the clonant looked to him for paternal attention and support?...

Finally, and perhaps most important, the practice of human cloning by nuclear transfer—like other anticipated forms of genetic engineering of the next generation—would enshrine and aggravate a profound and mischievous misunderstanding of the meaning of having children and of the parent-child relationship. Embracing the future by procreating means precisely that we are relinquishing our grip, in the very activity of taking up our own share in what we hope will be the immortality of human life and the human species. This means that our children are not our … property, nor our possessions. Neither are they supposed to live our lives for us, or anyone else's life but their own. To be sure, we seek to guide them on their way, imparting to them not just life but nurturing, love, and a way of life; to be sure, they bear our hopes that they will live fine and flourishing lives…. Still, their genetic distinctiveness and independence are the natural foreshadowing of the deep truth that they have their own and never-before-enacted life to live.

How much influence should parents be able to have over their children? Do you see any evidence that some adults treat their offspring as "possessions"?

Summary

Few topics in the realm of genetics arouse such passions as human cloning. Both writers here examine the scientific and social background to the procedure with relative dispassion—though both also incorporate more emotive scenarios into their arguments.

Robert Wachbroit relates possible ways in which human cloning could provide hope to people carrying a lethal recessive gene who wished to become parents. Donor DNA could free any offspring of the recessive gene. He also describes how a clone could provide perfect compatible bone marrow for transplant for a terminally ill child. But he ends with the powerful libertarian stance that the state has no right to intervene in human reproduction.

In the counter stance, in an extract from a much longer and influential article, Leon R. Kass examines cloning within the context of family, motherhood, fatherhood, and the links between generations. He suggests that cloning would allow parents to engineer the very identity of their offspring in ways that even overdominant parents cannot achieve through nurture alone. He sees the cloning of human infants as an exercise in adult control that will disrupt the very basis of human society. As well as highlighting the social problems, he also cites the risk of deformity and the grave risk of mishaps involved in cloning procedures.

FURTHER INFORMATION:

Books:

Alonso, Kenneth, *Shall We Clone a Man?: Genetic Engineering and the Issues of Life*. New York: Allegro Press, 1998.

Useful websites:

www.st-edmunds.cam.ac.uk/Papers/Paper1.html
Colin Honey, "Human Cloning: The Theological Issues."
www.navhindtimes.com/cybervoices/messages/230.htm
James P. Pinkerton, "The Human Clone."
www.globalchange.com/clonech.htm
Patrick Dixon, "Human Cloning."
www.ncpa.org/health/pdh/july98d.html
National Center for Policy Analysis site. Article on "Health Care Issues: Legal Status of Human Cloning."
www.humancloning.org/david.htm
"Human Cloning Should Be Permitted!" by B. David.
www.newscientist.com/nsplus/insight/clone/clone.htm
New Scientist, Cloning special.
www.princeton.edu/~wws320/Second%20Pages/06Reprotech/Cloning/Wisdom%20of%20repugnance.htm
Full text of Leon R. Kass's article "The Wisdom of Repugnance."

SHOULD IT BE LEGAL TO CLONE HUMAN BEINGS?

YES: Cloning could offer the possibility of parenthood to those who carry a lethal recessive gene or hereditary disease

YES: Cloning could have important ramifications for the shortage of organ donations

CHILDREN
Should cloning be used to help reduce infertility problems?

NO: There are enough problems feeding our population—removing this natural check would just exacerbate them

ORGAN TRANSPLANTS
Will cloning human beings help to provide life-saving donor organs?

NO: Even if scientists develop the technology to help infertile men and women, there is always the danger that it will be abused to create "designer babies"

NO: The technology is too unsafe, and there would have to be too many human "experiments" before cloning organs is deemed safe

SHOULD IT BE LEGAL TO CLONE HUMAN BEINGS?

KEY POINTS

YES: As a "delayed twin" a clone would be the sister, not the offspring, of its "mother," which could lead to social problems

YES: The clone would act independently of the being it is cloned from

NATURE V. NURTURE
Would nature rather than nurture determine how human clones acted?

NO: Nurture and socialization would shape the cloned person— nature alone does not make a human being

NO: A human clone could not be truly independent, and its behavior and mores would come from its family, parents, and friends

THE HISTORY OF CLONING

The history of cloning goes back only 50 years. Yet huge progress has been made since 1953, when geneticists James Watson and Francis Crick described the double-helix structure of DNA. Their discovery would eventually allow scientists to develop ways to manipulate the molecules of genes—a vital element in cloning. Today, after various successes and failures, the first clones have been born.

April 1953 Watson and Crick describe the three-dimensional structure of DNA. The genetic information for an entire organism is coded in DNA. This insight heralds the development of "molecular" genetics, as scientists are able to manipulate genes at the molecular level.

1961–1965 The genetic code is cracked. Researchers can decipher the information coded in DNA. If the sequence of a gene is known, it is now possible to translate the sequence of the DNA into the amino acid sequence of a protein. All life on Earth uses the same basic code.

December 1977 The first cloned gene. Using recombinant DNA techniques, scientists at Genentech Inc. in the United States clone the gene for the hormone somatostatin. The DNA sequence of the somatostatin gene was engineered into a viruslike carrier (a vector) and introduced into a bacterium. As the bacterium grew, the vector directed the synthesis of a fully functional hormone protein. This breakthrough is considered the dawning of the "age of biotechnology."

September 1981 Genes from other animals are transferred into the chromosomes of mice by scientists at Ohio University, thus creating the first "transgenic" organisms. Transgenic mice are now a standard laboratory method for studying mutations, gene expression, and human disease.

October 1985 FDA approval is given to Genentech Inc. to market human growth hormone. It is the first recombinant pharmaceutical product to be sold by a biotechnology company.

December 1990 The first transgenic dairy cow, used to produce human milk proteins for infant formula, is born. The cows produce human-lactoferrin protein in their milk.

May 1995 The first complete DNA sequencing of the genome of a free-living organism— the bacterium *Haemophilus influenzae*— is announced.

January 1997 Scientists in Oregon divide an eight-cell fertilized ovum of a rhesus monkey into single, genetically identical cells, remove the DNA from each cell, and reintroduce it into several fresh anucleate egg cells. The resultant two live births are clones of each other (but not of their parents). The research paves the way for producing unlimited, identical copies of primates. The technique is known as "embryo cloning."

April 1997 British geneticists clone Dolly the sheep. Chromosomes taken from frozen udder tissue of an adult sheep were inserted into an unfertilized egg that had had its nucleus removed. The fused cells were grown in the laboratory and then implanted into the uterus of a surrogate mother sheep. This was the first time cloning was achieved using cells other than reproductive cells. Only 30 out of 200 attempts at cell fusion worked, and they were implanted in ewes. Of 13 pregnancies, only one lamb, Dolly, was born. Dolly is a true clone of the adult sheep whose tissue was used in the experiment.

January 1998 Nineteen European nations, but not Britain or Germany, sign an agreement to prohibit human cloning. U.S. President Clinton calls for a five-year ban on human cloning experiments.

December 1998 Researchers at Kinki University, Japan, produce eight cloned calves from cells of an adult cow; four of the eight died at, or soon after, birth.

December 1998 The first complete sequence of a multicellular animal genome is presented for the microscopic nematode worm—*C. elegans*.

December 1998 Researchers at Kyunghee Hospital, Seoul, South Korea, are reported to have cloned a cell from an infertile woman to produce a four-cell embryo. The announcement causes a worldwide furor of public protest. For ethical reasons the researchers reportedly stop their work before implanting the embryo.

August 1999 An international team of scientists, including leading experts from the United States, attempt to clone an extinct animal—the woolly mammoth. DNA samples are obtained from a woolly mammoth frozen in the Russian tundra for over 23,000 years. The group attempts cloning an embryo implantation in a modern elephant. This fails because the genetic material is too damaged.

January 2000 The first animal born after the DNA of one species was put into the egg of another dies after just 48 hours. Named Noah, it was the clone of a rare wild ox,

the gaur, and was created by fusing skin cells from a gaur that died in 1993 with cow eggs stripped of their nuclei.

January 2000 Britain is the first country to legalize cloning of human embryos for research purposes. Embryo cloning is only permitted for medical reasons. Cloning of a developed individual remains illegal.

March 2000 An international group of fertility experts, including Italian obstetrician Professor Severino Antinori, announce plans to be the first scientists to clone a human being "in an effort to assist couples that have no other alternatives to reproduce."

June 2000 Celera Genomics and the NIH announce the completion of the Human Genome Project—the deciphering of the entire genome sequence of a human. The announcement is described as "the first great technological triumph of the 21st century."

August 2000 Pope John Paul II, in a public address to an international conference on transplant techniques, condemns human embryo cloning as "morally unacceptable."

December 2000 By the end of the year eight species of mammals have been cloned, including mice, cows, sheep, goats, pigs, and rats. More than 5,000 cloned animals have been produced.

January 2001 U.S. scientists announce first transgenic primate. Named ANDi, for "inserted DNA" read backward, the rhesus monkey carries a gene for a green fluorescent protein derived from a jellyfish.

June 21, 2001 The Bush administration announces that it favors a bill that would outlaw not only the creation of cloned children, but additionally the creation of cloned human embryos for research.

Topic 3
IS GENE MANIPULATION WRONG?

YES
"'PERFECT CHILDREN' WILL NO LONGER BE AN OXYMORON"
NATIONAL POST, MARCH 14, 2000
BRAD EVENSON

NO
"GENE HUNTERS EXTRAORDINAIRE"
NATIONAL POST, MARCH 16, 2000
MICHAEL LEGAULT AND MARGARET MUNRO

INTRODUCTION

Improvements in genetic engineering have made it possible to alter a child's genes before he or she is born. Some people see such a development as heralding an age when humankind can humanely eradicate diseases that have affected people throughout history. Opponents, however, argue that the current technology opens the door to a nightmare world in which parents can play God and effectively order children on demand. It is a slippery slope from altering a child's vulnerability to disease to the possibility that society will eventually prevent the creation of children who do not fit conventional molds—for example, people who are overweight or have the "wrong" sexual preferences.

For centuries people have used selective breeding to produce high-yield strains of crops or domesticated animals that provide more milk or meat. This "improvement," known as eugenics, is widely accepted. But what is the morality of applying the same techniques to human beings?

For five decades human eugenics has carried uncomfortable echoes of the racial policies of Hitler's Nazi Germany. Classifying other peoples as "inferior," the Nazis encouraged the selective breeding of an Aryan "master race." This is a nightmare vision of eugenics, but images associated with the racist experiments practiced in Nazi Germany continue to underlie popular responses to genetic technology.

In a sense, eugenics already plays a part in modern medicine. Negative selection of fetuses is practiced. Births of severely deformed children are reduced by scanning and other forms of prenatal diagnosis. Such diagnosis is often followed by abortion, but in some cases disease and deformity can be treated in the womb.

But genetic manipulation opens up the possibility that it could be employed not for medical reasons but to enhance attributes such as intelligence or beauty. Such procedures are sometimes referred to as "gene therapy." Where would the dividing line lie between a medical intervention and a genetic enhancement?

In "'Perfect Children' Will No Longer Be an Oxymoron" Brad Evenson—the Pro author—depicts a nightmare future in which gene manipulation has crossed medical lines and is instead used to create "perfect children." Evenson believes that this ability to genetically engineer will be a privilege of the rich, and not limited to cosmetic changes—such as eye or hair color—in already healthy babies. Children, in his view, could literally be "made to order."

> *"These new technologies will create a host of difficult, often unprecedented, ethical and legal controversies, many of which will find their way to the courts."*
> —PROFESSOR MAXWELL J. MEHLMANN, CASE WESTERN RESERVE UNIVERSITY

Evenson believes that transforming the body is only the start: The technology could be used to eradicate certain characteristics that researchers know are determined by our genetic makeup. These unwanted characteristics could include alcoholism, shyness, and risk-taking behavior, for example, as well as sexual disposition. Evenson argues that the ability to "fine tune" a person's character would result in a society divided between those who can afford to eradicate unwanted genetic material and those who cannot.

To strengthen his case, Evenson reminds us that the desire to mold perfect people can be seen in Hitler's attempts to create the Aryan race through the science of eugenics (see page 44). We have not, he argues, learned from history, and that is why gene manipulation is a dangerous science that is open to abuse.

Conversely, Michael Legault and Margaret Munro, in "Gene Hunters Extraordinaire," examine the achievements of Lap-Chee Tsui, the director of the Center for Applied Genomics at Sick Kids, in Toronto, Canada. Tsui has specialized in the investigation of faulty genes, in particular the gene mutation that causes cystic fibrosis (CF).

This condition affects one in 2,400 babies and kills half the sufferers before they reach adulthood. It is caused by genetic factors that result in the production of thick mucus in the lungs that causes severe breathing problems and other complications. Treatment, at present, is daily percussive therapy on the back and chest cavity to loosen and free mucus in the lining of the lungs. It is an exhausting, painful, and artificial way to accomplish what healthy lungs do naturally.

Through their investigations Tsui and his colleagues found the small segment of mutated DNA that is responsible for cystic fibrosis. It is hoped that this discovery will eventually lead to a permanent cure for this debilitating condition, and it is for this reason that the authors support gene manipulation as an important advance in medical science. In their view the ability to manipulate genes may bring about cures for a range of debilitating—and often fatal—diseases and is therefore a worthwhile pursuit.

"PERFECT CHILDREN" WILL NO LONGER BE AN OXYMORON
Brad Evenson

YES

Since his death in 1955, the public has been fascinated with the brain of Albert Einstein. What made it different? Was it bigger? Could the secret of his towering intellect be locked in his genes in the same way as his eye color, personality traits, and his grey haystack of hair?

If so, the genes that confer such genius may be hot commodities in the future.

How about actor Elizabeth Taylor's "violet" eyes? Or the extraordinary constitution of comedian George Burns, who smoked cigars for almost 100 years?

Cosmetic gene therapy

As the technology to transfer genes improves, it will become routine for technologists to alter our DNA, in much the same consumer fashion that people now undergo liposuction, take Prozac, and wear tinted contact lenses. In philosophical circles, this possibility is known as the "perfectibility of man." Most people don't realize that it has already begun.

In 1990, at London's Hammersmith Hospital, the first pregnancies that followed molecular testing for X-linked recessive diseases came to term. Cells were removed from an embryo and the DNA examined for such disorders as cystic fibrosis, one of about 4,000 known single-gene diseases. Only "healthy" cells were then implanted in the mothers' wombs.

More recently, doctors have used gene therapy to alter the development of embryos in the womb. For example, last year researchers at Toronto's Hospital for Sick Children showed how implanting a synthetic "decoy gene" could help newborns with congenital heart defects survive. It is a surprisingly short step from using gene therapy to treat medical defects to using it to "improve" an already healthy baby.

"You can design your own children," says Jeffrey Nisker, a University of Western Ontario professor of obstetrics and gynaecology. The implications make him uncomfortable. "We will be able to do in one generation what it took a million years of evolution to achieve."

Evenson introduces his subject with some familiar names to get the reader's attention.

Find out more about genetic disorders and possible cures at www.shef.ac.uk/~scharr/publich/research/genetics/impphi.html.

At a time when childless U.S. couples are offering up to $100,000 to female college students for their eggs, Nisker's fears that wealthy people will use this to "engineer perfect babies" are neither misplaced nor exaggerated.

Paediatricians may be among the first to confront the moral quagmire of perfectibility, but it won't take long before plastic surgeons, who live most comfortably in this ethical territory, will be asked to implant anti-ageing genes. A facelift sounds barbaric when one can buy the genes that make model Claudia Schiffer's skin so soft and clear. The pain and humiliation of hair plugs could be replaced by an infusion of genes that would grow hair to make Fabio weep with envy.

"People are already asking me these questions," says Julio Fernandez, a San Diego plastic surgeon. "One woman asked me for 'Mexican' genes. I asked, 'Why? For the accent?' She said she wants dark, tan skin but she was scared of going out in the sun. She's already had a few [benign skin cancers] removed."

Fernandez says as Baby Boomers enter their 50s, they are horrified at the prospect of looking—and performing—old. "Look what it's done for Viagra," he chuckles.

Would he do cosmetic gene therapy?

"I'm not trained in it, so I wouldn't. But if it was proven safe, why not? It's a question of personal choice, like shaving your head or getting a tattoo. Kids today, with the piercings and body mutilations, they're already comfortable with these ideas," he says.

Genetic personality traits

But transforming the body is only half the picture. For nearly 40 years, researchers have been examining the role DNA plays in personality. Shyness, risk-taking, panic disorder and depression are all understood to be hereditary traits. This year, psychiatric researchers in Ottawa announced they had found a gene mutation that makes people more vulnerable to suicide.

"This could even lead to gene therapy," Pavel Hrdina, a Royal Ottawa Hospital neurobiologist, suggested at the time.

Why treat a patient with antidepressants when the genes that regulate thought can be corrected? It may be impossible to confer Einstein's genius, but how about the fearlessness of Charles Lindbergh or Sir Edmund Hillary? Many people are uncomfortable with the idea that human beings are elastic vessels whose properties can be shifted at will. "Only the rich will have access to these possibilities," says Nisker.

Do you think that offering a woman money in exchange for her eggs is an ethically sound way of bringing life into the world?

What social pressures are there for the old to appear younger than they really are?

Find out more about DNA and personality traits at www.time.com/ time/magazine/ 1998/dom/980427/ science.the_person ality_8.html.

COMMENTARY: Prodigy

The nature/nurture debate surfaces in the case of child prodigies. It asks how much of their ability stems from inborn talent, and how much is because of the teaching of obsessive parents?

The Archbishop of Salzburg patronized Leopold Mozart, a very talented and successful violinist and composer who

Musical ability is a characteristic of some child prodigies.

wrote a treatise on violins. However, the world might never have heard of Leopold had it not been for his prodigiously gifted son, Wolfgang Amadeus Mozart (1756–1791), who could play the klavier at the age of three and was composing his own music a mere two years later. Leopold devoted much of his time to training his son and daughter, Nannerl, and has often been accused of exploiting their gifts. But no amount of training could have produced such a great composer as Wolfgang Amadeus Mozart if ability had not been present in the first place.

Child prodigies are very rare and tend to attract attention and achieve fame quickly. Some, such as the violinist Yehudi Menuhin, retain their fame as adults—their talent is not only precocious, but also greater than that of an ordinary adult. This is, however, quite unusual.

Which category will Kissandra Cohen fall into? As a small child she achieved fame as an actor, and as a 10-year-old Cohen had gotten the top grade in a UCLA calculus class. She later gained her diploma, in two majors, from Duke University when she was just 17. In Cohen's case the talent was there—she was reading Dr. Seuss at the age of two—and her mother struggled to keep up with the academic demands of her brilliant daughter.

One child prodigy who has achieved national fame is Piyush "Bobby" Jindal, who is 28. The first Indian American to be nominated by President George W. Bush for a senior administration position, Jindal graduated from high school when he was 16 and completed his college degree four years later. At 24 he was the secretary of the Louisiana Department of Health and Hospitals. Again, although he received great encouragement, the talent was inborn. But what would the future hold if genetic enhancement could "implant" such talent into the womb?

"We're defining the fittest in our society as the wealthiest. It's elitist selection based on finances."

When it's possible to drink from the fountain of youthful DNA, those who choose to live and age naturally could come to be viewed as freaks.

Yet our society could not survive without freaks.

Last year, researchers at London's Robarts Research Institute found a genetic mutation in the chemokine receptors of white blood cells that makes 1 percent of all Caucasians resistant to HIV. Based on genetic analysis, the scientists speculated the mutation evolved at least 700 years earlier, and may have protected carriers against smallpox. Without such variations in its genome, our species could not survive future plagues and pandemics.

Personality traits and creativity

Similarly, many of the greatest works of literature, art, and science have been created by manic-depressives (more correctly known as people suffering from bipolar disorder). In their hypomanic state, humans are capable of extraordinary leaps. Lord Byron, Samuel Coleridge, Vincent Van Gogh, Robert Lowell, John Berryman, Sylvia Plath, Theodore Roethke, Le Corbusier, and Virginia Woolf are but a few "bipolars" who helped change the world. Yet in their depressed state, these people may become self-destructive, such as the time when Van Gogh cut off his ear. Indeed, Einstein himself is believed to have suffered from depression.

Find out how this disorder affects people at www.nimh.nih.gov/publicat/manic.cfm.

It may be that using gene therapy as liquid paper to "white out" our perceived imperfections won't work. Perhaps it is our flaws that draw us toward perfection.

GENE HUNTERS EXTRAORDINAIRE
Michael Legault and Margaret Munro

Lap-Chee Tsui personifies the promise of science to undo cruel fate.

His team at Toronto's Hospital for Sick Children discovered the gene that causes the deadly lung disorder cystic fibrosis in 1989 and has been searching for a cure ever since.

"It's amazing to see how people crowd around him at conferences and meetings," says Stephen Scherer, one of Tsui's colleague at the hospital's Centre for Applied Genomics. "It's like he's a rock star or celebrity."

In a field of science known for its oversized egos, Tsui is anything but pretentious. He is informal, cheerful, and persistent. Tsui can often be found in his office long into the evening contemplating faulty genes. Or plotting ways to sell the importance of genetics to the likes of Paul Martin, the Finance Minister, who announced $160-million in financing for Genome Canada in the budget.

Find out about work carried out at a typical genome center at www.genome. washington.edu/ UWGC/.

"It's not quite what we were after but we're happy," says Tsui, who co-chaired the Genome Canada committee of academic and industry researchers that had been pushing the government to invest $250-million to set up genome centers across the country. The provinces have also pledged substantial investments in the five new centres that will be based in the Atlantic provinces, Quebec, Ontario, the Prairies, and British Columbia.

Technological requirements

Tsui and his colleagues note that many disease-related genes have been discovered in Canada or by Canadians. But many of the discoveries are being put to work in the United States, where scientists can get access to the costly machines and cash needed to develop tests and treatments.

Find out more about DNA sequencing at www.celera. com/genomics/news /whats_a_genome/C hp2_1.cfm.

Some gene-hunting facilities in the United States have hundreds of new high-speed DNA sequencing machines, while Tsui's group—one of the most advanced in Canada— has only two of the machines. This makes it increasingly hard to compete.

Details on the new Canada genomic centres are still being worked out, but the plan is to provide Canadian scientists with technical capabilities and services "that will greatly enhance the efficiency of their work and make possible projects that otherwise could not be undertaken." One or two centres will specialize in reading or sequencing genes, another in so-called proteomics, which is the simultaneous study of proteins produced by genes, while others will focus on how genes function.

Researching gene mutations

With Genome Canada launched, the affable Tsui is hoping to spend a little less time on politics and a bit more on genetics. His own work has evolved into a continuing study of the molecular genetics of cystic fibrosis. As director of the Center for Applied Genomics at Sick Kids, Tsui oversees five principal researchers and their work, much of it focused on identifying the genes on chromosome seven, known to be particularly rich with disease-causing mutations.

Find out more about cystic fibrosis at www.cff.org.

It is on chromosome seven that Tsui and his colleagues found the small segment of mutated DNA responsible for cystic fibrosis, which affects one in 2,400 babies and kills half the sufferers before they reach adulthood.

Treatment, at present, is a daily whacking on the back and chest cavity to loosen and free mucus in the lining of the lungs. It is an exhausting, painful, and artificial way to accomplish what healthy lungs do naturally. [And] as time goes by, the possibility increases that a virus or bacteria will find fertile breeding grounds in the clogged lungs, leading to an infection that is often fatal.

Tsui became intrigued with cystic fibrosis, which is one of the most common and deadly hereditary diseases, soon after arriving at the University of Toronto in 1981. (He was born in China, raised in Hong Kong, and educated as a molecular biologist in the United States.) He and his colleagues began their search for the gene with the help of about 50 Canadian families who had two or more children with the disease.

Discovering a cure

To speed up the search, he enlisted the help of Francis Collins, now director of the U.S. National Human Genome Research Institute, who had developed a more efficient technique for examining DNA. In August 1989 they announced they had found the gene, raising hope that a cure would be just around the corner.

Find out more about curing cystic fibrosis with gene therapy at www.school science.co.uk/ content/5/biology/ mrc/3/page5.html.

"After we found the CF gene, a lot of people jumped very quickly to the conclusion that we would have a cure in five years using gene therapy," Tsui says. "People thought, now you found [the problem with] the gene, so put the good gene

COMMENTARY: Eugenics

This undated file picture shows the dissected brains and skulls of some 400 Nazi victims of eugenic policies at the Baumgartner Hoehe—a psychiatric hospital in Vienna.

Eugenics—the science of genetic improvement through selective breeding—has long been a controversial issue. It carries inevitable suggestions either of racist thought or of intolerance of people who do not "fit" society's often created ideals. It particularly suffers from its association with the extreme behavior of the Nazis in 1930s Germany.

Interest in eugenics grew in early 20th-century Germany: People perceived as "good stock" were encouraged to breed, but those of "bad stock" were discouraged from doing so—sometimes forcibly. New societies were founded in Germany to promote the idea of creating a race of new and improved Germans for the New Reich. In 1933 the government passed a law for the compulsory sterilization of those with hereditary defects. Under the Nazis the provisions were extended to those with mental defects, sufferers of schizophrenia, manic depressives, epileptics, and even to alcoholics. The Nazis enthusiastically embraced not only medical "improvement," but also "racial hygiene," sterilizing gypsies and other people who didn't fit into the political, social, or ethnic makeup of Hitler's Germany. The logic behind such practices culminated in the Holocaust, which killed millions of Jews, gypsies, and homosexuals. Eugenics had been used to excuse genocide.

The Nazis did not have a monopoly on eugenics in Europe. Programs also existed in states more usually celebrated for their liberalness and social tolerance. The U.S. writer P. J. O'Rourke once observed that he never noticed any crazy people in Sweden: "Where are the mutterers, the twitchers, the loony importunate?" The truth of the absence of such eccentricity lay partly in the practice of state-controlled eugenics. Between 1934 and 1974 a national program in Sweden forcibly sterilized the mentally ill and others that the government judged to be unsuitable as parents. More than 62,000 people fell victim to this program. Such practices may come as a surprise in a country often praised as socially liberal—but there was nothing secret about the program in Sweden. Most Swedes knew it was going on but believed it was a way of creating a better society.

back. In reality, things aren't so simple." They are in fact incredibly complicated. So far a bewildering array of more than 850 different mutations have been found on the CF gene, some much more common than others. The most common mutation—which is common to about 90 percent of people with cystic fibrosis—is due to three nucleotides (pairs of molecules that form DNA) on the gene that are out of sequence. As a result, a key protein does not fold properly, says Tsui. "Because the protein is misfolded it gets trapped inside cellular compartments and is not able to perform its proper function in the cells of the lungs."

He likens it to a bureaucrat's refusal to release a report because it contains a spelling mistake. The analogy is appropriate, says Tsui, because once the protein reaches the right region of the cell membrane it will function as well as a perfectly formed protein.

Further investigations

Although much work remains to be done, the molecular biologists are confident they will eventually find better treatments, perhaps even a cure.

Find out more about Lap-Chee Tsui's work at www.sickkids.on. ca/research/profiles/ tsui.asp.

Tsui, who has been named a fellow of England's Royal Society for his work on cystic fibrosis, downplays his role in gene-related disease research, insisting that being the first to find the CF gene was more a result of dogged persistence and timing than any special talent or breakthrough science.

Summary

The two articles explore the pros and cons of genetic manipulation. Furthermore, the commentary boxes highlight how child prodigies can arise and also examine the other side of the coin—the use of eugenics to create a race of seemingly perfect people, but taken to an appalling extreme as seen in Nazi Germany between 1933 and 1945, and also in the sterilization policies of Sweden, which carried on until late in the 20th century.

Brad Evenson—the Pro author—believes that genetic manipulation is wrong because of the inevitable abuse of the technology in the future. He argues that cosmetic gene therapy will supersede its medical applications and create a society where those who can afford treatment will create perfect children. Evenson also reminds us of Nazi eugenic experiments, in which people with "undesirable" personality traits, such as homosexuality, were targeted.

Michael Legault and Margaret Munro—the Con authors—concentrate on the imminent use of gene manipulation and its ability to eradicate hereditary disease. They do not look to future abuse of the technology, but concentrate on the here and now. In their view the ability to cure people of debilitating, painful, and often fatal diseases outweighs the considerations put forward by Evenson. They cite the work of Lap-chee Tsui as an example of how this technology can be used for good.

FURTHER INFORMATION:

Books:

Russo, Enzo. *Genetic Engineering*, Oxford: Oxford University Press, 1998.

Wilmut, Ian, Keith Campbell, and Colin Tudge, *The Second Creation*. New York: Headline, 2001.

Useful websites:

www.ornl.gov/hgmis/publicat/judicature/article6.html
Maxwell J. Mehlman, "The Human Genome Project and the Courts, Gene Therapy and Beyond."

www.princeton.edu/~wws320/Second%20Pages/06Reprotech/Cloning/Wisdom%20of%20repugnance.htm
Leon R. Kass, "The Wisdom of Repugnance."

www.ncpa.org/health/pdh/july98d.html
National Center for Policy Analysis article "Health Care Issues: Legal Status of Human Cloning."

http://vector.cshl.org//
The DNA Learning Center, Genes in Education.

www.cancernet.nci.nih.gov/clinpdq/therapy/
National Cancer Institute article on gene therapy.

The following debates in the Pro/Con series may also be of interest:

In this volume:

IS GENE MANIPULATION WRONG?

YES: The risk of babies being born with painful or even fatal conditions would be eradicated

YES: Gene manipulation could eliminate genetically transmitted diseases forever and therefore reduce suffering

DISABILITY
Should any genes that cause disabilities be removed?

DISEASE
Should scientists be able to get rid of genes that pass on hereditary diseases?

NO: This could be abused—who determines what a disability is? For example, could it be seen as height, weight, or color of eyes?

NO: Some people would argue that sexual preference, such as being homosexual, is a disease— and this could be abused

IS GENE MANIPULATION WRONG?

KEY POINTS

YES: Why should parents not be able to give their offspring the best start in life?

YES: Enhancement would lead to a better adjusted, more healthy, and more intelligent population

ENHANCEMENT
If genes for improving artistic, intellectual, or sports prowess are identified, should society be able to "improve" future children?

NO: Only the rich will be able to afford genetic enhancement for their children

NO: Children should be wanted for their own sake and not as predesigned packages

Topic 4
SHOULD U.S. PRIVACY LAWS INCLUDE GENETIC TESTING?

YES
"NEW GENETIC TESTING METHODS REQUIRE STRONGER PRIVACY LAWS"
GEORGE LEWIS

NO
"GENETIC TESTING IN LIFE INSURANCE: TO BE, OR NOT TO BE"
KARI GREGORY, LANCE KAYFISH,
AND NORMA NIELSON

INTRODUCTION

Life is a lottery. No one knows if they will be involved in a car crash, will become unemployed, or will suffer an accidental injury in the home. It is possible, however, to assess the risks of any of these occurrences happening and to insure ourselves against injury or loss of income. Insurance against specific contingencies—financial protection for property or health, for example—is part of modern life. We need protection against injury, damage, or loss of income. We are willing to pay regular premiums to obtain protection. In some cases the risk can be assessed with some degree of accuracy. The value of our household goods or our car can be determined very easily. However, life and medical insurance can be more difficult.

Insurance companies routinely ask our physicians about our state of health. Medical tests are normal before an insurance policy is confirmed. An insurance company is not a philanthropic institution: It needs to know the chances that its customers might become ill owing to their health and previous medical history.

That medical history includes their medical inheritance. Insurance forms ask questions concerning the health of our parents and grandparents. They ask whether our immediate ancestors are still alive; if they suffer, or suffered, any serious health problems; and, if they are deceased, what caused their death. Many medical conditions are hereditary. Before an insurance company can make any decisions concerning the risk of insuring us, they have a right to know whether our parents suffered from, say, heart disease.

In some cases diseases or medical conditions are not in themselves genetically related, but the likelihood that we might succumb to these conditions is hereditary. Again, an insurance company would want to take such considerations into account.

The Human Genome Project (HGP) (see page 56) has the potential to alter the entire playing field. Our personal genetic charts will, for the first time, be able to be mapped. Our individual medical inheritance will be deciphered.

What are the implications of this advance in medical science? Many people are already frightened that insurance companies will use genetic information gathered in this way to refuse insurance cover. There is a fear that genetics will create an underclass of people—those who are to all appearances healthy, but who will be unable to obtain insurance because of damaging genetic information.

"Even at birth the whole individual is destined to die, and perhaps his organic disposition may already contain the indication of what he is to die from."

—SIGMUND FREUD, PSYCHOLOGIST

Could people lose their jobs because of their genetic profile? Could people be denied health insurance because of the results of genetic tests? The topic is a minefield strewn with issues of personal privacy and legal protection set against an insurance company's or employer's perceived right to know. At present, if one withholds from an insurance company information that might prejudice its decisions about a policy, the agreement becomes invalid.

If genetics were to give companies a much clearer picture of our health, or potential health, would withholding that information equally make any

insurance agreement invalid? And should the insurance industry have the right to demand genetic tests as a condition for providing insurance cover to any individual?

In many ways this issue is one for the future rather than for the present. The complete genome map does not mean that science will then be able to know everything about your future health. There are still imponderables and room for error. It will take many years for geneticists to understand what the genome map means. In the meantime, the knowledge that can be gained is partial and therefore not substantial enough to base financial decisions on. No insurance company yet uses genetic profiles, and it is the general feeling in the insurance industry that it will be a very long time before it will be in a position to do so safely.

The following articles examine the moral and commercial issues involved. George Lewis believes legislation is required. Worried by the loss of privacy, he warns that genetic testing might lead to the loss of a job or to the refusal of health insurance. Lewis outlines an argument for legal protection and states that your genetic chart should remain as private information between you and your physician.

In the second article—extracts from a paper prepared by Kari Gregory, Lance Kayfish, and Norma Nielson for Risk Management and Insurance—the authors take great care to reassure readers that the genetic information currently available is not yet reliable enough to form the basis of insurance decisions. But they say that when reliable genetic information is available, life insurers should be given access to that data. They outline the benefits for the insured as well as the insurers.

NEW GENETIC TESTING METHODS REQUIRE STRONGER PRIVACY LAWS
George Lewis

The Human Genome Project was begun in 1990. A joint effort by the U.S. Department of Energy and the National Institutes of Health, its main goal is to identify all of the approximately 30,000 genes in human DNA. The project is scheduled for completion in 2003 (see page 56). Visit the project's website at www.ornl.gov/ TechResources/ Human_Genome/ project/about.html.

Scientists working on the Human Genome Project are well on the way to identifying all the genes in DNA. DNA (deoxyribonucleic acid) and RNA (ribonucleic acid) are the two chemical substances involved in the genetic transmission of characteristics from parent to offspring, and in the manufacture of proteins. A genome is all the DNA in an organism, including its genes. Genes carry information for making all the proteins required by an organism. The proteins determine, among other things, how the organism looks, how well its body metabolizes food or fights infection, and sometimes even how it behaves. This means that once scientists are able to determine the sequences of the three billion pairs of chemical bases that make up human DNA, hereditary defects or predispositions that may lead to future illness will be able to be identified in people very early, often at the start of their lives. Such information could prove vital to the individual, but it will also be available to any other interested party, say an employer or insurance company, until more privacy laws or other forms of protection, are adopted.

Access to information about your DNA will be achieved in the following ways: through carrier screening, which involves identifying unaffected individuals who carry one copy of a gene for a disease that requires two copies for the disease to be expressed; prenatal diagnostic testing; newborn screening; and presymptomatic testing to predict adult-onset disorders such as Huntington's chorea, Alzheimer's disease, and cancer.

How realistic are the scenarios the author presents? Would legislation safeguard the privacy of the individual?

Implications

One of the future benefits of this advance is that medical science may be able to treat disorders before they get a grip on the body. It may also help prevent conditions that are life-threatening if not detected in good time. Yet many diseases may remain incurable, and perhaps the most significant implication of the Human Genome Project is that it might be possible to determine at birth the likeliest cause of a person's death (barring accident). However, we should remember that genes only show predispositions, not inevitable outcomes.

Genetic information acquired on each individual will be stored on databases so that eventually there will be an electronically retrievable genome dossier on almost everyone. There are already similar files that can tell moneylenders about your creditworthiness and the police about your criminal record. Doctors have long been able to look at your medical history, but soon they will be able to predict your future health with greater certainty than ever before.

The legal and social issues

This is an exciting breakthrough, but it also introduces many problems that will have to be addressed. The first is the legal issue. The Human Genome Project is currently run by the U.S. government. In view of the potential dangers of so many intimate personal details being available to the state, on February 8, 2000, President Bill Clinton signed an executive order that prohibited federal departments and agencies from using genetic information when hiring new staff or promoting existing employees.

When the Human Genome Project is completed, the results will be transferred to the private sector. This itself is a matter of controversy, but genetic information is red hot no matter who owns it—banks, courts, schools, adoption agencies, the armed forces. So far the main public concerns are about possible abuse by insurers and employers. If an insurance company knows that a certain disease runs in your family, it may either refuse to cover you or raise your premium to an unaffordable level. If it learns that you already had a certain illness when you took out your policy, even though you were unaware of it, it may invalidate your cover: "pre-existing conditions" are currently grounds for revoking any insurance.

The accessibility of genetic information can also influence social issues, such as discrimination. For instance, employers may try to avoid hiring anyone they believe likely to take excessive sick leave, retire early for health reasons, file for compensation, or use health care benefits a great deal. Some firms may even try to use genetic tests to discriminate against workers—including those who do not and may never show signs of disease—because management fears the cost consequences of keeping such employees on the payroll. Many people are worried that such discrimination may increase as further research makes DNA testing cheaper and more widely accessible. Genetic predispositions could lead to discrimination, even in cases where workers are healthy and unlikely to develop disease or where the genetic condition has no effect on their ability to do the work satisfactorily.

What is the difference between organizations having access to your criminal and credit records compared to their gaining access to your genetic information?

Should something as important as insurance be left to market forces like other products?

For further research into the issues caused by genetics and insurance see The Howard Hughes Medical Institute website at www.hhmi.org/genmedinsure.htm

Another legal concern is that firms might take DNA samples from their employees without permission—for example, by sending swabs from their coffee cups for laboratory analysis—in order to find out who might die of what. The only sure way to prevent this kind of practice is by effective privacy legislation.

What forms might discrimination on the basis of genetic makeup take?

The need for privacy protection

At present, U.S. law provides inadequate protection against employment discrimination based on genetic information. The only reliable way to ensure that genetic technology and research are used properly to address the health needs of the nation, rather than to deny individuals employment opportunities and benefits, is by comprehensive federal legislation supplemented by state laws.

Because DNA samples can be held indefinitely, there is the additional threat that test results will be used for purposes other than those for which they were originally gathered. There is, for example, a growing fear that pharmaceutical companies might send unsolicited drugs to treat illnesses that they know the addressee might contract because of his or her genetic profile.

To what other uses could a person's genetic information be put if it were made available to everyone?

Thus obtaining or disclosing genetic information about employees or potential employees should be prohibited, except in cases where it is necessary to provide medical treatment to employees, ensure workplace health and safety, or provide data for occupational and health researchers. In every case where genetic information about employees is obtained, it should be subject to legally enforcable federal and state privacy protections.

Toward appropriate legislation

These were among the main findings of a 1988 report to the Clinton Administration that recommended legislation to ensure discoveries made possible by the Human Genome Project are used to improve health, rather than to discriminate against workers or their families. The report also stated that employers should not require or request employees or potential employees to take genetic tests or to provide genetic information as a condition of employment or benefits; that employers should not use genetic information to discriminate against, limit, segregate, or classify employees in any way that would deprive them of employment opportunities; and that employers should not obtain or disclose genetic information about employees or potential employees, except under special circumstances.

Without federal legislation, future genetic tests may not be adequately controlled for accuracy and reliability. It is perfectly possible that some people will be genetically programmed for a particular illness yet never develop it—there are still uncertainties associated with gene tests for susceptibilities and complex conditions, such as heart disease, because we still have insufficient evidence about the significance of various interactions between multiple genes and their environment. If genome information is widely available without any statutory limitation, people may be stigmatized for some condition that they do not have and will never get.

The moral and philosophical issues

The Human Genome Project also gives rise to numerous ethical concerns. Is it right to perform a DNA test when no treatment is available for the disease that it identifies? Should parents be at liberty to let their children be tested for adult-onset diseases? What, if anything, does genomic information tell us about minority communities—does the increased susceptibility of certain groups to particular diseases, such as that of Africans, Afro-Caribbeans, and some Asians to sickle cell anemia, make them different in other ways too? Without adequate legislation, it will be impossible to ensure that health care personnel counsel parents properly about the risks and limitations of genetic technology. Patients must be made aware of all the relevant data before deciding whether to give doctors the go-ahead for complex and potentially controversial procedures. For example, even with the most up-to-date fetal testing, it is still impossible to be sure that an unborn child with the genes for a fatal adult-onset illness will develop it. If parents have to decide whether to terminate a pregnancy, it is imperative that they are clear whether they are acting in anticipation of a likelihood or a certainty.

How might the results of such DNA testing for incurable or adult-onset diseases influence the life of the individual?

The Human Genome Project also has many conceptual and philosophical implications regarding responsibility, free will versus genetic determinism, and concepts of health and disease. Do people's genes make them behave in a particular way? Can people always control their behavior? What does our society regard as acceptable diversity? Where do we draw the line between medical treatment and enhancement? These questions are probably unanswerable, but the absence of certainty in these areas makes it all the more important to put in place legislation that prevents us from abusing our newly acquired knowledge and helps us avoid the temptation to become involved in social engineering.

GENETIC TESTING IN LIFE INSURANCE
Kari Gregory, Lance Kayfish, and Norma Nielson

NO

Since the late 1980s, scientists have been trying to identify more than 6,500 genetic diseases that humans now suffer, and up until now about one-half have been identified. A person's DNA (deoxyribonucleic acid) can determine with high accuracy their chances of getting some specific hereditary diseases. Therefore, through analysis of a person's DNA, individuals and insurance companies may be able to better predict a potential insured's mortality.

This presents the problem of adverse selection because genetic testing is something that is currently available in some areas…. If people have access to these tests, and are getting them done, the insurance companies could be victims of adverse selection. People who are getting these tests, and are receiving results that are positive for predispositions to genetic diseases, may then [be] insuring themselves at rates which are not representative of the risk they hold (because the potential insured is not at this time required to disclose such information). If this were to happen frequently it could compromise the mortality calculation and pooling principles that insurers use to calculate their risks, which could eventually lead to insolvency.

The DNA molecule contains all the information needed to construct and operate a human body. Each person's DNA is—for all practical purposes—unique.

Understanding genetic blueprints

Results of genetic tests [usually] elicit normal findings with only a minority having abnormal results. Through further understanding of these genes, those with abnormal results retain the possibility of changing their lifestyle, undergoing special treatments, or trying emerging gene therapies to attempt avoiding the consequences of their genetic blueprints. With these points in mind it seems that the insurance industry would not change as drastically as once suspected because normal results would be a majority. Depending on the size of the majority, rates could even drop. Also, the possibilities that avoiding the results of predispositions to illness as identified by genetic testing through alternative and preventative methods may even demonstrate insurability for those individuals with negative test results.…

Do you agree that a better understanding of people's genetic makeup would enable them to modify or change their lifestyle to avoid potential health problems?

Genetic testing today

"No insurance companies are now using DNA tests in underwriting unless it's already in someone's medical record. Insurers of course do use things like blood tests and cholesterol tests, which can be considered a type of genetic testing." This statement made by Roberta Meyer, senior counsel for the American Council of Life Insurance, provides insight into how current testing techniques can be seen as having genetic testing undertones. Current underwriting practices have become very good at deriving information from sources that insurance companies are legally allowed to tap. Common tests include saliva, urine, blood, and cholesterol testing as mentioned above. Medicals with a licensed doctor can be requested by the insuring company. The life insurer, with written permission from the potential insured, also has the option of contacting their current physician to inquire about any information that may pertain to life insurance being issued. All of these methods allow underwriters to take a fairly elaborate look at the medical status of a potential insured. The accessibility the insurer has to medical information now is quite astounding.

Who benefits from genetic testing?

The access to such information has put insurers in a good position to make well-informed decisions about a potential insured's suitability for coverage, which has often benefited consumers in the past. This point is demonstrated by the statistic that 55 percent of applications from people with cardiovascular problems were declined in 1952 but only 25 percent were turned down in 1992. What's more, in 1958 only 2 percent of individual life insurance policies were issued to individuals over 55 years of age, but in 1993 that number became 11 percent. From this we can see that increased technology in recent years has allowed underwriters to make better use of information at their disposal. In the past, along with improvements in medical testing, insurance has become more affordable and, as demonstrated above, more widely available....

The advent of genetic testing may undermine the value of underwriting in the insuring process causing astronomical changes to the industry. In life insurance the underwriting process that has so far been in place based on historical mortality data is a tried method of dealing with risk classification. Genetic testing could dramatically change the underwriting process and reconfigure the manner in which the principal of pooling is currently applied to insuring life.

"Underwriting" an insurance policy means that a person or company agrees to become liable in case of certain losses specified in that policy.

Do you think that these tests are fundamentally different from genetic testing?

With the wide variety of medical data already available to insurance companies, is it necessary that they should also have access to DNA profiling?

COMMENTARY: The Human Genome Project

A U.S. scientist examines DNA gel as part of genetic engineering research.

The Human Genome Project (HGP) was formally begun in October 1990. The project is an international effort set up to discover and map all of the approximately 30,000 to 35,000 human genes and also to determine the complete sequence of the 3 billion DNA subunits. At least 18 countries are involved in the project, and work is expected to continue until at least 2003. The U.S. has one of the largest contributing roles, and the joint coordinators are the U.S. Department of Energy and the National Insititutes of Health. Aside from the purely technical and medical aspects, the project is also charged with addressing the ethical, legal, and social issues that may arise from its work.

The main purpose of the Human Genome Project is to gain knowledge about the effects of DNA variations among individuals, which, it is hoped, will lead to revolutionary new ways to diagnose, treat, and ultimately to prevent thousands of the diseases and disorders that affect us all.

Such changes may turn out positively for insureds and insurers alike. Advocates in favor of using information provided by genetic testing believe it could allow coverage to become more affordable because of the specific information it provides. They feel it would take the guessing game out of underwriting. For instance, genetic testing could reveal that a person who would normally have been thought to be a bad risk to insurance companies because of family medical history might be proven to carry none of the destructive genes, thus making an uninsurable person, insurable. The ratio of how many people are currently accepted for life insurance to the number declined is not expected to change with genetic testing. Also, the ratio of how many people applying are offered standard rates to those offered higher rates is not expected to change.

With genetic testing making its debut, the face of insurance would change in many other ways as well. The pooling principle that today's insurance industry is so solidly based on would be altered:

"Insurance is based on the complementary principles of solidarity and equity in the face of uncertain risks. Solidarity implies the sharing by the population, as a whole or in broad groups, of the responsibility and the benefits in terms of cost, while equity means that the contribution of an individual should be roughly in line with his or her known level of risk."

Basically, the method that is followed today is everyone is pooled together and pays premiums according to their scientific test results and personal information. Examples of scientific tests are blood, cholesterol, and saliva testing. These tests reveal only a limited amount of information. Personal information would include the following: age, family history of illness, and so on. This way everyone pays premiums reflecting the probability of a claim being made at a future date. By pooling everyone together, the law of averages helps to disperse the risk of the policies among everyone. However, once genetic testing is started, everyone becomes more their own risk because the probability of death of any one person would be more easily identified. Understanding when and how an individual will die would be in their genetic blueprints, unless, of course, it is accidental.

Hence, underwriting would become more accurate. Premiums could reflect each individual's risk and would not have to be priced to take into account other insureds' risks. That is, the low risk insureds would not be subsidizing the high risk insureds. From the point of view of most insurance companies, they feel being able to fully assess risks is a positive thing because it makes insurance more fair for everyone.

> The authors seem to be completely positive of the benefits of genetic testing. Can you see any major problems?

> The authors give no source for their quote. Quotes should always be attributed.

> Is this a fairer system? Might this mean that some people will have to pay more than they can afford for insurance?

Summary

These two articles contrast not only in position but also in style. In the first article George Lewis is troubled by the invasion of privacy that genetic testing for health insurance—and for other reasons—would bring. He worries that genetic data could be abused or misused, both intentionally and accidentally. This article advocates legal protection and the necessity of obtaining permission from an individual before his or her genetic profile is used for insurance or any other purposes.

The second article—extracted from a much longer paper prepared by Kari Gregory, Lance Kayfish, and Norma Nielson writing within the insurance industry—takes a dispassionate, almost legalistic, look at the present and future. It gives reassurance that the current state of genetic knowledge prevents insurance companies from making any adverse decisions regarding, for example, health insurance. It states that the insurance industry is unlikely to change drastically, since the majority of results from genetic testing would, in any case, be normal. It goes on to highlight what it sees as the benefits of testing to the insured. Since people pay premiums that reflect the probability of a claim being made, genetic testing would bring reduced premiums for those with "clear" results.

The pros and cons of both sides of this issue are summarized in the diagram opposite.

FURTHER INFORMATION:

Books:

Davies, Kevin, *Cracking the Genome: Inside the Race to Unlock Human DNA*. New York: Free Press, 2001.
Frank-Kaminetskii, Maxim D., *Unraveling DNA: The Most Important Molecule of Life*. London: Perseus Press, 1997.
Tudge, Colin, *The Impact of the Gene*. New York: Hill and Wang Publishing, 2001.

Useful websites:

www.kaiserpermanente.org/medicine/permjournal/winter98pj/gentest.html
"The Coming Tidal Wave," by Al Weiland.
www.geneletter.org/10-0200/features/insuranceimpact.html
"The Impact of Genetics on Insurance and Insurability," by Charles C. Cantor.
www.time.com/time/magazine/article/0,9171,1101990111-17689,00.html
"Playing the Odds: Health Insurers Want to Know What's in Your DNA," by Christopher Hallowell.
www.managedcaremag.com/archives/0006/0006.ethics.html
"Roll Over, Beethoven Your Genetic Profile's In," by Michael S. Victoroff.
www.uwm.edu/~strlab1/points_to_think_about.htm
Strickler Laboratory, "Points to Think About."
www.cnn.com/HEALTH/bioethics/9808/genetics.part2/template.html
"Genetic Testing and Insurance," by Jeffrey P. Kahn.

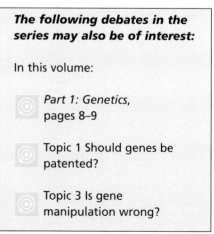

SHOULD U.S. PRIVACY LAWS INCLUDE GENETIC TESTING?

YES: DNA profiling may provide information that could be used to discriminate against people in the workplace or in other ways

YES: No one except the individual should know his or her genetic makeup unless he or she authorizes it

RESTRICTING ACCESS
Should legislation restrict access to a person's genetic test results?

THE RIGHT TO PRIVACY
Is genetic testing an invasion of privacy?

NO: A great deal of medical information is already available to groups such as insurance companies. DNA test profiles are no different than many other medical test results that it is currently legal to access.

NO: It is in a person's best interests that their DNA profile be known. Existing medical procedures already provide a wealth of data, and genetic testing is simply an additional tool for gaining information.

SHOULD U.S. PRIVACY LAWS INCLUDE GENETIC TESTING?

KEY POINTS

YES: An insurance company should be able to utilize any source of information before offering coverage since it stands to lose a lot of money in paying out the claims of its customers

YES: A genetic test may prove that a person previously thought to be uninsurable is, in fact, worthy of insurance coverage. A genetic test may help people modify their lifestyles to prevent potential health problems from occurring in the future.

GENETICS AND INSURANCE
Should insurance companies have the right to demand genetic testing before agreeing to provide insurance cover?

NO: A person has a right to privacy and should not be required to provide such personal information

NO: People who are thought to have detrimental DNA profiles will be forced to pay higher premiums

CRITICAL THINKING

Critical thinking is an approach to problems that involves the careful questioning of accepted beliefs or assertions, in order to distinguish which of them are logical and reasonable and which have no evidence or foundation. The technique is helpful in all areas of study.

1. WHAT SHOULD CRITICAL THINKING QUESTION?

Thinking in an analytical way will help you keep any discussion or argument focused. Stimulate your thinking with intelligent questions and reasoning, and always end with a rational conclusion. Critical thinking should help you focus on and question the following issues:

• ends and objectives

• sources of information/facts

• type of reasoning used

• assumptions underlying the concepts

2. SOME FUNDAMENTAL QUESTIONS

Asking some of the questions below will help you have a more structured and analytical way of thinking. Ask yourself:

• What is the fundamental issue here?
• Can I just assume the information here is correct?
• Should I check the statistics/dates?
• From what point of view should I approach this question/problem?
• Is this consistent with what has gone before?
• Is this a credible source of information?
• Should I double-check the statistics?

ORDINARY V. CRITICAL THINKING: DIFFERENCES

ORDINARY	CRITICAL THINKING
Guessing	Estimating
Preferring	Evaluating
Grouping	Classifying
Believing	Assuming
Inferring	Inferring logically
Associating concepts	Grasping principles
Supposing	Hypothesizing
Offering opinions without reasons	Offering opinions with reasons
Making judgments with no criteria	Making judgments with criteria

3. HOW CRITICAL THINKING EVOLVED

The ancients
Critical thinking is a well-established academic technique that has its roots in an ancient philosophical tradition. It was developed about 2,500 years ago by the Greek philosopher Socrates (469-399 B.C.). Other noted ancient Greek thinkers—including Plato (c.428-c.348 B.C.), Aristotle (384-322 B.C.), and the Skeptics, a group that questioned the truth of everything—similarly believed that only a trained and finely tuned mind can see beyond the surface to determine the real truth behind matters.

European thought
In the Middle Ages Thomas Aquinas (1225-1274) reiterated the need for society to challenge accepted thinking and attitudes. He showed that thinking critically did not necessarily mean the rejection of all established beliefs, just those that lack reasonable foundation. The European scholars Erasmus (about 1466-1536) and Thomas More (1478-1535) were influenced by these ideas and shared the view of their predecessors that critical analysis could be applied to most areas of life. More, in particular, in his book *Utopia* applied critical analysis to the existing social order in England to show how it might be improved. Macchiavelli's book *The Prince* (see *Government* volume, pages 176-181) also assessed modern politics, and he laid the foundation for modern critical political thought.

The thinkers of the French Enlightenment in the 18th century also contributed to the development of critical thinking, among them Montesquieu (see *Government* volume, pages 16-19), Voltaire, and Diderot. Their premise was that the mind is better equipped to deal with the social and political world if it is disciplined by reason and analysis. They believed that everyone and everything should be scrutinized through reasonable critical examination.

During the 18th century the conception of critical thinking developed further and produced such texts as Immanuel Kant's *Critique of Pure Reason* (1781) and Adam Smith's *Wealth of Nations* (1776). In the 19th and 20th centuries critical thinking spread to other disciplines, including politics, anthropology, and sociology.

Today critical thinking is a useful and essential skill that will help you in every area of life. Apply some of the above approaches to reasoning to the topics in this series, and it will help you have a more reasoned way of thinking. For further help see the following articles in the *Pro/Con* series:
- *Individual and Society*, pages 112-113, *The Value of Debate*
- *Government*, pages 58-59, *Research Skills*
- *Economics*, pages 60-61, *Argumentation Skills* and pages 210-211, *Speaking Skills*
- *Environment*, pages 186-187, *How to Write an Essay*

MEDICINE AND HEALTH

INTRODUCTION

Huge advances in medicine and health were made during the 20th century, from the development of antibiotics to organ transplantation and gene therapy. In the developed world fewer children die in infancy, life expectancy is longer, and the population in general is healthier than at the beginning of the 20th century. But with these benefits come added problems and dilemmas.

Alternative medicine

Although alternative medicine has been practiced for many centuries, its use today attracts much debate. Critics argue that alternative medicine does not work and is just a popular trend. However, increasing numbers of people have turned to alternative therapies since World War II. The World Health Organization has estimated that as many as 80 percent of the world's population use alternative medicine. With the massive growth in the trade of herbal medicines, the regulation and registration of alternative medicine are of major concern (see Topic 5).

In time herbal medicine may become as big a business as the orthodox drug industry. Pharmaceutical companies spend a lot of money researching new treatments for disease. They recoup this money by selling the resulting drugs for a large profit. But this means that some patients may be unable to afford medication. Topic 6 asks *Should Governments Limit the Price of Drugs?*

That would benefit sick people, but would it reduce the amount of money available for research on other new drugs?

Organ transplants

A relatively recent medical concern has been the use of organs in transplants. Although the first organ was transplanted in the 1950s, it is only since the 1970s that transplants have become more successful. As transplant operations have become more common, the supply of organs simply does not meet the demand of patients waiting for transplants. There are serious ethical issues surrounding the supply of organs for transplants. Organs need to be transplanted as soon as possible after the death of the donor, and many grief-stricken families find it difficult to consent to the use of their deceased loved ones' organs. Topic 7 asks *Should Organ Replacement Be a Commercial Enterprise?* If a person can receive payment for donating their blood, then should they not be able to do the same with one of their organs?

Origin of HIV/AIDS

The emergence of the HIV/AIDS virus was one of the most devastating health issues of the 20th century. Scientists and researchers have worked continually on tracing its origins. One theory is that it originated with polio vaccine testing in Africa in the 1950s.

African green monkeys were discovered to be the natural hosts of a virus similar to AIDS, simian immunodeficiency virus (SIV). The link with the polio vaccine was made because some vaccine was produced in kidney tissue from rhesus monkeys. The debate about this possible link continues, while some people argue that the origin of AIDS is

with euthanasia to bring about an early death. Is the doctor's role to preserve life at all costs or to alleviate suffering? Topic 10 asks *Should Doctors Be Able to Assist in Euthanasia?* These important questions are part of a greater dilemma of who has the right to make decisions about the individual: the doctor, the patient, or the family.

"In medicine, as in statecraft and propaganda, words are sometimes the most powerful drugs we can use."
—DR. SARA MURRAY JORDAN, GASTROENTEROLOGIST

---

not as important as finding a cure (see Topic 8).

Medical ethics have been an issue for as long as medicine has been a profession. The Hippocratic oath, attributed to Hippocrates in about 400 B.C., was adopted by the medical profession in the Middle Ages, but in the last half century its relevance has been questioned as doctor-patient relationships have changed. Malpractice cases against doctors have risen steadily in the United States, and this has led to calls for a stricter form of monitoring of doctors. One implication of such monitoring is that doctor-patient confidentiality could be at risk (see Topic 9).

A difficult issue central to the doctor-patient relationship is euthanasia. Should people with terminal illnesses be given nonpalliative treatment? They may be able to be treated, but at what cost to their quality of life? Should their symptoms simply be alleviated and they be allowed to die? Some people think that doctors should be allowed to assist

Religion v. medicine

Topic 11 asks *Should Religion Affect Parents' Medical Decisions?* Parents with strong religious beliefs sometimes refuse to allow some types of medical treatment needed by their child. In extreme cases this can lead to the child's death. This situation is difficult for nonbelievers to understand, but the parents often do not see their religious faith conflicting with the love for their child. Do parents have rights over the life or death of their child? Or should doctors or the courts overrule them when significant harm may result?

Drug testing has traditionally been carried out on animals, but this is now seen by some people as inflicting cruelty on animals and unnecessary now that alternative testing methods are available. Topic 12 asks *Should Medical Research on Animals Be Allowed?* Should medical experiments on animals be stopped? That may lead to delays in development, but the public may feel happier using cruelty-free treatments.

Topic 5
DO COMPLEMENTARY AND ALTERNATIVE MEDICINE WORK?

YES
"ALTERNATIVE MEDICINE AND THE TRUTH ABOUT BEING 'SCIENTIFIC' AND 'PROVEN'"
WWW.ALTERNATIVEMEDICINE.COM
BURTON GOLDBERG

NO
"HOMEOPATHY: THE ULTIMATE FAKE"
WWW.QUACKWATCH.COM/01QUACKERYRELATEDTOPICS/HOMEO.HTML
STEPHEN BARRETT, M.D.

INTRODUCTION

There are numerous treatments, known in the West as complementary and alternative medicine (CAM), which are now commonly used by many people. They include elements from some highly developed systems such as Chinese medicine; some elements of herbal medicine; and some therapies developed in the West. The World Health Organization (WHO) defines alternative medicine as a means of "protecting and restoring health that existed before the arrival of modern medicine."

Some of the most popular alternative treatments used in the West include massage (manipulation of the muscles), osteopathy (manipulation of the bones), homeopathy (using highly diluted doses of medication that produce similar symptoms as the ailment to stimulate the body's own defense and repair system), herbal medicine, faith healing, and acupuncture (stimulating pressure points on the body with needles). CAM

practitioners believe that it is their job to support and stimulate the natural healing ability inherent in each patient. Conventional medicine, or "biomedicine," tries to base the healing process on a series of physiological, physical, and chemical reactions that can be measured by modern science.

The use and application of alternative medicine has, however, led to much debate. Critics argue that alternative medicine does not work and that users are being deceived. They further assert that alternative medicine sometimes actually prevents patients from getting well and keeps them from undergoing life-saving biomedical treatment.

Yet advocates argue that although CAM medicine has only become increasingly popular in the West since World War II, its remedies served traditional communities for centuries before modern biomedical techniques became available to them. However, we can now judge the effectiveness of alternative medicine by the standards of conventional medicine. Has alternative medicine, for example, achieved the overwhelming successes of biomedical medicine, such as the eradication of smallpox, or the discovery of antibiotics to treat a vast range of infections?

"The trend of increased CAM therapy use across all cohorts since 1950, coupled with the strong persistence of use, suggests a continuing increased demand for CAM therapies that will affect all facets of health care delivery over the next 25 years."

—REPORT, HARVARD MEDICAL SCHOOL AND CENTER FOR ALTERNATIVE MEDICINE RESEARCH AND EDUCATION

Medicinal plants are the oldest known healthcare products and form the basic material in the composition of most drugs used in both CAM and biomedical treatments. The legislative controls for medicinal plants vary from country to country, resulting in different licensing, dispensing, safety, quality, and trade controls. Thus the establishment of international regulation and registration procedures is currently of major concern, especially with the growth in the international trade in herbal medicines. In 1996 a WHO scientific group of 100 international experts from around the world adopted a list of the medicinal plants that are widely used in healthcare, thus creating a formal register.

In 2001 WHO estimated that as much as 65–80 percent of the world's population relied on alternative medicine as their primary form of healthcare. WHO also stated that Chinese medicine, which relies heavily on herbal or "naturally based" remedies, should be promoted as a viable means of treating medical conditions. Other recent studies have shown that more and more people in the United States are turning to CAM remedies to treat their medical conditions. Alternative Medicine Online claims that one out of every three Americans has used some form of alternative medicine during their lifetime, and around 84 percent say they would use it again.

Nonbiomedical treatments are also becoming increasingly accepted by the medical profession. The American Medical Association (AMA) encourages its members to be "better informed regarding alternative (complementary) medicine and to participate in appropriate studies of it." Around a third of U.S. medical schools, among them Harvard, Yale, and John Hopkins, offer course work in alternative methods. Yet many doctors are also calling for formal regulation and legislation to prevent the abuse and misuse of CAM medicine. Its growing popularity has increased concern that it is now more liable to overblown hype and false claims.

The following two articles look at the CAM debate. The first argues that alternative medicine is finally getting the notice it deserves. The second article looks at homeopathy, arguing that it does not work and also needs proper regulation.

ALTERNATIVE MEDICINE AND THE TRUTH ABOUT BEING "SCIENTIFIC" AND "PROVEN"
Burton Goldberg

YES

Acupuncture is a Chinese method of puncturing the body with small needles at specific pressure points to alleviate pain or cure disease. "Fibromyalgia" is a muscle disorder that usually causes widespread muscle pain and tenderness. It has no obvious cause, but is thought to develop during periods of stress.

The U.S. government has belatedly confirmed a fact that millions of Americans have known personally for decades—acupuncture works.

A 12-member panel of medical "experts" recently informed the National Institutes of Health (NIH), its sponsor, that acupuncture is "clearly effective" for treating certain conditions, such as fibromyalgia, tennis elbow, pain following dental surgery, nausea during pregnancy, and nausea and vomiting associated with chemotherapy. The panel was less persuaded that acupuncture is appropriate as the sole treatment for headaches, asthma, addiction, menstrual cramps, and others.

The NIH panel reported that, in their view, "there are a number of cases" in which acupuncture works. As the modality has fewer side effects and is less invasive than conventional treatments, "it is time to take it seriously" and "expand its use into conventional medicine."

These developments are, naturally, welcome, and the field of alternative medicine should, by rights, be pleased with this progressive step. Underlying the NIH's endorsement and qualified "legitimization" of acupuncture is a deeper issue that must come to light. I refer to a presumption so deeply ingrained in Western society as to be almost invisible to all but the most discerning eyes. The presumption is that the "experts" of conventional medicine are entitled and qualified to pass judgment on the scientific and therapeutic merits of alternative medicine modalities. They are not.

Recounting a commonly accepted viewpoint and then using evidence to discredit it is a good way to establish your argument.

The matter hinges on the definition and scope of the term "scientific." The mainstream media is continually full of carping complaints by supposed medical experts that alternative medicine is not "scientific" and not "proven." Yet we never hear these experts take a moment out from their vituperations [condemnations] to examine the tenets and assumptions of their cherished scientific method to see if they are valid. They are not.

Medical historian Harris L. Coulter, Ph.D., author of the landmark four-volume history of Western medicine called *Divided Legacy*, first alerted me to a crucial, though unrecognized, distinction. The question we should ask is whether conventional medicine is scientific. Dr. Coulter argues convincingly that it is not.

The author uses evidence from a medical expert to lend credence to his opinion.

Evidence

Over the last 2,500 years, Western medicine has been divided by a powerful schism between two opposed ways of looking at physiology, health, and healing, says Dr. Coulter. What we now call conventional medicine (or allopathy) was once known as Rationalist medicine; alternative medicine, in Dr. Coulter's history, was called Empirical. Rationalist medicine is based on reason and prevailing theory, while Empirical medicine is based on observed facts and real-life experience—[of] what works.

Dr. Coulter makes some startling observations based on this distinction. Conventional medicine is alien, both in spirit and structure, to the scientific method of investigation, he says. Its concepts continually change with the latest breakthrough. Yesterday, it was germ theory; today, it's genetics; tomorrow, who knows?

Is the observation that medical thought in conventional medicine changes with fashion unfair? Look at ama.org—site of the American Medical Association—and try to see if you can find evidence to prove or disprove this statement.

With each changing fashion in medical thought, conventional medicine has to toss away its now outmoded orthodoxy and impose the new one, until it gets changed again. This is medicine based on abstract theory; the facts of the body must be contorted to conform to these theories or dismissed as irrelevant.

Doctors of this persuasion accept a dogma on faith and impose it on their patients, until it's proved wrong or dangerous by the next generation. They get carried away by abstract ideas and forget the living patients. As a result, the diagnosis is not directly connected to the remedy; the link is more a matter of guesswork than science. This approach, says Dr. Coulter, is "inherently imprecise, approximate, and unstable—it's a dogma of authority, not science." Even if an approach hardly works at all, it's kept on the books because the theory says it's good "science."

On the other hand, practitioners of Empirical, or alternative medicine, do their homework: they study the individual patients; determine all the contributing causes; note all the symptoms; and observe the results of treatment.

Homeopathy and Chinese medicine are prime examples of this approach. Both modalities may be added to because physicians in these fields and other alternative practices

See page 70 for a definition of "homeopathy."

It is important to define specific or unfamiliar terms.

constantly seek new information based on their clinical experience. This is the meaning of empirical: it's based on experience, then continually tested and refined—but not reinvented or discarded—through the doctor's daily practice with actual patients. For this reason, homeopathic remedies don't become outmoded; acupuncture treatment strategies don't become irrelevant.

Alternative medicine is proven every day in the clinical experience of physicians and patients. It was proven ten years ago and will remain proven ten years from now. According to Dr. Coulter, alternative medicine is more scientific in the truest sense than Western, so-called scientific medicine.

The FDA is the U.S. Food and Drug Agency. It is a consumer protection agency and monitors the safety of alternative medicines, among other things.

Sadly, what we see far too often in conventional medicine is a drug or procedure "proven" as effective and accepted by the FDA and other authoritative bodies only to be revoked a few years later when it's been proven to be toxic, malfunctioning, or deadly.

The double-blind study

The conceit of conventional medicine and its "science" is that substances and procedures must pass the double-blind study to be proven effective. But is the double-blind method the most appropriate way to be scientific about alternative medicine? It is not.

The guidelines and boundaries of science must be revised to encompass the clinical subtlety and complexity revealed by alternative medicine. As a testing method, the double-blind study examines a single substance or procedure in isolated, controlled conditions and measures results against an inactive or empty procedure or substance (called a placebo) to be sure that no subjective factors get in the way. The approach is based on the assumption that single factors cause and reverse illness, and that these can be studied alone, out of context and in isolation.

The double-blind study, although taken without critical examination to be the gold standard of modern science, is actually misleading, even useless, when it is used to study alternative medicine. We know that no single factor causes anything nor is there a "magic bullet" capable of single-handedly reversing conditions. Multiple factors contribute to the emergence of an illness and multiple modalities must work together to produce healing.

Equally important is the understanding that this multiplicity of causes and cures takes place in individual patients, no two of whom are alike in psychology, family medical history, and biochemistry. Two men, both of whom are 35 and have similar flu symptoms, do not necessarily and automatically have the same health condition, nor should they receive the same treatment. They might, but you can't count on it. The double-blind method is incapable of accommodating this degree of medical complexity and variation, yet these are physiological facts of life. Any approach claiming to be scientific which has to exclude this much empirical, real-life data from its study is clearly not true science. In a profound sense, the double-blind method cannot prove alternative medicine is effective because it is not scientific enough. It is not broad and subtle and complex enough to encompass the clinical realities of alternative medicine. If you depend on the double-blind study to validate alternative medicine, you will end up doubly blind about the reality of medicine.

Although Goldberg dismisses the double-blind study, he proposes no alternatives. Are there practical alternative methods to test the safety of drugs? Do drugs need to be tested at all?

Misconceptions

Listen carefully the next time you hear medical "experts" whining that a substance or method has not been "scientifically" evaluated in a double-blind study and is therefore not yet "proven" effective. They're just trying to mislead and intimidate you. Ask them how much "scientific" proof underlies using chemotherapy and radiation for cancer or angioplasty for heart disease. The fact is it's very little.

Try turning the situation around. Demand of the experts that they scientifically prove the efficacy of some of their cash cows, such as chemotherapy and radiation for cancer, angioplasty and bypass for heart disease, or hysterectomies for uterine problems. The efficacy hasn't been proven because it can't be proven. There is no need whatsoever for practitioners and consumers of alternative medicine to wait like supplicants with hat in hand for the scientific "experts" of conventional medicine to dole out a few condescending scraps of official approval for alternative approaches. Rather, discerning citizens should be demanding of these experts that they prove the science behind their medicine by demonstrating successful, nontoxic, and affordable patient outcomes. If they can't these approaches should be rejected for being unscientific. After all, the proof is in the cure.

HOMEOPATHY: THE ULTIMATE FAKE
Stephen Barrett, M.D.

Samuel
Hahnemann
(1755–1843), a
German physician,
formulated
homeopathy's basic
principles in the
late 1700s. He
developed a "law
of similars,"
arguing that
diseases could be
cured by extremely
small amounts of
natural substances
that produce
similar symptoms as
the ailment itself.

NO

The word "homeopathy" is derived from the Greek words *homoios* (similar) and *pathos* (suffering or disease)…. Because homeopathic remedies were actually less dangerous than those of 19th-century medical orthodoxy, many medical practitioners began using them. At the turn of the 20th century, homeopathy had about 14,000 practitioners and 22 schools in the United States. But as medical science and medical education advanced, homeopathy declined sharply in America, where its schools either closed or converted to modern methods. The last pure homeopathic school in this country closed during the 1920s.

Many homeopaths maintain that certain people have a special affinity to a particular remedy (their "constitutional remedy") and will respond to it for a variety of ailments. Such remedies can be prescribed according to the person's "constitutional type"—named after the corresponding remedy in a manner resembling astrologic typing. The "Ignatia Type," for example, is said to be nervous and often tearful, and to dislike tobacco smoke. The typical "Pulsatilla" is a young woman, with blond or light-brown hair, blue eyes, and a delicate complexion, who is gentle, fearful, romantic, emotional, and friendly but shy. The "Nux Vomica Type" is said to be aggressive, bellicose, ambitious, and hyperactive. The "Sulfur Type" likes to be independent. And so on. Does this sound to you like a rational basis for diagnosis and treatment?…

See www.homeo
pathic.com/intro/hes
homeo.htm for
more information
on these types.

Unimpressive research

A "placebo"
is medication
prescribed more for
the mental relief of
the patient rather
than its physical
influence.

In 1990, an article in *Review of Epidemiology* analyzed 40 randomized trials that had compared homeopathic treatment with standard treatment, a placebo, or no treatment. The authors concluded that all but three of the trials had major flaws in their design and that only one of those three had reported a positive result. The authors concluded that there is no evidence that homeopathic treatment has any more value than a placebo.

In 1994, the journal *Pediatrics* published an article claiming that homeopathic treatment had been demonstrated to be effective against mild cases of diarrhea among Nicaraguan children. The claim was based on findings that, on certain days, the "treated" group had fewer loose stools than the placebo group. However, Sampson and London noted:

1. the study used an unreliable and unproved diagnostic and therapeutic scheme
2. there was no safeguard against product adulteration
3. treatment selection was arbitrary
4. the data were oddly grouped and contained errors and inconsistencies
5. the results had questionable clinical significance
6. there was no public health significance because the only remedy needed for mild childhood diarrhea is adequate fluid intake to prevent or correct dehydration...

In December 1996, a lengthy report was published by the Homoeopathic Medicine Research Group (HMRG), an expert panel convened by the Commission of the European Communities.... Its aim was to evaluate published and unpublished reports of controlled trials of homeopathic treatment. After examining 184 reports, the panelists concluded:

The author uses a published report to discredit homeopathic treatment.

1. only 17 were designed and reported well enough to be worth considering
2. in some of these trials, homeopathic approaches may have exerted a greater effect than a placebo or no treatment
3. the number of participants in these 17 trials was too small to draw any conclusions about the effectiveness of homeopathic treatment for any specific condition.

Simply put: Most homeopathic research is worthless, and no homeopathic product has been proven effective for any therapeutic purpose. The National Council Against Health Fraud has warned that "the sectarian nature of homeopathy raises serious questions about the trustworthiness of homeopathic researchers."

Having spelled out the conclusions of the report, the author reiterates the evidence to make sure the reader is in no doubt about the conclusions.

The London example

In 1997, a London health authority decided to stop paying for homeopathic treatment after concluding that there was not enough evidence to support its use. The Lambeth, Southwark, and Lewisham Health Authority had been referring more than 500 patients per year to the Royal Homoeopathic Hospital. Public health doctors at the authority reviewed the published scientific literature as part of a general move toward purchasing only evidence-based treatments. The group concluded that many of the studies were methodologically flawed and that recent research produced by the Royal Homoeopathic Hospital contained no convincing evidence.

The author brings in international evidence to support and strengthen his evidence.

Homeopaths are working hard to have their services covered under national health insurance. They claim to provide care that is safer, gentler, "natural," and less expensive than conventional care—and more concerned with prevention. However, homeopathic treatments prevent nothing, and many homeopathic leaders preach against immunization. Equally bad, a report on the National Center for Homeopathy's 1997 Conference described how a homeopathic physician had suggested using homeopathic products to help prevent and treat coronary artery disease. According to the article, the speaker recommended various 30C and 200C products as alternatives to aspirin or cholesterol-lowering drugs, both of which are proven to reduce the incidence of heart attacks and strokes.

Illegal marketing

In a survey conducted in 1982, the FDA found some over-the-counter products being marketed for serious illnesses, including heart disease, kidney disorders, and cancer. An extract of tarantula was being purveyed for multiple sclerosis; an extract of cobra venom for cancer. During 1988, the FDA took action against companies marketing "diet patches" with false claims that they could suppress appetite. The largest such company, Meditrend International, of San Diego, instructed users to place 1 or 2 drops of a "homeopathic appetite control solution" on a patch and wear it all day affixed to an "acupuncture point" on the wrist to "bioelectrically" suppress the appetite control center of the brain.

Does the U.S. government have enough consumer protection legislation in place? Look at the FDA's website at www.fda.gov and find out what precautions the FDA takes.

America's most blatant homeopathic marketer appears to be Biological Homeopathic Industries (BHI) of Albuquerque, New Mexico, which, in 1983, sent a 123-page catalog to 200,000 physicians nationwide. Its products included BHI Anticancer Stimulating, BHI Antivirus, BHI Stroke, and 50 other types of tablets claimed to be effective against serious diseases. In 1984, the FDA forced BHI to stop distributing several of the products and to tone down its claims for others.

Greater regulation is needed

If the FDA required homeopathic remedies to be proven effective in order to remain marketable—the standard it applies to other categories of drugs—homeopathy would face extinction in the United States. However, there is no indication that the agency is considering this. FDA officials regard homeopathy as relatively benign (compared, for example, to unsubstantiated products marketed for cancer and AIDS) and believe that other problems should get enforcement priority. If the FDA attacks homeopathy too vigorously, its proponents might even persuade a lobby-susceptible Congress to rescue them. Regardless of this risk, the FDA should not permit worthless products to be marketed with claims that they are effective. Nor should it continue to tolerate the presence of quack "electrodiagnostic" devices in the marketplace.

In August 1994, 42 prominent critics of quackery and pseudoscience asked the agency to curb the sale of homeopathic products. The petition urges the FDA to initiate a rulemaking procedure to require that all over-the-counter (OTC) homeopathic drugs meet the same standards of safety and effectiveness as nonhomeopathic OTC drugs. It also asks for a public warning that although the FDA has permitted homeopathic remedies to be sold, it does not recognize them as effective.

The FDA has not yet responded to the petition. However, on March 3, 1998, at a symposium sponsored by *Good Housekeeping* magazine, former FDA Commissioner David A. Kessler, M.D., J.D., acknowledged that homeopathic remedies do not work but that he did not attempt to ban them because he felt that Congress would not support a ban.

The FDA monitors homeopathic drugs. See www.fda.gov/ fdac/features/ 096_home.html for an article on homeopathic medicine.

"Quackery" is the practice of someone who pretends to have knowledge that they actually do not have.

Summary

During the second half of the 20th century complementary and alternative medicine became a popular method of medical treatment. But some people have criticized it, arguing that CAM remedies do not work. In the first article Burton Goldberg, founder and publisher of AlternativeMedicine.com, argues that the U.S. government has finally confirmed that traditional medicine works. He argues that conventional medicine is not, in fact, scientifically based and that the "proof is in the cure." Conversely, medic Stephen Barrett looks at homeopathy and calls it the "ultimate fake." He asserts that homeopathy became popular during the 19th century, when it was safer than most conventional medicine, but that today that is far from the case. Dr. Barrett further argues that most homeopathic medicine today is dangerous and should be subject to specific safety guidelines.

FURTHER INFORMATION:

Books:

Fugh-Berman, Adrianne, *Alternative Medicine: What Works*. New York: Williams and Wilkins, 1997.

Pelletier, Kenneth R., *The Best Alternative Medicine: What Works, What Doesn't*. New York: Simon and Schuster, 2000.

Reader's Digest Guide to Alternative Medicine. London: Reader's Digest, 1991.

Useful websites:

www.alternativemedicine.com/AMHome.asp?cn=Catalog&act=GetProduct&crt=ProductKey=10001&Style=/AMXSL/EssayDetail.xsl
Burton Goldberg, "Alternative Medicine and the Truth about Being 'Scientific' and 'Proven.'"

www.quackwatch.com
Site on health fraud and health news.

www.oncodev.securedata.net/scripts/index.asp
Jeffrey Jump, et al., "Physicians' Attitudes toward Complementary Medicine and Alternative Medicine."

www.healthy.net/asp/templates/article.asp?id+510
Mary and Michael Morton, "Ten Most Commonly Asked Questions about Alternative Medicine."

www.homeopathic.com/intro/heshomeo.htm
Dana Ullmann, "Homeopathic Typologies: The Bodymind Personalities."

www.fda.gov/bbs/topics/NEWS/2001/NEW00765.html
Article on FDA site on banning certain herbal remedies.

The following debates in the Pro/Con series may also be of interest:

In this volume:

DO COMPLEMENTARY AND ALTERNATIVE MEDICINE WORK?

YES: Many people are influenced by the media; and when they are told that alternative medicines work, they believe it

YES: Most CAM remedies are untested, and further testing and regulation of use are needed to ensure safety

MYTH V. REALITY
Is complementary and alternative medicine just a passing fad?

REGULATION
Do CAM remedies need regulation?

NO: WHO reported that in 2001 between 65 and 80 percent of the world's population relied on alternative medicine—that is more than a passing fad

NO: There are enough regulatory bodies around to ensure safety of product—look at the FDA alone

DO COMPLEMENTARY AND ALTERNATIVE MEDICINE WORK? KEY POINTS

YES: Statistics show that CAM remedies are safe, otherwise more people would reject them, and WHO would not endorse them

YES: That is why complementary and alternative medicine is better since it deals with the individual rather than dealing with a disease in general terms

SAFETY
Are CAM remedies safe?

YES: Traditional economies have used alternative medicines for centuries before biomedical treatment became available

PHYSIOLOGY
Does medical treatment vary according to a person's physiology?

NO: Sometimes CAM gets in the way of biomedical treatment—for example, in the case of cancer patients who could benefit from more scientifically based medicine

NO: More testing is necessary before their safety can be proved

NO: Biomedical treatment, based on a course of medicines, has helped millions of people suffering from serious diseases, such as cancer, HIV/AIDS, etc.

Topic 6
SHOULD GOVERNMENTS LIMIT THE PRICE OF DRUGS?

YES
"THE PRICE ISN'T RIGHT"
THE AMERICAN PROSPECT, VOL. 11, ISSUE 20, SEPTEMBER 11, 2000
MERRILL GOOZNER

NO
"WHY DO PRESCRIPTION DRUGS COST SO MUCH MORE"?
WWW.PHRMA.ORG/PUBLICATIONS/PUBLICATIONS/BROCHURE/QUESTIONS/TOC.PHTML
PHARMACEUTICAL RESEARCH AND MANUFACTURERS OF AMERICA

INTRODUCTION

Prescription drug prices were an issue during the 2000 presidential election. One older woman who had to go without basic items just to pay for her medication briefly became a national celebrity. And stories emerged from across the nation of people who had had to cut their medication in half to make it go further or had to choose between continuing to take their prescription drugs and maintaining a reasonable standard of living for their families. Medicare reform came to the forefront of the political agenda.

It has often been said that drug prices are much lower across the border in Canada, and during the fall of 2000 television cameras followed seniors from Detroit and Seattle across the border into Canada as they joined the growing number of "medication tourists."

The 2000 campaign also momentarily threw a spotlight on the situation in most of Western Europe, where state healthcare systems reduce the price of medication for everyone and provide medication free for seniors, infants, and those who suffer chronic incurable illnesses.

Pharmacy bills are a considerable drain on the finances of many U.S. families. The worry is particularly acute for the 37 percent of Americans who do not have prescription coverage. Now more voices in the United States call for a thoroughgoing reform of the present system—but no one can agree on what could or should be done.

If the cost of medication in the United States is a major public concern, the cost of medication in developing nations became a burning global issue in 2001. Multinational pharmaceutical companies stood accused of profiteering at the expense of AIDS patients in Third World countries. Medication prices that seem high in the Western world are prohibitive in poor African and Asian nations. Some developing nations tried to circumvent the problem by manufacturing their own generic drugs at much lower prices. The pharmaceutical giants went to court to prevent this practice and protect their patent monopolies.

> "No American should have to choose between fighting infections and fighting hunger, between skipping doses and skipping meals, between staying healthy and paying the rent. We can do better than that. We are now prosperous enough to do better than that."
>
> —BILL CLINTON, 42ND U.S. PRESIDENT, JUNE 1999

Activists both here and in Europe protested when the 40 largest multinational drug companies filed a lawsuit in South Africa in an attempt to challenge the Pretoria government's Medicines Act, which would have enabled the production of low-cost generic drugs and introduced compulsory licensing. And in February 2001 protesters occupied the New York City offices of one multinational drug company's public relations firm and threw "blood money."

Legal measures delayed the implementation of the Medicines Act for more than three years. During that time about 400,000 South Africans died of AIDS-related illnesses, most of them unable to benefit from low-cost drugs. More than 35 million people worldwide face death from AIDS-related disease, the majority in developing nations. The perceived profit motive of the drug multinationals was widely condemned, particularly since poor nations account for a tiny percentage of the global medication market, and the drug giants could afford to ship medication at cost to countries like South Africa and India without financial loss. Eventually the multinationals backed down, but not before their public image had suffered. Cheaper generic drugs can now be manufactured in South Africa. Similar agreements have now been reached with the authorities in a growing number of developing countries. The unfolding news story focused attention back to the U.S., where medication prices again came under fire.

The following two articles consider medication prices in the United States. First, Merrill Goozner points out that Americans pay the highest drug prices in the world. He looks at the plight of those, mostly seniors, who are unable to benefit from discounted prices. He investigates the costs of pharmaceutical research and remains unconvinced by the multinationals' arguments.

The second article is an official publication of the Pharmaceutical Research and Manufacturers of America. It states that the cost of a medicine is not simply the cost of its ingredients. Like other products that result from research, medicines are really made of knowledge—knowledge that prevents and cures disease and relieves suffering. Research is costly, and price control would be a disincentive to research.

THE PRICE ISN'T RIGHT
Merrill Goozner

Americans pay the highest prices in the world for prescription drugs. Drug expenditures in the United States have doubled since 1993 and are expected to double again by 2004, according to a study by the Health Insurance Association of America. Elderly people now spend more on medicine than on doctor bills. Many health plans have cut back on other benefits because of their rising drug bills. About one-third of seniors have no insurance and are therefore paying the highest, nondiscounted retail prices.

The pharmaceutical industry has one defense for the skyrocketing price of drugs: private-sector laboratories are chiefly responsible for the breakthroughs in prescription drugs. Any efforts to limit drug prices, especially under a Medicare drug benefit, will short-circuit the medical revolution now underway.

Alan Holmer, president of the Pharmaceutical Research and Manufacturers of America (PhRMA), told the Senate Finance Committee that the industry's cost of developing a new drug has now reached a staggering $500 million. Controlling the prices Medicare pays for drugs would mean the industry "would attract less investment money that could be used to discover and develop new medicines."

> The Medicare government program for persons aged 65 and over was launched in 1965 under the Johnson administration.

The truth about pricing

It's a tidy story, but it falls apart under scrutiny. Every independent study [of] the sources of medical innovation has concluded that research funded by the public sector—not the private sector—is chiefly responsible for a majority of the medically significant advances that have led to new treatments of disease. Moreover, the drug industry's expense for bringing those advances from lab to market is well below the $500-million claim. If one discounts the research clearly aimed at marketing and producing drugs whose contribution to public health does not exceed that of drugs already on the market, the assertion collapses on its face.

The government can structure a drug benefit that limits drug prices—without jeopardizing the search for tomorrow's cures. But that will require overcoming the power of one of Washington's most potent lobbies.

> The author points the finger at the lobbying system. Do you think that lobby groups have too much power in U.S. politics?

Cancer drug costs

Taxpayer-funded research is responsible for many chemotherapy agents. According to the National Cancer Institute (NCI), the NCI sponsored the investigational new drug applications for 50 of 77 anticancer drugs on the market as of the end of 1995. That work often extended right through to clinical trials. For instance, NCI sponsored 140 clinical trials for tamoxifen, which is produced by AstraZeneca for treating breast cancer.

Goozner moves the argument from the general to the specific.

> *"We believe Congress should devote its time and attention to expanding prescription drug coverage for seniors."*
>
> —ALAN F. HOLMER,
>
> PhRMA PRESIDENT

The most frequently cited cancer drug story … is the development of paclitaxel (Taxol). The NCI spent 15 years and $32 million of taxpayers' money to develop what is now the world's most popular anticancer drug, used to treat breast, lung, and ovarian cancers. Bristol-Myers Squibb claims it spent $1 billion to bring it to market. The drug generated an estimated $1.7 billion in sales for Bristol-Myers Squibb last year alone. Jamie Love of the Consumer Project on Technology (CPT), an indefatigable researcher on this subject and the main source for most press accounts that criticize the industry's assertions about its research-and-development costs, has estimated the manufacturing cost of Taxol at around $500 per patient for up to an 18-month course of treatment. Yet Bristol-Myers sells Taxol to patients and their insurers for more than 20 times its manufacturing cost.

If you quote an authority, explain clearly who they are and why their opinion is valuable.

Who really made AZT?

Most drugs for treating AIDS also owe their existence to government-funded research. Samuel Broder, the former head of NCI, and four government scientists laid out the government case in a bitter letter to the *New York Times* in September 1989 after the president of Burroughs Wellcome, now part of Glaxo Wellcome, asserted that his company had discovered and developed azidothymidine (AZT) on its own. AZT was the first effective treatment for slowing the AIDS

In December 2000 Glaxo Wellcome merged with SmithKline Beecham to form GlaxoSmithKline.

Activists from Oxfam protest the price of drugs outside the premises of GlaxoSmithKline. Oxfam works for famine relief and medical aid in developing countries.

virus's impact. Broder [now chief medical officer at Celera Genomics in Maryland] declined to discuss the sentiments he expressed while a member of the public sector, but Broder and fellow scientists wrote in the *Times* letter that:

"[t]he company specifically did not develop or provide the first application of the technology for determining whether a drug like AZT can suppress live AIDS virus in human cells, nor did it develop the technology to determine at what concentration such an effect might be achieved in humans. Moreover, it was not first to administer AZT to a human being with AIDS, nor did it perform the first clinical pharmacology studies in patients. It also did not perform the immunological and virological studies necessary to infer that the drug might work, and was therefore worth pursuing in further studies.

All of these were accomplished by the staff of the National Cancer Institute working with the staff of Duke University.... They were doing investigator-initiated research in response to a public health emergency. Indeed one of the key obstacles to the development of AZT was that Burroughs Wellcome did not work with live AIDS virus nor [did it] wish to receive samples from AIDS patients."

One reason the drug industry must rely on the public sector is that its own scientists play a bit part in basic biological research, which uncovers the building blocks of modern medicine. A 1997 National Science Foundation study of biomedical patents found that only 17 percent of key discoveries came from industry. The vast majority were generated by public, not-for-profit, and foreign labs.

No one doubts that the pharmaceutical industry has played a crucial role in the development of the drugs that are transforming medicine and prolonging many lives. Many pathbreaking medicines came solely from industry labs.... The industry is instrumental in bringing the discoveries of government-funded researchers ... to market.

But that doesn't mean they can't do their jobs more efficiently and without imposing undue financial hardships. A good start is recently enacted legislation ... to restore "reasonable pricing" clauses on any NIH-funded research that leads to patents and commercialization of drugs and medical devices.... The problem, however, is that these clauses were never adequately enforced. We need legislation to ensure that publicly funded innovations are broadly available at moderate prices.

Because all scientists rely on the work of others, how is it possible to distinguish which is responsible for which discovery? Can any individual claim to "own" such knowledge? Can any company?

The case for discounts

Government, or insurers who handle any new drug benefit for the elderly, should be given the power to negotiate bulk discounts with pharmaceutical firms.... Why should seniors pay the highest price for drugs when pharmacy-benefit managers and insurance companies are already negotiating discounts for their clients? In addition, drug companies should be required to conduct clinical trials for proposed new drugs, comparing the safety and effectiveness of these drugs against both placebos and existing alternatives.

Over the past century, the pharmaceutical industry's evolution toward science-based medicine has largely been driven by public research and careful government regulation. It's time for a new set of rules that will give Americans both affordable medicine and research priorities genuinely devoted to developing the next generation of cures.

Supporters of bulk discount programs say they would save government money, and the loss of revenue to drug giants would be offset by the greater number of people able to buy the drugs.

WHY DO PRESCRIPTION DRUGS COST SO MUCH?
Pharmaceutical Research and Manufacturers of America (PhRMA)

NO

The unprecedented medical progress we have made over the past few decades is nothing short of remarkable. Much of this progress—past and future—is due to the discovery and development of new medicines. Today, prescription drugs play a leading role in health care. Innovative medicines available today can ease the symptoms of arthritis, help reduce the risk of osteoporosis and breast cancer, extend the lives and improve the quality of lives for people with congestive heart failure, make life easier for people with diabetes and, generally, prevent the disability that was once considered a normal part of the aging process. Medicines have turned many diseases that were once virtual death warrants into treatable conditions. We can't stop now.

The prospects for better health at all stages of life have never been brighter. Scientists now have greater knowledge of how disease works and the high-tech tools needed to design more effective medicines. Pharmaceutical research companies are constantly increasing their commitment to R&D; this year alone, companies will invest more than $26 billion to discover and develop new medicines.

Private sector insurance is best

Against this backdrop of progress and promise, there is a debate about the cost of these medical miracles and how to ensure access to the fruits of its research. Anytime someone has difficulty affording their life-saving medicines, it is of concern to us. America's seniors, in particular, should have access to what 150 million Americans—and Members of Congress—now enjoy. Given the benefits of prescription drugs to patients and to society, there is no doubt that Medicare should cover them. For this reason, we have dedicated our industry to work toward private sector insurance coverage of prescription drugs. Some politicians, at the federal and state levels, are proposing legislative bills that rely on government price controls to contain costs. This

Arthritis and osteoporosis are diseases linked primarily to aging. The latter affects some 28 million Americans.

would only hurt innovation and result in fewer breakthrough medicines in the future. Price control proposals do not offer what is needed: insurance coverage for medicines. That is where we should focus the debate.

The cost of drugs

Just as the price of a textbook is not determined by the cost of the paper of its pages and the cost of surgery has little to do with the price of the surgeon's scalpel, the cost of a medicine is not simply the cost of its ingredients. Like other products that result from research and creativity, medicines are really made of knowledge—knowledge that prevents and cures disease and relieves suffering.

To be effective, a good analogy needs to be immediately comprehensible. Something familiar, like a textbook, is often a good choice.

> *"Do you want a shortage? Have the government legislate a maximum price that is below the price that would otherwise prevail."*
>
> —MILTON FRIEDMAN, ECONOMIST

The knowledge needed to discover and develop new medicines does not come cheap. Discovering, developing, testing, and gaining regulatory approval for new medicines is expensive, time consuming and risky:

Using brief bullet points is a good way to communicate statistics clearly without interrupting the flow of your argument.

- Of every 5,000 medicines tested, on average, only 5 are tested in clinical trials and only 1 of those is approved for patient use. Revenues from successful medicines must cover the costs of the "dry holes."
- The average cost of bringing one new medicine to market is $500 million.
- It takes an average of 12–15 years to discover and develop a new medicine. Most of that time is spent testing the drug to make sure it is safe.
- On average, only 3 of every 10 prescription drugs … generate revenues that meet or exceed average R&D costs.

Although the cost of developing drugs is soaring, the time that companies have to recoup their investment is shrinking due to stepped-up competition from generic drugs.

Companies fund research on future medicines and improvements to existing medicines with revenues from medicines on the market. One out of every five dollars in

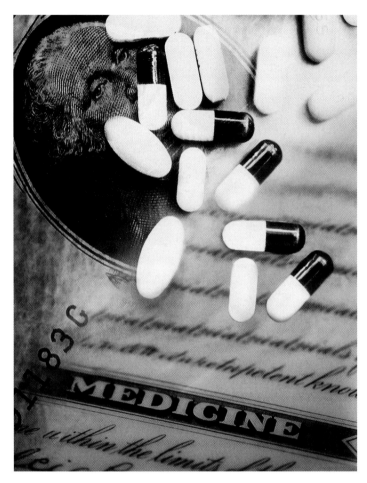

Most people recognize that pharmaceutical research can prevent suffering and disease. But at what cost?

Do we need so many new drugs? Would more cooperation in research yield better results, or is it competition that leads to major medical breakthroughs?

revenues is poured back into research and development. Currently, pharmaceutical companies are working on more than 1,000 new medicines—for Alzheimer's, stroke, cystic fibrosis, arthritis, and many other diseases. For cancer alone, there are more than 350 medicines in the pipeline.

The cost of medicines reflects their enormous value—to patients, to society, and to the health-care system. If we focus too much on cutting the costs of medicines, we may lose sight of their value, and we may jeopardize the value of pharmaceuticals that could be developed in the future.

Against price controls

Price controls have been tried numerous times over the past 4,000 years but have never worked. Instead, they produce shortages and black markets. Price controls on oil and natural gas in the 1970s led to widespread artificial shortages and long lines at the gasoline pump. Price controls on rental property lead to housing shortages and the deterioration and neglect of existing housing.

Price controls would discourage investment in drug research; unless there is a possibility of a return on that investment commensurate with its high risk at the end of the pipeline, investors will probably put their money elsewhere. Even the threat of price controls can push down research spending just when we need new treatments most. In fact, every year since 1980, pharmaceutical companies have increased research spending by double digits—except in 1994 and 1995, just after price controls were proposed as part of the Clinton health care reform plan.

The United States is the world leader in pharmaceutical innovation—at least in part because of its relatively free market for pharmaceuticals. Nearly half of the world-class medicines developed over the past two decades originated in the United States. It is no accident that the United States, where free market competition is allowed to determine prices, produces the most innovation and that countries with price controls on pharmaceuticals produce the least.

The healthcare reform proposal caused stock prices to tumble, and many of the drug giants were obliged to downsize. Eli Lilly announced it would lose 4,000 workers, Johnson & Johnson lost 3,000, and Searle, 2,250.

Meeting the needs of an aging population

The stage is set for a new era of pharmaceutical breakthroughs, but price controls would jeopardize this promise of progress, [which] must continue in order to meet the needs of a rapidly aging population. At the beginning of [the 20th] century, only 3.1 million Americans were over 65. As we enter the 21st century, there [are] 35 million older Americans. By 2030, nearly 70 million Americans will be over 65. Unless we can control or cure the diseases of aging, we may be overwhelmed by the costs of giving custodial and palliative care to people with these diseases. By keeping free market incentives strong, we can give a green light to the innovation that will lead to better health.

With life expectancy rising, population aging is a global problem. Because the birth-rate is also falling, the proportion of seniors will rise while the numbers of workers who can support them will fall.

Summary

The two sides in this debate seem far apart. In the first piece, a series of extracts from a much longer article by Merrill Goozner, the writer firmly nails his colors to the mast with the title, "The Price Isn't Right." He claims that every independent study that has ever investigated medical research sources has concluded that research funded by the public sector—not big pharmaceuticals—is chiefly responsible for the majority of the medically significant advances that have led to new treatments for disease. He cites marketing costs and profits as being responsible for the high prices charged for prescription drugs in the United States.

The industry underlines the commitment of the pharmaceutical companies to increasing research and development, and quotes an annual $26 billion investment to develop new medicines. The PhRMA believes that Medicare should cover the costs of prescription drugs and reemphasizes the commitment of the industry to involving the private sector in that coverage. Prices, they maintain, are an unavoidable consequence of research and development costs. And they argue forcefully against price control as unworkable, in that it has never worked in the past and would discourage investment in new drug research—a fatal trend, given the increasing proportion of seniors in the population.

FURTHER INFORMATION:

Books:

Danzon, Patricia, *Pharmaceutical Price Regulation: National Policies Versus Global Interests.* Washington, D.C.: AEI Press, 1998.

Useful websites:

www.depaul.edu/ethics/icpfpi.html
Ronald R. White and Sean Fraley, "Imperfect competition, price-fairness, and the pharmaceutical industry."
www.prospect.org/print/V11/20/goozner-m.html
Merrill Goozner, "The Price Isn't Right."
www.phrma.org/
The site of the Pharmaceutical Research and Manufacturers of America has a lot of useful information on price control in the form of press cuttings, briefings, and mission statements.
www.aegis.com/news/wsj/2000/WJ001003.html
Mark Schoofs and Michael Waldholz, "Drug Companies, Senegal Agree to Low-cost HIV Drug Pact," *Wall Street Journal*, 2000.
www.cooperinstitute.org/prescription.htm
"The Cents and Nonsense of High Cost Prescription Drugs" by Jeanne Findlater for the Cooper Institute.
www.cepr.net/wto/realdrugcrisis.htm
Dean Baker, "The Real Drug Crisis."
www.securethefuture.com
Seeks to find solutions for HIV/AIDS in women and children.

The following debates in the Pro/Con series may also be of interest:

In this volume:

Topic 5 Do complementary and alternative medicine work?

Topic 8 Can the origins of HIV/AIDS be traced to the polio vaccine?

SHOULD GOVERNMENTS LIMIT THE PRICE OF DRUGS?

YES: The huge prices of successful drugs recoup R&D costs very rapidly

RESEARCH COSTS
Are drugs giants making a profit on the pretext of covering R&D costs?

NO: It takes years to perfect a drug and millions of dollars; that massive investment justifies the high price

YES: An acceptable compromise on price control, this would make drugs available to more patients

BULK BUY
Should government buy pharmaceuticals in bulk to obtain a discount?

NO: That's just a way for government to scrimp on healthcare expenditure—though by enlarging the client base, it may offset the reduced profit margin

SHOULD GOVERNMENTS LIMIT THE PRICE OF DRUGS? KEY POINTS

YES: It works in other developed countries in Europe and elsewhere

YES: If big pharmaceutical companies spent less on marketing and profit seeking, their drugs would be affordable

PRICE CONTROL
Can price control be made to work?

NO: Many countries where prices are fixed have seen their pharmaceutical research companies weaken or head abroad

NO: What about the small pharmaceutical companies? They will go to the wall if price control is introduced.

Topic 7
SHOULD ORGAN REPLACEMENT BE A COMMERCIAL ENTERPRISE?

YES
"ARGUMENTS IN FAVOR OF ORGAN SELLING:
AN EXAMINATION OF ORGAN SELLING AND SPERM AND EGG SELLING"
LAUREN GOLDSTEIN AND VIKAS KHANNA

NO
"I'D SELL YOU MY KIDNEY IF I COULD"
ECONOMY.COM, SEPTEMBER 13, 1999
BRIAN NOTTAGE

INTRODUCTION

The removal and reuse of organs from living people for commercial gain has only become a major issue in the relatively recent past. Before even the late 1970s the practice of organ transplantation was not common enough to require a supply of donor organs for operations.

The history of organ transplantation began in the 1950s, when a kidney was transplanted from a living donor to a recipient. Following transplantation, the recipient body detects a "foreign" object and tries to reject it. In this case, however, the donor and recipient were identical twins; their genetic similarities reduced the risk of rejection. However, it was only in 1978 that doctors discovered the drug cyclosporin, which suppresses the body's immune system and prevents rejection, making organ transplantation a more feasible proposition. By the late 1970s kidney transplants from living donors were relatively common.

Meanwhile, the South African surgeon Christiaan Barnard performed the first heart transplant in 1967. Few of the first recipients lived long after surgery. Advances in surgical techniques in the late 1970s and 1980s made such transplants not only possible but relatively routine. Today nearly 90 percent of recipients live normally for at least 18 months after surgery.

Advances in surgical techniques now make it possible to transplant a range of vital organs, from eyes to kidneys, livers, hearts, and combined hearts and lungs. Such transplants can bring great benefits to recipients. However, the main source of organs for transplantation—the bodies of deceased people—poses new problems for surgeons and society alike.

The main complication is that for successful transplantation organs need to be used as soon as possible after the death of the donor. This raises serious logistical problems, such as the creation of information networks that can rapidly connect available organs with suitable patients and transportation networks that can move organs to the hospital where they are needed. There are also profound ethical issues. When is the donor dead, for example? And who has the right to decide whether or not to remove a patient's organs?

In all countries where transplantation is routinely practiced there is a chronic shortage of suitable organs. In most of those countries supporters of transplantation argue that programs should educate the public about its advantages to increase the number of donors. Such programs encourage people to carry cards declaring that their organs can be used in the case of their death; they also encourage people to discuss their wishes with their family and friends. Families have the legal right to release or withhold the organs of the dead person.

"It is infinitely better to transplant a heart than bury it to be devoured by worms."

—CHRISTIAAN BARNARD, TRANSPLANT SURGEON

There is another way in which more organs might be procured. Supporters of transplants—who include many doctors and, naturally, the relatives of sick people waiting for organs to become available—question whether families should have the right to refuse to allow the organs of a dead relative to be removed. They argue that such people are always highly upset and

grieving, and may not be thinking rationally. There is also the possibility that they had not discussed the topic with the dead person and so are expressing their own wishes rather than those of the deceased. Many people instinctively shy away from the thought of the body of a loved one being dissected and parts removed. Under "presumed consent" some countries assume that organs are available when patients have not specified otherwise.

A more controversial suggestion to raise the number of available organs is the commercial exploitation of the human body as a "natural resource." Advocates contend that a living person has the right to sell an organ (or organs) to the highest bidder for transplantation purposes. They argue that if one can receive payment for a donation of blood, the same principle should apply to organs, such as a kidney. If a person has ultimate legal ownership of his or her body, then he or she has the right to do with that body as they wish.

In the first of these two articles Lauren Goldstein and Vikas Khanna argues that there is a strong economic case for permitting organ selling and describes ways in which the commercial aspects can be regulated. It further argues that since the surgeon and hospital involved in the transplantation process benefit financially, it is only fair that the donor should also be rewarded. In the second article Brian Nottage comes down against the sale of organs. Rich people with health problems would benefit more than the less wealthy, he argues, and poorer people might be tempted to sell their organs to the detriment of their own long-term health.

ARGUMENTS IN FAVOR OF ORGAN SELLING
Lauren Goldstein and Vikas Khanna

All economic arguments in favor of organ selling start by noting that there is a current shortage of organs that could be eliminated if financial incentives were offered for the organs. Some statistics confirming this shortage are:

The waiting period for an organ transplant varies greatly. Kidneys have been found in as few as 18 or as many as 648 days. To date, the longest wait for a liver, the most difficult organ to find, is 858 days.

- Nationally, more than 64,000 people are awaiting an organ transplant; approximately 12 will die each day without receiving one.
- More than 42,000 people await a kidney transplant.
- One organ, tissue, and eye donor may help between 200 and 400 people.

Economic arguments

Proponents of the economic argument for organ selling also point out that between 10,000 and 12,000 people die annually who are considered medically-suitable for organ donation, yet only an estimated 5,200 donate. Financial incentives, they claim, will urge a substantially higher amount of people to donate.

If organ selling were, in principle, an acceptable commercial activity, why would it be necessary to introduce regulations or modify the free market in any way?

Not all proponents of organ selling feel that there should be a completely free market for organs. Below are some proposals that give incentives for organs without putting organs on the free market:

- Organ Trading: Live donation rates could be increased by allowing an unrelated person to donate a mismatched kidney to a "pool" in exchange for a matching kidney. This would also increase the chances of an individual getting a perfect match for the kidney he/she needs.

Organizing your points in a list can be highly effective. A similar list also makes a good script for a spoken debate.

- Preferred Status: Those who agree to become organ donors would have preferential access to organs if the need were to arise.
- Death Benefits: The families of cadaveric donors would receive estate tax deductions or funeral expense reimbursements, the latter coming possibly from the organ recipient(s).
- Prospective Sale: Individuals would sign a contract

ensuring payments to designated persons upon harvesting of the organs. Payment amounts would be based on the type and number of organs harvested or used. The beneficiary could also be a charity or any nonprofit organization.

• Regulating only the Demand Side: We could apply market principles to the supply side while still maintaining control over the demand side of the market. Thus, we could still control how the organs are distributed.

Below are some more traditional free market ways of providing incentives for organs:

• Paid Donation: Living organ providers are directly paid for one of their kidneys, bone marrow, etc. The donor receives cash and free health care following the operation. This has been tried in other countries ... where the supply of organs substantially increased after payment for organs was allowed.

• Free Market: Cadaveric organs would be sold like other commodities, with proceeds going to the family of the deceased. To prevent abuse, the deceased would have had to include such provisions in his will.

> *This system was successful in India, a country with a large population, the majority of whom are on low incomes.*

Other arguments

• Many proponents of organ selling argue that, since every aspect of the transplant procedure besides the organs themselves is subjected to free-market norms, organs should be as well. For example, organ procurement organizations get $25,000 per organ for retrieving kidneys from cadavers. Transplant surgeons [and] hospitals profit so much from organ transplants that they are willing to pay for organs if organs [c]ould be sold. The profit they make is shown by the fact that liver transplant operations go for an average of $300,000, and that doesn't include the money earned from follow-up care. Kidney transplant operations are $100,000, plus $12,000 per year follow-up care. Why should everyone besides the donor profit from the transplant?

• Responding to claims that only the rich will be able to get organ transplants if organ selling is allowed, proponents of organ selling claim this will surely not be the case. They have many arguments to support their claim:

> *Do you agree that the process of organ transplantation is now a legitimate commercial activity, and that, therefore, the donor should be permitted to benefit in the same way as everyone else involved?*

1. The price of organs is already included in much of the current price of the operation, but organ procurement agencies and doctors receive the money instead of the donors. If selling organs is allowed, some of the money made by doctors and organ procurement agencies will be transferred to the donors and thus the overall price of the operation will increase slightly.

COMMENTARY: Heart transplant pioneer

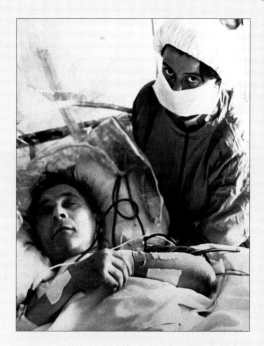

A nurse attends to the world's first successful heart transplant patient, Louis Washansky.

Even today the process of removing a diseased or damaged heart and replacing it with a strong one from a donor is so complex that it is viewed as last-resort surgery. On December 3, 1967, Dr. Christiaan Barnard performed the first successful human heart transplant on Louis Washansky, a businessman, in Cape Town, South Africa.

Born in 1922, Barnard studied at the University of Cape Town and the University of Minnesota. He later became a specialist in cardiac and cardiothoracic (heart-lung) surgery. Returning to Cape Town, he pioneered open-heart surgery at the Groote Schuur Hospital and conducted heart-transplant experiments on dogs.

Washansky, a 55-year-old grocer, suffered from diabetes and terminal heart disease. When Denise Darvall, a young woman who shared his blood type, was brought into Groote Schuur with injuries from which she soon died, Barnard gave Washansky her heart. The five-hour operation was a success, but Washansky died just 18 days later from pneumonia brought on by immunosuppressant drugs.

For Barnard, who died in 2001, the operation brought global fame. He conducted more heart transplants, gradually achieving greater life expectancy, and the procedure was adopted by other specialists. Today a heart-transplant recipient can expect to live on for many more years.

2. Medicare, Medicaid, and private insurance already cover most transplant operations. The costs of the operation will not increase so much if organ selling is legalized that Medicare, Medicaid, and private insurance will stop covering these life saving operations.

3. In some operations such as kidney transplants, the cost of the transplant operation is less than the cost of dialysis.

Thus, with a greater supply, Medicare, Medicaid, and private insurance may actually save money, which could cause them to cover even more transplant operations.

Commerce or altruism?

• Many supporters of organ selling don't see a problem with it even if the rich are the ones who receive more organ transplants. They claim that donations are motivated by altruism. Thus, donations will not go down if organ selling is allowed, and the poor will get the same amount of transplants. Therefore, why should we allow more rich people to die by disallowing organ selling, if saving their lives isn't a burden on poor people.

When it comes to life or death, should money be the deciding factor? Is there a moral element to the issue of organ selling?

James Blumstein, a proponent of organ selling, argues that the practice should be allowed because it would be no different than the selling of many other similar healthcare products. We currently allow rich people to have more access to life-saving drugs like AZT for AIDS so why can't we allow rich people to have more access to organs, which save lives just like any life-saving drug?

• Proponents of organ selling also appeal to the issue of human rights. By preventing the sale of body parts, some say we are denying people's fundamental rights to own themselves. Of all the things in life that we ever own, the only thing we truly own throughout is our body, and yet we have no legal ownership of it. Why can we harm our bodies by smoking or drinking or help our bodies by exercising, and not sell parts of our bodies as we please? Why is it that only one use of our bodies is restricted, while in every other case our bodies are seen only as our own.

• In conclusion, many who favor egg selling claim that the public is, at least partly, in favor of allowing sales of organs. For example, they cite surveys such as one conducted by UNOS, the current agency in charge of organ distribution, showing that currently half of Americans are in favor for allowing some incentives to be given to organ donors. This is clearly enough people, proponents claim, to start some experimental studies to see how a system of offering incentives for organs would turn out.

The United Network for Organ Sharing (UNOS) is a nonprofit organization whose aims are to advance organ availability and transplantation. Visit its website at www.unos.org.

I'D SELL YOU MY KIDNEY IF I COULD
Brian Nottage

NO

eBay, the best known of the growing number of online auction websites, has recently endured a string of problems from unusual and illegal items for sale. Just over a week ago, one item made national, headline news. A Florida man offered to sell one of his kidneys, setting a minimum asking price of $25,000 and asking for "serious bids only." Buyers were also told, "Of course, only one for sale, as I need the other one to live." A bid of $5.75 million was posted before eBay shut this auction down, as the 1984 National Organ Transportation Act punishes the purchase or sale of human organs by up to five years in prison or a $50,000 fine.

Although further investigation of the seller and top bidder suggest that neither was actually serious, numerous copycat auctions continue to sprout up. One supposedly serious "seller" offered a "fully functional kidney, 30s, male, with daily intakes of springwater, vitamins and exercise," asking for hospital and travel expenses, and a written agreement that does not break any laws.

Moral and economic issues

Most interesting are the moral and economic questions raised by these auctions: Should these transactions be illegal? Would everyone be better off if people could trade organs as they wish?

The economic consequences of policies restricting such transactions are straightforward. The current U.S. system of screening and matching for organ transplants mandates a price of zero to the donor. Therefore, supply is effectively constrained, as more people would certainly donate if compensated. According to one estimate, a $20,000 price for a kidney would elicit a 50 percent increase in the number donated. And naturally at zero price, substantial excess demand is created. Accordingly, over 40,000 people sit on the national list for kidneys. If allowed to trade freely, an equilibrium quantity that is higher than this amount would surely result, eliminating most of the shortage and waiting time.

The cost to society of the legal restriction is the potential net gain of the transactions that are foregone. This is referred to as the deadweight welfare loss and it represents inefficiency from banning mutually beneficial trades. In the case of kidney transplants, using reasonable assumptions about the elasticity of demand, this deadweight loss or inefficiency could be as high as $100 million. Some believe that the efficiency losses are likely even greater because organs are generally not allocated according to ability to pay and so may not be allocated to those who value them most.

The financial implications

While the somewhat conservative $100 million figure is small relative to GDP, or even total healthcare spending in the U.S., it represents a huge imposition on those waiting for organs who are willing (and able) to pay. The incentives to make additional beneficial trades are so strong that black markets of various sorts have developed. Many so-called organ brokers even advertise on the Internet. There is also evidence that Americans are at a disadvantage to wealthy foreigners. A *New York Times* investigation in the mid-1980s claimed some hospitals were performing as many as a third of their kidney transplants on wealthy foreigners who jump the waiting list by paying higher hospital fees.

Naturally, there are serious offsetting concerns about selling organs. Such plans would tend to be more appealing to those with lower incomes, potentially leading to poorer people making health decisions that might turn out to be detrimental later based on current income constraints. This clearly happens with payments for blood; at least those donations do not have long-term consequences. There may even be incentives to reduce end-of-life treatment on the part of some families. Further, a donor or his family may be tempted to conceal negative health information that might disqualify the sale of their organs. And of course, on moral grounds, the ability to pay may not be an appropriate way to allocate organs. Conventional economic reasoning gives little, and maybe no insight on that front, but it does tell us we must be aware of the costs of legal restrictions on desired medical procedures.

The ongoing debate

Cognizant of these costs, the public policy debate appears to be moving forward (although the debates are rarely framed in terms of economic efficiency and deadweight losses). For example, in May, Pennsylvania proposed offering $300 to families of organ donors. To prevent running afoul of the 1984 law, and to stanch concerns about paying for organs, the payment would not be made to the family but to a funeral

Gross Domestic Product (GDP) means the amount of wealth created by a nation.

Do you think that money gives people the right to jump hospital waiting lists?

What other arguments are there against organ selling?

COMMENTARY: Presumed consent

In the United States it is a legal condition under the Uniform Anatomical Gift Act (1968) that hospitals may remove organs only from people who have given "explicit consent." The act "gives all competent adults legal authority to decide for themselves whether or not they wish to become organ donors after death." This policy is also called "opt-in."

Not all countries adhere to the same policy. Many European nations, and some in South America, follow a policy known as "presumed consent," or "opt-out," in which it is assumed that your organs may be removed after death unless you have specifically chosen otherwise. In Belgium, for example, people who do not wish to donate their organs after death must actively register their request. When the Belgian government introduced this policy, the country's organ donation rate doubled to become one of the world's highest. Today fewer than 2 percent of Belgians opt out.

Taking liberties

Some opponents of presumed consent say that it presumes too much. It assumes, for example, that everybody understands the principles on which it operates and has used every opportunity to learn their rights. There are also certain religious laws—Islamic Shariah included—under which it is unlawful to bequeath one's organs for donation after death. Under opt-out the burden of responsibility has shifted from the health service to the individual, and the altruistic notion of "donation" has become degraded.

One of the revelations from the Alder Hey scandal in Britain, in which a Liverpool children's hospital harvested more than 2,000 organs and tissue samples from 800 dead patients without parental knowledge, was the manner in which consent had been obtained. Parents had signed a permission form for postmortem examination without noticing a clause: "tissues may be retained." This was, in effect, presumed consent. For decades the hospital had been removing most or all of the organs from the children's bodies and using them, along with tissue samples, for medical research. In addition, 1,500 miscarried or stillborn fetuses had been stored. Further revelations of organ harvesting at hospitals in Birmingham and Bristol then emerged. Beyond the severe distress caused to immediate relatives of the children, there was a nationwide loss of public faith in the organ donor system.

A special inquiry into Alder Hey found that, ironically, staff had withheld information from parents in order not to distress them. The inquiry recommended new laws and new codes of practice to ensure that parents and patients receive informed consent. It found the hospital's policy of presumed consent to be "unethical and illegal," a view shared by many American experts. Both at home and abroad, however, clinicians still face a dilemma: how to uphold medical ethics while at the same time supporting initiatives in medical research that desperately need human material on which to work.

home to defray burial expenses. But even this small step may violate the law because, while the payments are modest, they are no different in practice from directly paying the family, i.e., in most cases the payment is effectively the same as having a hospital cut a check for the family. The same concerns about selling organs remain.

The world view of organ selling and donation

The rest of the world is pursuing other alternatives. In some countries, organ sales, if not explicitly legal, are de facto permitted and encouraged. There is evidence that some of the concerns about international organ trade, particularly as related to fairness, are warranted. For instance, the Chinese government appears to run a substantial business from "voluntary" donations from executed prisoners.

In some European nations, the government takes a more aggressive stand on organ donation, providing an appealing middle ground. Recognizing that a sizable majority of their citizens claim to favor organ donations, with few taking action, passive consent laws have been legislated. Under this arrangement, upon death, consent for organ donation is assumed; citizens must act affirmatively to prevent donation.

Does the system of passive consent present a threat to a person's freedom of choice?

In the countries where this system has been tried, the availability of organs has predictably gone up, and substantially so in many cases. This may be a way to preserve and enhance a system that disallows payments, but still increases organ availability, which is the most important factor in terms of economic efficiency.

Determining whether the European system is the best, or even appropriate for the U.S., is a difficult matter to resolve. There are obvious concerns about impingement on freedom from a passive consent arrangement. What is far less uncertain is the fact that, as the population ages and related health problems increase, organ shortages are only likely to worsen. Pressure for change in the current organ donation system seems as unstoppable as death and taxes.

Summary

Both articles agree that there is a problem, a shortage of organ donors. Both also agree that great benefits flow from transplantation and that organ transplant is to be encouraged. But when it comes to how the cause can be furthered, the agreement breaks down.

Lauren Goldstein and Vikas Khanna take a pragmatic view of organ selling. The right of a living person to sell his or her organs, and the right of families to sell the organs of a deceased relative, would greatly increase the number of organs that would be available for transplant, they say. They argue that transplantation is already a commercial enterprise, with hospitals and surgeons making vast profits. Why then, they ask, should the donor not also benefit financially? They conclude by stating that half of all Americans now believe donors should receive some monetary reward and ask that studies should be undertaken to explore the feasibility of this.

Brian Nottage sees the potential for the exploitation of the poor, who would be tempted to risk their own health to earn money. He sees the danger that families might hasten the death of a relative in order to cash in on the organs that could be harvested from the cadaver. He says that other systems around the world provide alternative methods of collecting organs and, in some cases, lead to higher rates of collection than "organs-for-sale."

FURTHER INFORMATION:

Books:

Caplan, A. L., and D. Coelho (editors), *The Ethics of Organ Transplants: The Current Debate*. Amherst, N.Y.: Prometheus Books, 1998.

Chabot-Long, Lynn, *A Gift of Life: A Page from the Life of a Living Organ Donor*. Milwaukee, WN: Le-Lynn Publications, 1996.

Fox, R. C., and J. P. Swazey, *Spare Parts: Organ Replacement in American Society*. New York: Oxford University Press, 1992.

Williams, Phillip G., *Life from Death: The Organ and Tissue Donation and Transplantation Source Book*. Oak Park, IL: P. Gaines Co., 1989.

Articles:

Gallup, Inc., "The American Public's Attitudes toward Organ Donation and Transplantation." Boston, MA: The Partnership for Organ Donation, 1993.

Useful websites:

www.acponline.org/journals/annals/01jul96/inbalan1.htm

Aaron Spital, "Mandated Choice for Organ Donation." www.transweb.org/partnership/press.html

Press releases from The Partnership for Organ Donation.

The following debates in the Pro/Con series may also be of interest:

In this volume:

 Part 2: Medicine and Health, pages 62–63

Topic 11 Should religion affect parents' medical decisions?

In *Individual and Society*:

Topic 16 Is surrogate motherhood wrong?

SHOULD ORGAN REPLACEMENT
BE A COMMERCIAL ENTERPRISE?

YES: Families should have the right to sell organs as a way of defraying funeral expenses. Poorer families would benefit.

YES: Living donors benefit financially, and the deceased clearly have no further need of the organs. In both cases why not use the organs to save lives?

AFTER-DEATH SALES
Should families be allowed to sell the organs of their dead relative?

MEDICAL ETHICS
Is it incumbent on a doctor to use organs—however they have been procured—to save lives?

NO: Families may be going against the wishes of the deceased simply to make money. End-of-life care might be withheld in order to speed death.

NO: Unauthorized removal of organs is a violation of the deceased's rights; it is no better than graverobbing. Neither should physicians take any part in a commercial transaction that could risk the long-term health of a living donor.

SHOULD ORGAN REPLACEMENT BE A COMMERCIAL ENTERPRISE? KEY POINTS

YES: This system enables many more people to get the organs they need to solve their health problems

YES: The transplantation "industry" makes large sums of money for the services it provides. The organ donor should also profit.

ORGAN SELLING
Is it morally and ethically right to sell one's own organs for commercial gain?

NO: The ability to pay should not be the major factor in deciding who will and will not receive life-saving treatment

NO: A human body is not a commodity and should not be exploited. Poorer people may be tempted to put their health at risk in order to earn money.

Topic 8

CAN THE ORIGINS OF HIV/AIDS BE TRACED TO THE POLIO VACCINE?

YES

"AIDS: A PLAGUE THAT HUMANKIND
HAS INFLICTED UPON ITSELF"?
FLOYD MANN

NO

"THE RELATIONSHIP BETWEEN
AIDS AND THE POLIO VACCINE: TRUTH V. MYTH"
STAN HANCOCK

INTRODUCTION

The abbreviation "AIDS" stands for acquired immunodeficiency syndrome. It is caused by infection with a virus called the human immunodeficiency virus (HIV). People developing HIV infections will most probably contract full-blown AIDS as a result. The virus is passed from person to person through blood-to-blood contact and the exchange of bodily fluids—blood, semen, vaginal fluid, and other bodily fluids containing blood—during sexual intercourse. Women can also pass HIV on to their babies during pregnancy or delivery and through breast-feeding.

HIV destroys certain kinds of blood cells that are essential to the normal functioning of the human immune system. Recent studies have shown that people with HIV can carry the virus for several years before enough damage is done to the immune system for AIDS to develop. Reducing the amount of the HIV virus with drugs can slow down the immune destruction and stave off the development of AIDS.

Today the international community is concerned about the incidence of AIDS in the world. According to the Joint United Nations Program on HIV/AIDS, in December 2000 about 21.8 million people have died from AIDS since 1981, when the disease first came to public attention—including 4.3 million children under the age of 15. In 2000 alone about three million people died of the virus. A further 36.1 million people are estimated to be living with HIV/AIDS, about 47 percent of whom are women.

The organization also estimates that about 95 percent of those infected by the virus live in the developing world. The Centers for Disease Control and Prevention (CDC) estimate that about 800,000 to 900,000 people in the United States are living with HIV/AIDS and predict that about 40,000 new HIV infections will occur every year. In order to stop the rapid growth of HIV/AIDS, scientists and researchers need to find out the origins of the disease. Various theories have been put forward. They include suggestions that AIDS originated in Africa among the homosexual community, that it is a human-made disease stemming from chemicals or biological warfare experiments, or that the virus began with polio vaccine testing in Africa in the 1950s. This latter theory has resulted in much debate among the scientific community, but is there really any credibility in the argument that HIV/AIDS is linked to the polio vaccine?

"AIDS obliges people to think of sex as having, possibly, the direst consequences: suicide. Or murder."

—SUSAN SONTAG, WRITER

AIDS first came to the world's attention in 1981, when the Centers for Disease Control in Atlanta, Georgia, discovered some unusual cancers and infections occurring among homosexual men in New York, Los Angeles, and San Francisco. By the fall of 1981 the disease had moved beyond the gay community, and cases were reported among heterosexual intravenous drug users, some prison inmates, Haitians, hemophiliacs, and recipients of blood transfusions. In October 1983 French doctors reported that a disease similar to AIDS was raging through equatorial Africa, and some people believe that the disease originated there.

In February 1983 scientists noted that the monkeys at the University of California Primate Research Center and Harvard's New England Primate Center were suffering from diseases similar to those seen in AIDS patients. The diseases had been noted in monkeys since 1969 but had been largely ignored until the emergence of AIDS. A retrovirus 40 percent identical to HIV, called the simian immunodeficiency virus (SIV), was isolated in a macaque monkey. It was thought that it had been infected with the virus while in captivity, since African green monkeys were discovered to be the natural hosts of the virus. Since some batches of polio vaccine were produced in kidney tissue obtained from rhesus monkeys, scientists began to look at the links between HIV/AIDS and polio, especially when some West Africans were infected with a disease resembling SIV.

Polio vaccine research took place in the Congo in the 1950s. From 1957 to 1959 the vaccine was given to hundreds of thousands of people in the former Belgian Congo. However, the validity of the links between polio and HIV/AIDS are still being debated; and while some researchers believe that human AIDS has its origin in the cross-species transfer of African monkey viruses to humans, others believe that the transfer took place via contaminated vaccines.

In the first article, Floyd Mann examines the polio vaccine research done in the 1950s and points to strong evidence suggesting that the vaccine is linked to HIV/AIDS. Stan Hancock in the second article examines the facts and myths surrounding the polio-HIV/AIDS debate, with particular reference to the dialogue between Dr. Hilary Koprowski and journalist Tom Curtis.

AIDS: A PLAGUE THAT HUMANKIND HAS INFLICTED UPON ITSELF?
Floyd Mann

YES

✓ AIDS is one of the best known and most feared illnesses on the planet. But despite the attention it has achieved from experts all over the world since it was first reported in the United States in 1981, the disease remains elusive. Researchers know how it is transmitted but have not managed to develop a cure, despite some successful drugs to control its symptoms. And while they think they know when and where it originated—in equatorial Africa around 1959 or 1960 many now believe—they still do not know how. But one current theory about the origin of AIDS presents it as a scourge humankind has inflicted upon itself. During the 1990s numerous scientists and observers developed an explanation for the origin of the disease that suggests that the human immunodeficiency virus (HIV), the cause of AIDS, was accidentally transferred from chimpanzees to humans during tests to develop a new polio vaccine.

The scientific establishment has largely failed to accept the theory. Perhaps this should come as no surprise. Accepting this theory would inevitably lead to a tremendous degree of soul searching on the part of scientists and a reappraisal of the whole methodology of medical research. But the case remains strong. One of its most influential expressions came in a 1992 paper by B. F. Elswood and R. B. Stricker, "Polio Vaccines and the Origin of AIDS." That same year, an article in *Rolling Stone* magazine by journalist Tom Curtis brought a high profile to what had previously been a rather arcane academic controversy. Those two sources provide much of the evidence presented in this article.

A case to answer

It is a tremendous irony that AIDS, the plague of the 21st century, owes its existence to well-intentioned attempts to rid the world of a great killer of previous centuries, polio. But there are a number of facts that make this highly likely:

• AIDS is endemic in central Africa in an area that corresponds almost exactly with the area where early polio

> Not everybody believes AIDS first appeared in Africa. There are theories, for example, that the virus was cultivated in laboratories for chemical warfare.

> Polio is an infectious disease that causes paralysis and sometimes leads to death by asphyxiation. Today the disease has been eradicated from large parts of the world, but it persists in South Asia and sub-Saharan Africa.

vaccines were given to nearly half a million people between 1957 and 1960.

- The first occurrence of AIDS in what was then the Belgian Congo and is now Zaire came in 1959; this coincides almost exactly with the timing of the polio vaccine tests.
- Polio vaccines are grown on monkey kidneys; monkeys are now know to carry a simian immunodeficiency virus (SIV) which can be up to 84 percent identical to HIV.
- A different monkey virus, Simian Virus 40 (SV40), is already known to have contaminated early polio vaccines and thus to have jumped species to infect humans.

Although it might be possible to dismiss any one of these facts as coincidence, all four together create a formidable case that transcends any chance of accident; instead, it points the finger of responsibility squarely at the polio vaccine trials.

Geographical evidence

The primary epidemic of AIDS radiated out from a region located in what is now Zaire and Rwanda. This was precisely where researchers were working on the development of the polio vaccine in the 1950s. Discovering a vaccine was a big prize and a number of respected researchers were racing for the honor. Among them were Jonas Salk, Albert Sabin, and Hilary Kopowski.

For more information on the Salk Institute visit the website at www.salk.edu.

The first efforts to develop a polio vaccine began in 1952 with intensive growing of poliovirus on monkey kidneys. The virus was then killed with formaldehyde and used to inoculate laboratory animals; this was followed by a mass public testing in 1954. From 1956 another vaccine, this one a live one which had not been treated with formaldehyde, was tested in the Soviet Union and Eastern Europe. It was administered on sugar cubes soaked in syrup to more than 77 million people, and taken up in the United States and in most of the world.

At the time, scientists knew little about the simian viruses that infected monkeys. They also worked in an environment with little or no federal regulations about what tissue types viruses could be grown in. It was a shock, then, when it became apparent in 1960 that both polio vaccines were contaminated. Hundreds of millions of people had been exposed to SV40, a simian virus that caused tumours in laboratory animals. For a long time it was thought that SV40 was not active in humans. In the 1970s, however, researchers discovered an increased occurence of certain types of tumors among people who had received contaminated vaccines.

Then in 1988 researchers looked again at the results of a text of more than 58,000 pregnant women in the United States between 1959 and 1965. The number of children of those women who had received the polio vaccine who later developed brain tumors was thirteen times the rate of the children whose mothers had not. Tests on stored blood from the women originally tested suggested that SV40 was not the culprit—but that an as yet unidentified virus had been transferred by the polio vaccine. The vaccine had, it turned out, been contaminated with a number of simian viruses. Under U.S. guidelines, all SV40-contaminated vaccines were forbidden from use in the United States. Meanwhile, the Asian monkeys used to grow polio vaccine—which were virtually all infected with SV40—were no longer used; they were replaced by African green monkeys, which did not naturally harbor the virus.

In 1967 a new, highly infectious disease broke out in Germany and Yugoslavia among people working on polio vaccine research. The 31 victims of the "Marburg" virus had one thing in common: All had been in contact with monkeys or their blood or tissue.

> For further information on the SV40 monkey virus see the website www.chronicillnet.org/online/bensweet.html.

The link with HIV

Medical researchers first began to take notice of AIDS in 1981, when the first cases occurred in the United States, primarily among homosexual males. The disease spread through western societies, mostly through sexual and other contact, and was largely confined to high-risk groups such as gays, intravenous drug users, and the sexual partners of infected people. This was not the sort of general eruption of the disease that might have been expected if AIDS were directly related to the polio vaccine. But such an eruption did occur; and significantly, it happened in central Africa.

French physicians noted in 1983 that a deadly disease virtually identical to AIDS was raging in equatorial Africa. Within a year scientists in France and the United States had succeeded in identifying the human immunodeficiency virus that caused the disease. It appeared to be an African virus, and it appeared to be a new one. No evidence of HIV infection in humans exists before 1959; a serum sample collected that year in Leopoldville, in the Belgian Congo (now Kinshasha, Zaire), contains the earliest known antibodies against HIV.

The link with the Congo is interesting. In the late 1950s another American researcher was testing weakened strains of the polio virus on monkeys and chimps. His early tests included giving his vaccine in chocolate milk to a group of mentally defective children in a New York State hospital. At a research facility in Lindi Camp in the Belgian Congo, he experimented with giving the vaccine to a colony of chimpanzees. At the same time, he successfully gave the vaccine to the animals' keepers. That success led to the rapid innoculation of up to 250,000 Africans and, later, another 75,000 children in Léopoldville.

What ethical issues are raised by testing drugs on "mentally deficient" children and those born in institutions?

When the researcher published his findings, he included a map showing the areas where the testing had been concentrated, including Léopoldville. Thirty years later, researchers published another map showing areas where they had discovered strikingly high levels of HIV infection. They also suggested that HIV infection among adults in the region probably began in childhood. The two maps coincided almost exactly. What was more, another researcher discovered that the polio vaccine being tested was contaminated with a virus that was *not* poliomyelitis. The original researcher acknowledged that all vaccines made in monkey tissue were probably contaminated with unknown simian viruses.

Conclusion

Might one of those viruses that contaminated the vaccines have been HIV? Evidence is piling up that AIDS did indeed originate in monkeys. Epidemics of AIDS-like diseases were noted in monkeys since 1969. The World Health Organization (WHO) tested the polio vaccine in 1985—and found no link with HIV. In the meantime, however, another form of HIV was identified in some West Africans. It was called HIV-2 and it very closely resembled SIV.

HIV-2 was discovered in 1986 and mainly infects people living in West Africa. Those infected with HIV-2 usually show no symptoms for many years, and few develop full-blown AIDS.

But how might a monkey virus have crossed species and occurred in humans? And why, if polio vaccine were indeed responsible for introducing HIV to humans, was the early occurrence of AIDS so localized? Numerous questions remain to be answered about the exact mechanics of the exchange. The bare bones of the story, however, are clear, and they make for stark reading. It is more than likely that doctors themselves are responsible for infecting humans with a virus that originated in monkeys.

Tom Curtis concluded his controversial *Rolling Stone* article with a chilling observation: "There is evidence that all three pioneers used vaccines inadvertently contaminated with viruses from a species dangerously close to our own. If the Congo vaccine turns out not to be the way AIDS got started in people, it will be because medicine was lucky, not because it was infallible."

THE RELATIONSHIP BETWEEN AIDS AND THE POLIO VACCINE: TRUTH V. MYTH
Stan Hancock

NO

Hancock begins his essay with a strong statement.

Jonas Salk (1914–1995) was a U.S. virologist. Salk was first sponsored by the U.S. Army to find a vaccine for flu. He began research into polio in 1949, using "killed" viruses, and successfully tested the vaccine on around 1 million U.S. children in 1954. Salk set up the Salk Institute for Biological Sciences in La Jolla, CA, in 1963.

To see the complete text of "The Origin of AIDS" by Tom Curtis, go to www.uow.edu/au/arts/bmartin/dissent/documents/AIDS/Curtis92.html.

The idea that AIDS originated from experiments to produce a vaccine against polio threatens to tarnish one of medical science's great achievements: the successful development of an effective vaccine to one of the world's most pernicious diseases. It is also potentially dangerous. It makes parents reluctant to provide their children with an essential defense against sickness. The plaudits for the breakthrough of creating a polio vaccine went to U.S. researcher Jonas Salk in 1954, but Salk was only one of a number of researchers working at the time to develop a polio vaccine with poliovirus extracted from monkeys. All have now found themselves and their methods questioned by critics ranging from fellow scientists to journalists.

The accusations against the polio pioneers are largely circumstantial. Briefly, they are based on the claim that HIV and AIDS originated in monkeys or other primates, and that monkeys were the hosts used to grow cultures of the poliovirus used in the vaccine. There is also, critics allege, a direct correlation between the region and timing of early tests of the vaccine—the Belgian Congo, from the 1950s to the early 1960s, and particularly from 1957 to 1960—and the date and location of the first appearances of HIV in humans. In other words, the polio vaccine was responsible for transferring AIDS from monkeys to human beings simply because critics' logic tells them that this probably should have been the case. But this is no real proof. The evidence does not support the conclusion.

The most articulate spokesman of the claims linking poliovirus to AIDS is the man at the center of much of the debate. Physician Hilary Koprowski conducted a mass polio innoculation in equatorial Africa between 1957 and 1960. Koprowski has been forced to defend himself and his reputation repeatedly in print, notably in rejecting the arguments of reporter Tom Curtis, printed in *Rolling Stone* magazine in 1992.

Koprowski rebuts Curtis's specific points one by one, arguing that evidence is flawed. One of the main arguments is that the areas where Koprowski carried out his tests virtually match the areas of greatest HIV infection today, particularly the area of the Ruzizi Valley in northwestern Burundi. However, Curtis makes errors in his analysis, including mislocating the Ruzizi Valley in the Kivu district of Zaire, which is where he claims Koprowski carried out most of his tests.

Not only that, the alleged high rates of HIV infection in the area may not themselves be established beyond doubt. Researchers in the Kivu district have found a high prevalence of antibodies against AIDS, though no trace of the disease itself. This is explicable by the generally accepted fact that the ELISA (enzyme-linked immunosorbent assay) tests used at the time tend to show a high rate of nonspecific positive reactions. In other words, a positive result does not necessarily point to the presence of AIDS. Indeed, the researchers who carried out the report later recognized this fact and reduced their estimate of the prevalence of AIDS in Kivu, from between 12 and 24 percent down to a figure closer to 4 percent, which is supported by further research on blood donors in Kivu.

ELISA tests are used to detect HIV antibodies in blood. Western Blot analysis tests for proteins found in the AIDS virus.

Distribution discrepancies

The discrepancies in the close correlation claimed by researchers between the area of Koprowski's tests and the areas with high incidences of HIV simply do not bear examination. Repeated epidemiological studies in the rural populations of northeast Zaire, Burundi's Ruizizi Valley, and Rwanda have in fact established relatively low incidences of HIV: 0.7 percent in Burundi, 1.3 percent in Rwanda, and 3.7 percent for Zaire. Were the vaccine directly to blame for spreading AIDS to children in these rural areas in the late 1950s, these figures might have been expected to be much higher. In fact, it is the region's cities—where Koprowski carried out relatively few tests—that have the higher incidence of the virus, from 25 to 30 percent, suggesting that infection has spread from the cities to the countryside, and not the other way around.

Koprowski did give polio vaccinations in one city, Léopoldville, capital of the Belgian Congo (today Kinshasha in Zaire). The rate of HIV infection there today is high, up to 30 percent. But that high incidence cannot be linked directly to the polio vaccination tests: The same pool of virus material was also used for the vaccination of children in Poland—and Poland has one of the lowest incidences of AIDS in Europe. Even what may have been the earliest cases of AIDS in

There are around 13,000 adults with HIV/AIDS in Poland. For further information look at www.undp.org/hiv/poland/pdf.

107

Africa—they occurred before the disease had been identified—were diagnosed thousands of kilometers away from the site of Koprowski's main tests.

The timing of the disease also counts against the polio vaccine theory. The first proved case of AIDS occurred in a British sailor who began to show symptoms of the disease in 1958—at a time before Koprowski had even begun a program of mass vaccination—but died in 1959.

Rebutting other charges

Curtis suggested that researchers had used species of monkeys that might harbor a simmunodeficiency virus (SIV) or HIV. Another critic, journalist Edward Hooper, alleged in his 1999 book *The River* that researchers had used kidneys from chimpanzees, a far more likely source of HIV than other species because of similarities between HIV and chimp SIV. Koprowski has stated categorically that, apart from one early batch produced in cotton rats, all the type II polio vaccine was produced in kidney tissue from rhesus monkeys (*Macaca mulatta*) from Asia, particularly the Philippines. And, contrary to Curtis's implication of unregulated practices, importers of the rhesus monkeys were closely scrutinized by the U.S. government.

Curtis also suggested that the Congo vaccine might have been contaminated by a "cell-killing virus" discovered by Albert Sabin. Koprowski has argued that "many monkey kidney vaccines infected with different strains of polio virus, including strains developed by Sabin, contained 'vaccuolating agents' cytopathic for tissue culture and contained foamy viruses."

The presence of these viruses, he argues, does not mean that the polio vaccine is not suitable or safe for distribution. Careful monitoring of the children he vaccinated includes not only the 76,000 children in Léopoldville but also more than 7 million in Poland, 34,000 in Switzerland, and 1.5 million—a quarter of the entire population—in Croatia. All research on these people shows that the vaccine is safe and is not associated with any major illness.

Perhaps the strongest case against the possible source of the AIDS virus lying in the polio vaccine is the failure of AIDS to reach epidemic proportions in the European areas where Koprowski conducted his tests. That would suggest that the epidemics of the disease in equatorial Africa must have a different explanation. The linking of the vaccine on the one hand and the disease on the other is the result of what Koprowski calls "the wildest of lay speculation." Other

Albert Sabin (1906–1993) was a U.S. physician and microbiologist. He conducted research on viral and other infectious diseases. In 1959 he developed a live-virus vaccine for immunization against polio.

"Cytopathic" means "causing disease symptoms in cells."

relatively simple explanations of how HIV may have transferred from monkeys and other primates to humans— a process most, but by no means all, scientists now believe took place—include the possibility that a hunter was bitten or scratched by a chimpanzee when capturing it or cut himself while he was butchering it.

Laboratory support

Koprowski is not a lone voice. Independent laboratory tests of the very kind called for by Curtis and other critics have found no evidence linking the polio virus to AIDS. In September 2000 researchers from laboratories including the Max Planck Institute in Leipzig, Germany, and the Pasteur Institute in Paris, France, announced the findings of their investigation into the CHAT vaccine used by Koprowski. First, they confirmed that the vaccine was grown on monkey kidneys, rather than chimpanzee kidneys. The vaccine was also found to be negative for both SIV and HIV.

While critics of the vaccination policy continue to protest and wave their smoking guns, new theories about the origin and spread of AIDS also undermine their case. A number of experts, including Dr. Stanley Plotkin of the University of Pennsylvania and Dr. Bette Korber of the Los Alamos National Laboratory in New Mexico now suggest that the spread of HIV actually began in the 1930s, long before the polio vaccination programs got under way. Korber's genetic analysis suggests that the virus spread only slowly at first and then increased, which is completely inconsistent with the link with polio vaccine. At the same conference where the results of the investigation into the CHAT vaccine were announced, Plotkin made a plea that is a stark reminder of the serious damage that can be done by mischief-makers among the lay press. He said: "It is now time for the scientists to reassure the public of the safety of vaccination in general and to move on to the important issues and how to prevent AIDS through vaccine development." Thus, while critics are playing at conspiracy theories, parents around the world are too frightened to allow their children to receive medicine's best defense against the curse of poliomyelitis: a safe vaccine.

In 2001 Nature *and* Science *magazines both reported that four independent teams had failed to find any evidence of SIV or HIV in the original stocks of the polio vaccine.*

Do you agree that the "lay press" is irresponsible to spread what may be misinformation? But should reporting such developments always be left to experts?

Summary

Since 1981, when HIV/AIDS came to be globally recognized, scientists have speculated about the origins of the virus. Theories have included the virus being a homosexual or African plague or a human-made disease originating from biological warfare tests or from contaminated vaccines, such as those used to cure hepatitis B and polio. In the first article Floyd Mann looks at the history of the virus and its link to the polio research undertaken by Koprowski, Salk, and Sabin in the Congo in the 1950s. He argues that at that time scientists knew little about monkey viruses, and there were few or no federal regulations about what types of tissues viruses could be grown in. He concludes with a quote by journalist Tom Curtis that if HIV/AIDS did not originate with the polio vaccine trials, it would be thanks to luck more than anything else.

Stan Hancock, in "The Relationship between AIDS and the Polio Vaccine: Truth v. Myth," examines the accusations that Tom Curtis made in *Rolling Stone* concerning Dr. Hilary Koprowski and other researchers' polio vaccine work. He systematically examines the arguments Curtis used to link Koprowski's research to HIV/AIDS and discredits them. Hancock concludes that misinformation has meant that parents "are too frightened to allow their children to receive medicine's best defense against the curse of poliomyelitis: a safe vaccine."

FURTHER INFORMATION:

Books:

Cantwell, Alan, *AIDS and the Doctors of Death: An Inquiry into the Origin of the AIDS Epidemic*. Los Angeles: Aries Rising Press, 1992.
Grmek, Mirko D., *History of AIDS: Emergence and Origin of a Modern Pandemic*. Princeton, NJ: Princeton University Press, 1990.
Hooper, Edward, *The River: A Journey to the Source of HIV and AIDS*. New York: Back Bay Books, 1999.

Useful websites:

www.uow.edu/au/arts/sts/bmartin/dissent/documents/AIDS/Elswood94/html
B. F. Elswood and R. B. Stricker, "Polio Vaccines and the Origins of AIDS."
www.msnbc.com/news/458600.asp
"HIV Not Tied to Polio Vaccine."
www.cnn.com/2000/HEALTH/AIDS/09/12/polio.vaccine/index/html
"No AIDS-related Viruses Found in 1950s-era Polio Vaccine."
www.news.bbc.co.uk/hi/english/health/newsid920000/920496.stm
Article on scientists and polio links to HIV/AIDS.
www.virusmyth.net/aids/data/rcracism.htm
Rosalind Harrison-Chirimuuta, "AIDS from Africa: Western Science or Racist Mythology?"
www.cumicro2.cpmc.columbia.edu/PICO/Chapters/History.html
Article on history of polio.

The following debates in the Pro/Con series may also be of interest:

In this volume:

Topic 9 Should the conduct of doctors be monitored?

Topic 14 Should scientists be responsible for the effects of their inventions?

CAN THE ORIGINS OF HIV/AIDS BE TRACED TO THE POLIO VACCINE?

YES: Finding out where the virus originated will help scientists/researchers come up with a cure more quickly

YES: It will help scientists prevent similar deadly viruses occurring

YES: Statistics show that millions of people have been vaccinated with the polio vaccine without contracting HIV/AIDS

BACKGROUND
Does it matter where AIDS originated?

NO: A map of the areas of polio inoculation in equatorial Africa coincides with the highest incidence of HIV/AIDS

MYTH V. REALITY
Is the polio link just another myth?

NO: It is a waste of money to research the history of the disease when money should be directed to HIV/AIDS prevention and awareness

NO: There is strong evidence to link the polio vaccine to HIV/AIDS

CAN THE ORIGINS OF HIV/AIDS BE TRACED TO THE POLIO VACCINE?

KEY POINTS

YES: Since the research was not monitored at the time, corners could have been cut

YES: The researchers and scientists were permitted to do live trials with the polio vaccine. That would not happen today.

SAFETY
Could lack of safety regulations have led to misconduct in the polio vaccine research?

NO: Even if corners were cut, the end justifies the means, and millions of people have been saved from contracting polio

NO: The scientists were well intentioned and would not have taken unnecessary risks

Topic 9
SHOULD THE CONDUCT OF DOCTORS BE MONITORED?

YES
"DOCTORS OFTEN NOT PRACTICING WHAT CLINICAL GUIDELINES PREACH"
WWW.HOOKMAN.COM/HC0009.HTM
AMERICAN MEDICAL NEWS, SEPTEMBER 2000

NO
"DOCTORS, PATIENTS FILE CLASS ACTION SUIT TO BLOCK FEDERAL PUNISHMENT
FOR MEDICAL MARIJUANA"
ACLU PRESS RELEASE, JANUARY 14, 1997
AMERICAN CIVIL LIBERTIES UNION

INTRODUCTION

Even before the formulation in about 400 B.C. of the oath, the code of practice attributed to the Greek physician Hippocrates (c.460–377 B.C.), doctors tried to work to a system of medical ethics acceptable to their profession. Such a code has always been seen as necessary to prevent medical malpractice or abuses of power, and it acts as a safety net to protect both patient and doctor.

Although the Hippocratic oath mentions the doctor-patient relationship, abortion, and other important issues, its relevance has been questioned since its wide-scale adoption by the medical profession in the Middle Ages. At the time of Hippocrates most people believed that disease was caused by an imbalance of the four "humors"—blood, phlegm, black bile, and yellow bile—thought to constitute the human body. However, in the 19th century, as scientific knowledge increased very

quickly, the oath became unpopular among those physicians who believed that knowledge and competence should dictate medical ethics. It gained popularity again at the beginning of the 20th century, when it became evident that the medical profession still needed a moral code by which to work.

In the past 50 years or so the oath's relevance has once more been questioned, especially since physician-patient relationships have changed, with patients having more control and say in their medical care. In the United States the introduction of health insurance, and with it business ethics, into medical practice led many people to look at the oath again.

A survey of 157 deans of allopathic and osteopathic schools in Canada and the United States carried out by Robert Orr, M.D., and Norman Pang, M.D., found that whereas in 1928 only 26 percent of the schools used some form of the Hippocratic oath, in 1993 that figure had risen to around 98 percent, although only one of the schools concerned used the original oath. That seems to support the premise that the medical profession recognizes that it requires some code by which its practices can be monitored.

> *"Into whatever houses I enter, I will go into them for the benefit of the sick and will abstain from every voluntary act of mischief and corruption."*
>
> —HIPPOCRATIC OATH (400 B.C.)

In the United States the American Medical Association is one of the bodies that helps monitor important issues concerning physicians. It has reported on, among other matters, the rise in malpractice suits (legal cases resulting from alleged instances of improper professional conduct) against doctors. This increase and the consequent questioning of doctors' conduct and ability have brought into question whether doctors need a more stringent and formal method of monitoring, both to protect the physicians themselves from false allegations and, more importantly, to protect the rights of the patient.

One of the consequences of President Lyndon B. Johnson's Medicare and Medicaid programs, which aimed to improve healthcare for the poor and elderly (see *Government*, page 70), is that the U.S. medical system underwent a change in emphasis from simply providing patient care to worrying about the financial implications of providing treatment to people. Because certain medical procedures are more in demand, the prices charged for those procedures rise as demand outstrips supply. Because people have to pay for certain medical procedures, their expectations of the service they should receive increase. If a patient does not get the service he or she expects, it is not uncommon to sue the doctor, hospital, or health authority concerned. Critics argue that an official monitoring organization or code of practice would help prevent a lot of the cases that go to trial in the United States.

A number of organizations and websites already provide guidelines for members of the medical profession and for patients, and this in itself suggests that some kind of policing is needed. On the other hand, some people argue that doctors are already becoming increasingly restricted in their work practices as big insurance companies, big businesses, and heavy bureaucracy prevent them from doing their jobs properly. Fears also exist that patient-doctor confidentiality might have to be breached if doctors' activities are continually monitored.

The following two articles examine this complex issue. In the first article *American Medical News* looks at how patients are not always receiving the care that they expect or for which they pay. In the second article the American Civil Liberties Union examines the contentious issue of marijuana use in medical treatment. The ACLU argues that the right of doctors to discuss the subject confidentially with their patients is protected under the First Amendment.

DOCTORS OFTEN NOT PRACTICING WHAT CLINICAL GUIDELINES PREACH
American Medical News

Yet another study confirms that actual clinical practice often doesn't live up to recommended care.

A decade after professional organizations began pushing for implementation of clinical practice guidelines to ensure patients receive needed care, significant deviation from those guidelines is still prevalent, new data from the Michigan-based Medstat Group show. Many now think pressure will have to come from outside the medical profession before that gap can be closed.

A Medstat analysis of two years of claims data pooled by numerous employers and plans revealed serious shortfalls in basic treatment for patients with common chronic conditions. For example, only 29 percent of almost 16,000 patients diagnosed with diabetes received recommended annual eye exams; less than half received total cholesterol tests. Among the 3,949 patients with heart failure included in the study, only 40 percent received an echocardiogram within three months of their initial diagnoses. And less than half received a chest x-ray within the first year. Only about a quarter of the 6,404 patients with asthma whose cases were reviewed received inhaled anti-inflammatory drugs.

Similar shortfalls in recommended practice were seen for patients with otitis media, low back pain, peptic ulcer, breast cancer, hypertension and systemic heart disease said Medstat Senior Vice President Dennis J. Becker.

An echocardiogram is a test carried out on the heart that uses ultrasound waves to record heart activity.

"Otitis media" is inflammation of the middle ear. "Hypertension" is abnormally high blood pressure.

Gaps between the optimal and the actual

Countless studies show similar trends, and the Medstat data offer sobering confirmation that unexplained clinical variation is still widespread, said David B. Nash, MD, an outcome expert at Thomas Jefferson University Hospital.

"What we're really learning is just how difficult it is to achieve change in behavior," he said. "Even where we have grade A evidence, like in asthma, there's very little in the way of reportable success at decreasing variation. We're seeing pockets of improvement here and there. But there's no national effort to address this problem." In fact, in Dr. Nash's view efforts to address quality problems have been pushed to a back burner by the current managed care backlash.

At the same time, physicians and other providers often cite patients as the reason needed care is not always given. No-show rates indeed do keep many patients with chronic conditions from receiving treatment.

Yet the Medstat data also punched some holes in that excuse. For example, closer examinations of claims data of the patients with diabetes showed that most had been seen by their primary care physicians frequently during the two-year period and still had not received routine blood test or eye exams.

"What we're witnessing here is lost opportunity," said David Schutt, MD, Medstat's associate medical director: "People actually are accessing the health care system, but the system's failing them."

Problems at the system, patient and provider levels have allowed the gaps between optimal and actual practice to continue, he added. Patients typically are uninformed about the care they should be receiving. Physicians and hospitals seldom step back to assess overall treatment of broader populations of patients. And the health care system currently lacks the information infrastructure to track and change clinical behavior, noted Dr. Schutt.

Employers step in

Major employers, however, have begun to recognize the impact that failure to receive needed care can have on their employees' quality of life and productivity. And many now are seeking data tools to track performance and demand change among plans and providers.

"Once this becomes as much of a business issue as a clinical issue, and as it is helped along by the current wave of consumerism, I believe this will get much more attention than it has over the past few years," Becker said. "That's also going to require those on the payer side to be willing to pay for the care that's recommended."

Dr. Nash agreed. "Large employers, and the employees they represent, are really the only group now with the leverage to make a difference. Demanding monetary refunds for failure to meet a target is the only way to make a business case for quality."

There are some indications indeed that some employers and plans are serious about making the necessary investment. A related report on innovative models of care, released last month by the American Accreditation Healthcare

If doctors' shortcomings are to be monitored, should patients' behavior also be checked and punished?

What do you think the speaker means by becoming "a business issue"?

Launched in 1990, the American Accreditation HealthCare Commission (URAC) is a nonprofit charitable body that provides accreditation for organizations in the managed care industry.

COMMENTARY: Hippocrates and the oath

The ancient Greek physician and medical teacher Hippocrates is believed to have been born on the island of Cos in about 460 B.C. and to have died at Larissa in Thessaly on the Greek mainland in about 377 B.C. Widely considered to be the founder of modern medicine, he is credited with having removed the explanation of illness from the realms of superstition and placed it on a scientific footing. To most people he is best known for the oath, the text of which follows. Although he almost certainly did not write it himself, the oath bears the mark of his influence, as does the body of medical and philosophical writings known as the Hippocratic collection, which is thought to have been written partly by Hippocrates himself and partly by other adherents to his views on medicine, who were known as the Coan school, Hippocrates having practiced and taught on his home island of Cos.

The oath

"I swear by Apollo the physician, and Aesculapius, and Health, and All-heal, and all the gods and goddesses, that, according to my ability and judgment, I will keep this Oath and this stipulation—to reckon him who taught me this Art equally dear to me as my parents, to share my substance with him, and relieve his necessities if required; to look upon his offspring in the same footing as my own brothers, and to teach them this Art, if they shall wish to learn it, without fee or stipulation; and that by precept, lecture, and every other mode of instruction, I will impart a knowledge of the Art to my own sons, and those of my teachers, and to disciples bound by a stipulation and oath according to the law of medicine, but to none others. I will follow that system of regimen which, according to my ability and judgment, I consider for the benefit of my patients, and abstain from whatever is deleterious and mischievous. I will give no deadly medicine to any one if asked, nor suggest any such counsel; and in like manner I will not give to a woman a pessary to produce abortion. With purity and with holiness I will pass my life and practice my Art. I will not cut persons laboring under the stone, but will leave this to be done by men who are practitioners of this work. Into whatever houses I enter, I will go into them for the benefit of the sick, and will abstain from every voluntary act of mischief and corruption; and, further from the seduction of females or males, of freemen and slaves. Whatever, in connection with my professional practice or not in connection with it, I see or hear, in the life of men, which ought not to be spoken of abroad, I will not divulge, as reckoning that all such should be kept secret. While I continue to keep this Oath unviolated, may it be granted to me to enjoy life and the practice of the Art, respected by all men, in all times! But should I trespass and violate this Oath, may the reverse be my lot!" (version of oath translated by Francis Adams; see www.classics.mit.edu/).

Commission, highlighted almost 100 initiatives that have helped promote adherence to guidelines. The majority were driven by business coalitions and plans.

For example, Blue Cross and Blue Shield of the Rochester Area was able to increase its eye exam rate for patients with diabetes from 42.8 percent to 58 percent between 1996 and 1998 by providing data reports and guideline information to physicians, utilizing nurse case managers and disseminating educational materials to patients. More than 80 percent of those with diabetes employed by Black & Decker Corp. receive annual eye exams now that it's enlisted outside care coordinators to educate patients and contact primary care physicians to verify that patients receive needed tests.

> *Congestive heart failure (CHF) is a condition in which the heart can no longer pump blood adequately.*

Year long care plans for patients with congestive heart failure are developed in conjunction with patients' primary care physicians through a program devised by Evanston (Ill.) Northwestern Healthcare. The initiative helped the physician-hospital organization cut 30-day readmission rates for CHF from 19 percent to 2.7 percent.

In the report, Caren Heller, MD, acknowledged that gaps exist between the use of clinical interventions demonstrated to be effective and current practice. She noted that successful efforts to enhance "evidence-based practice" universally use guidelines that physicians or multidisciplinary teams have customized for local use, tools to integrate guidelines into daily practice and information systems to provide reminders and feedback on best practices. "Physicians are critical to implementing evidence-based clinical practice to improve quality and manage costs," she wrote. "However, they need support to achieve this goal systematically."

> *Evidence-based practice is a form of care provision in which a doctor not only relies on clinical experience when treating a patient but also consults current research and the patient's wishes.*

DOCTORS, PATIENTS FILE CLASS ACTION SUIT TO BLOCK FEDERAL PUNISHMENT FOR MEDICAL MARIJUANA
American Civil Liberties Union

NO

LOS ANGELES—A group of physicians and patients today filed a class action suit in federal court in San Francisco seeking an injunction blocking federal officials from taking any punitive action against physicians who simply recommend the medical use of marijuana to their patients.

The lawsuit names as defendants: Gen. Barry McCaffrey, Director of the White House Office of National Drug Control Policy; Thomas Constantine, Administrator of the U.S. Drug Enforcement Administration (DEA); Janet Reno, Attorney General of the United States; and Donna Shalala, Secretary of the Department of Health and Human Services (HHS).

Representing the plaintiffs are the San Francisco firm of Altshuler, Berzon, Nussbaum, Berzon & Rubin and the American Civil Liberties Union of Northern California.

An unconstitutional move

Graham Boyd, an attorney with Altshuler, Berzon, Nussbaum, Berzon & Rubin, said, "Our view is that the federal effort to gag physicians is blatantly unconstitutional. Discussion between a physician and patient about the risk and benefits of medical marijuana constitute protected speech under the First Amendment."

Boyd sets out the basis of the lawsuit, contending that since doctor-patient conversations are protected speech under the First Amendment, it would be unconstitutional to punish doctors for discussing medical marijuana use with their patients.

"The Supreme Court," Boyd continued, "has said that the government may not bar physicians from discussing contraception or abortion, both controversial topics in their day. By the same logic, federal officials may not use controversy over marijuana as an excuse to intrude into the sanctity of the physician-patient relationship."

Dr. Marcus Conant, a San Francisco specialist in AIDS treatment and the lead plaintiff in the lawsuit, said, "The Federal government has threatened me and doctors like me with dire consequences for simply discussing medical marijuana with my patients. My colleagues and I have seen marijuana work to relieve nausea and stimulate appetite where other drugs fail, and scores of studies support our observations."

"The medical community," Dr. Conant continued, "deserves more respect than having a retired General in Washington tell us how to practice medicine. Physicians should be allowed to discuss medical marijuana without having to risk arrest or other punishment by the federal government."

Dr. Arnold Leff, a Santa Cruz AIDS specialist who served in the White House Drug Abuse Office under President Richard Nixon, added, "By approving Proposition 215, California voters have endorsed the right of patients to use marijuana medically under a physician's care. To give force to that right, physicians also must be protected."

Jo Daly, a former police commissioner of San Francisco and a patient who uses marijuana medically, said, "The federal government is trying to intimidate the doctors who treat me for cancer. Marijuana literally saved my life by stopping the horrible vomiting caused by my chemotherapy. Bureaucrats like Barry McCaffrey want to get in between me and my doctors and make me another victim of their drug policies. This began as a war on drugs. Now it's become a war on doctors."

In general terms Proposition 215 was the political campaign to legalize medical marijuana use. It took effect on November 6, 1996, and became law as California Health and Safety Code Section 11362.5, the Compassionate Use Act of 1996.

Doctors face punishment

The lawsuit is a direct response to the Clinton administration's December 30 announcement of its plan to fight implementation of Proposition 215 by threatening doctors with a range of punishment if they are found to be recommending medical marijuana to their patients. The defendants named in the suit are the key federal officials involved in drafting and implementing the Clinton administration strategy.

Proposition 215 altered California law by creating a new exemption for a specific group of people—seriously ill patients who are using marijuana on the "recommendation or approval" of a physician. If an arrested patient is to be exonerated, he or she must prove that a physician advised that marijuana was medically appropriate for that patient.

However, given the new threats of federal action against physicians who recommend marijuana, doctors face a difficult choice when they observe that marijuana appears to be medically appropriate for a patient. Doctors can inform patients of their truthful medical opinion, and expose themselves and their practice to punitive action that could destroy their livelihood, or censor their discussions with patients, depriving them of useful treatment alternatives and eroding the trust and confidence essential to effective medical care.

Do you think it is right that the government should use federal laws to oppose changes in state law?

Do you believe that medical use of marijuana should be allowed?

COMMENTARY: Medical marijuana

Marijuana is obtained from the leaves and flower tops of the Indian hemp plant, *Cannabis sativa*. Its active ingredient, tetrahydrocannabinol (THC), is a psychoactive agent—that is, it acts on the mind—and it is in this substance that at least some of marijuana's therapeutic value seems to rest. In modern times marijuana is best known as an illegal recreational drug, having been prohibited in the United States since the passage of the Marijuana Tax Act of 1937. However, toward the end of the 20th century campaigns gathered momentum in the United States to have the drug accepted in medical treatment.

Uses for medical purposes

Although the full list of conditions that have been treated with marijuana is long, much research revolves around its use by AIDS and cancer patients. In the case of the former the drug may help treat the wasting associated with AIDS by stimulating the patient's appetite, whereas in cancer sufferers marijuana may bring relief from pain and from the nausea and vomiting that can come with chemotherapy. Marijuana seemingly can also alleviate muscle spasms in people with multiple sclerosis; and in glaucoma internal eye pressure has been relieved by marijuana, although patients had to smoke so regularly that they were permanently under the influence of the drug; the condition can now be treated effectively with other drugs.

Medical use of marijuana is not new—the Chinese made reference to it in an ancient book of remedies that may date from as far back as 2700 B.C.; and even while marijuana was a banned substance, research was undertaken into its possible therapeutic properties. The first U.S. states to decriminalize marijuana for medical use were California and Arizona, which passed referenda in November 1996 (Propositions 215 and 200 respectively). The Arizona initiative was later invalidated; but California's stood, and several other states have passed medical marijuana ballot initiatives since.

Taking marijuana as medicine

The traditional way to use marijuana is to smoke it, but research suggests that in the long term at least, this method brings with it similar, or possibly worse, health risks than does smoking tobacco. Other means of introducing marijuana's active ingredient into the body include Marinol, THC in pill form, which was approved by the U.S. Food and Drug Administration (FDA) as long ago as 1986. Natural marijuana pills are also available, and research has been undertaken into developing a marijuana inhaler. Even so, it seems that medical marijuana is not for everyone, with some people suffering side effects from THC, and others finding that marijuana smoking makes their symptoms worse. On the other hand, marijuana can be the drug of last resort for those people for whom other treatments do not work.

The lawsuit filed today argues that such a choice is no choice at all, and that the threat against doctors is in fact an unconstitutional intrusion into communications between doctor and patient with the potential to harm both. The doctor's recommendation to the patient, and his or her public acknowledgement of that recommendation in the context of a criminal proceeding against the patient, both constitute protected speech for which any penalties at all would be impermissible, the suit argues.

Boyd, the attorney helping with the suit, said, "there must be a means available to punish those who would abuse the new law, whether they be bogus 'patients' or profiting doctors. And our lawsuit is carefully phrased to provide no comfort to a doctor who recommends marijuana without having a good-faith diagnosis, based on a bona fide physician-patient relationship."

…"This lawsuit," said Dr. Conant, the San Francisco AIDS care physician, "directly challenges the federal government's declaration that any doctor making any recommendation for marijuana is committing a punishable act—and it offers real hope of protection for responsible physicians in this state."

Statement of Ann Brick

[Ann Brick of the] American Civil Liberties Union of Northern California [said,]

"The federal government's current efforts to insert itself between doctors and their patients when it comes to recommending medical marijuana is contrary to our most fundamental First Amendment values. The central purpose of the First Amendment is to protect dissent from the government's version of the facts on any particular issue, including the issue of medical marijuana."

The doctors who are plaintiffs in this lawsuit are asserting their right to tell patients, when they believe it is medically appropriate to do so, that the medical use of marijuana may help in the treatment or management of their disease. The government's recent threats to go after doctors who give such advice is a heavy-handed attempt to silence a group that is particularly well-placed to speak with authority in delivering a message that is different from the government's official line. It is the purpose of this lawsuit to see that the government does not succeed in silencing these physicians.

Doctors have a First Amendment right to speak on the issue of medical marijuana, not only when speaking to the public, but when speaking to their patients as well.

On April 30, 1997, Judge Fern Smith granted a preliminary injunction that restricted the ability of the federal government to punish doctors for recommending marijuana for medical use.

121

Summary

The issue of whether doctors' conduct should be monitored is fraught with difficulty. On the one hand, the patient-doctor relationship is important and should be protected. On the other, doctors should not get away with providing inadequate or inappropriate healthcare, although in the United States litigation in medical matters has arguably gotten out of control. Would a more formal system of policing the medical profession work?

The first extract, from *American Medical News*, states that "A decade after professional organizations began pushing for implementation of clinical practice guidelines to ensure patients receive needed care, significant deviation from those guidelines is still prevalent...." It provides recent statistics to support its argument. By contrast, the American Civil Liberties Union (ACLU) article examines the use of marijuana in healthcare. It argues that doctors have lived in fear of punishment for simply discussing the issue. The ACLU argues that the Supreme Court protected the right of physicians to discuss issues such as abortion and that marijuana treatment should come under the First Amendment freedom of speech statute.

FURTHER INFORMATION:

Books:

Mack, Alison, and Janet E. Joy, *Marijuana as Medicine?* Washington, D.C.: National Academy Press, 2001.

Useful websites:

www.hol.gr/greece/medicine.htm
Article on Hippocrates that provides background to the oath.
www.ama-assn.org/sci-pubs/amnews/pick_00/prca0501.htm
"Why Do Freshly Minted Doctors still Recite the Hippocratic Oath?" American Medical Association article on the modern relevance of the Hippocratic oath; second scenario, reply by Karen E. Geraghty.
www.imagerynet.com/hippo.ama.html
"The Modern Oath of Hippocrates." Article that discusses the Hippocratic oath in a modern context. Looks at the British Medical Association proposed revisions in 1997.
www.civilrights.com/medical.html
Article on actionable medical malpractice.
www.drugsense.org/mmj.htm
DrugSense site on medical marijuana.

SHOULD THE CONDUCT OF DOCTORS BE MONITORED?

YES: A doctor is bound by the Hippocratic oath to do his or her best for the patient concerned. No further intervention is necessary.

YES: If a doctor is in fear of being sued, that will inevitably affect his or her decision on whether to provide more risky but possibly beneficial treatment to patients

ETHICS
Should doctors be able to practice without intervention?

MALPRACTICE
Can the fear of litigation prevent adequate healthcare?

NO: Doctors are human and can be influenced by other factors such as money or politics. There has to be some system of monitoring their conduct.

NO: If a doctor is competent, he or she has nothing to worry about

SHOULD THE CONDUCT OF DOCTORS BE MONITORED?
KEY POINTS

YES: In the event of investigation doctors would have to reveal every aspect of a case in order to present all the facts

YES: Insurance companies and hospitals that stand to lose large of sums of money in litigation cases deserve to have all the facts

CONFIDENTIALITY
Would the patient-doctor relationship be affected by monitoring?

NO: Trust is essential to the doctor-patient relationship, and confidentiality must not be affected

Topic 10
SHOULD DOCTORS BE ABLE TO ASSIST IN EUTHANASIA?

YES
"GIVE ME LIBERTY, GIVE ME DEATH"
WWW.IMPACTPRESS.COM/ARTICLES/FEBMAR97/DEATH.HTM
MIKE HAIT

NO
"WHOSE RIGHT TO DIE"?
THE ATLANTIC MONTHLY, NO. 3, VOL. 279, MARCH 1997
EZEKIEL EMANUEL

INTRODUCTION

Euthanasia, which comes from Greek words meaning "easy death," refers to the practice of a person, usually a physician, assisting another person to commit suicide. Supporters see it as mercy killing, opponents as legalized murder. But for society it raises fundamental issues: Who has the right to choose whether a person should live or die? How is it possible to know that a very sick person really does wish to die? And how is euthanasia compatible with the duty of a physician to maintain rather than destroy life?

Such questions are far more than theoretical moral debates. For care workers they are sometimes real dilemmas that have to be faced. For two years in the mid–1990s euthanasia was legalized in the Northern Territory in Australia. The practice is still legal in the Netherlands. The trial and imprisonment of Dr. Jack Kevorkian in Michigan in 1999 showed that the issue is very much alive in the United States.

The rights and wrongs of physician-assisted suicide are a separate issue from suicide itself. Some see suicide as a personal decision made and executed by an individual. Although it was condemned for centuries as self-murder by the church, it is now often regarded as an individual's right. Voluntary euthanasia, on the other hand, involves several other people: the person's family, legal representatives, the physician who helps them end the life, and the other doctors who are required to approve the decision. Physician-assisted suicide is not a decision made by one person and assisted by another—in the few places where the practice is legal, there is a whole system of checks and balances to prevent abuse. Some critics assert that physician-assisted euthanasia compromises the role of the doctor, who has taken an oath to preserve life.

The role of the doctor is central to voluntary euthanasia. Where the practice is allowed, such a killing can be carried out only when death is judged to be medically beneficial to the patient. That benefit must be proved to more than one physician on more than one occasion. In no system is the simple request of the individual to end his or her life sufficient. The wish to die

> *"Legalization of assisted suicide and euthanasia is not the answer to the problems of people who are terminally ill. The Netherlands has moved from assisted suicide to euthanasia, from euthanasia for people who are terminally ill to euthanasia for those who are chronically ill, from euthanasia for physical illness to euthanasia for psychological distress, and from voluntary euthanasia to involuntary euthanasia."*
> —HERBERT HENDLIN, AUTHOR OF
> *SEDUCED BY DEATH* (1996)

is not enough. And if any of the doctors concerned with the case believe that the patient has any chance of recovery or even some sort of worthwhile life without recovery, then there are no grounds for euthanasia. Only when the doctors are convinced that no worthwhile life is possible can the

request even be considered. Even then the desire for life to be ended must be shown over a period of time. No system allows a hasty wish, expressed only once to be acted on. There must be evidence that all the implications of the deed have been thought through and that the individual fully realizes the enormity and finality of the decision.

But who defines a "worthwhile life"? And if the state recognizes the right of a person who does not have a "worthwhile life" to terminate life at their own request, what are the implications for people, also judged not to have "worthwhile lives," who have expressed no such wish? Some members of the Royal Dutch Medical Association seem to be moving toward advocacy of limited nonvoluntary euthanasia in the case of terminally ill patients who are in great pain.

Some estimates put the annual number of deaths through euthanasia in the Netherlands at as many as one in 12—and there are suggestions that more than one-quarter of those deaths were unrequested "mercy killings."

Both sides of the debate coopt compassion. Advocates of euthanasia say that the compassionate course is to end the suffering of a patient who is in terrible pain. Those who oppose it believe that true compassion is in the nursing and care of the terminally ill.

Mike Hait, in his article "Give Me Liberty, Give Me Death," suggests that euthanasia gives the suffering control of their lives. It lets them die with dignity.

The second article by Ezekiel Emanuel, "Whose Right to Die"? cites the example of the Netherlands, where he claims the guidelines that govern euthanasia are often abused.

GIVE ME LIBERTY, GIVE ME DEATH
Mike Hait

YES

The famous quote
Hait uses for his
title—"Give me
liberty or give me
death"— was
spoken in 1775 at
the Continental
Congress by Patrick
Henry, who became
the first governor
of independent
Virginia. Hait's
suggestion that it
referred to suicide
is tongue-in-cheek.

When Patrick Henry issued his legendary cry, was this the patriotic war call of a revolutionary, or the stifled plea of a suicidal? Though the modern euthanasia, or assisted suicide, movements did not find their way into the United States until 1938, suicide has long lived in the hearts of men desiring freedom.

The American society at large is noticeably uncomfortable with death. So when, in 1991, a high percentage of people found themselves faced with the news that Dr. Jack Kevorkian, a respected physician, had begun assisting terminally ill people to end their lives respectably, the American society at large shouted in outrage. Though all of Dr. Kevorkian's "victims" have been competent adults who sought him out, he soon came to bear the derogatory moniker "Dr. Death" and has, to date, been charged with the murders of eleven people, due to the Michigan bans on physician-assisted suicide. Fortunately, the courts have seen fit to acquit Dr. Kevorkian on all of these unconstitutional charges. On the flip side, the same courts have declared that the ban on assisted suicide stands....

Hait's piece was
written before
Kevorkian was
imprisoned in
Michigan in 1999.
See the box on
page 128 for a
fuller discussion
of Kevorkian.

Dying a good death

Exactly what is this issue that so offends the government? Euthanasia, which usually involves the prescription and possible administration of lethal dosages of drugs to the terminally ill by physicians of their choice, means, literally, "good death." The movement also bears another name: death with dignity. Since the advent, in the last decade, of the Living Will, the terminally ill have been able to control their death by demanding the unplugging of all life support machines. The only step past this is to bypass the hospital altogether. Many terminally ill people do not want the last memories of themselves to be those of a weak, dying decrepit. The assisted suicide and euthanasia movements provide for these situations. They allow people to control their life, and their death, and allow those final memories to be those of a strong, living character. This fear of dying without dignity must weigh heavily on the older generation, as they have the highest suicide rate of any other age group.

The AMA—for or against?

Physician-aided suicide seems the least harmful means to end a life of suffering. Even now, however, the American Medical Association disapproves. Not surprising, considering that until the U.S. Supreme Court ruled to the contrary, the AMA disapproved of abortion. Then, following the decision, they miraculously saw the error of their ways and reversed their position. Thusly, the AMA consistently backs down from controversy. In the case of physician-assisted suicide, their

For more information on how the AMA feels on this issue look at www.Mar ketingPower.com.

"To die proudly when it is no longer possible to live proudly. Death of one's own free choice, death at the proper time, with a clear head and with joyfulness, consummated in the midst of children and witnesses: so that an actual leave-taking is possible while he who is leaving is still there."

—FRIEDRICH NIETZSCHE (1844–1900),

GERMAN PHILOSOPHER

position, according to a letter written by AMA general counsel, Kirk Johnson, to Michigan Attorney General, Frank Kelley, on October 10, 1995, states that, "physicians must not act with the intent of causing the death of their patients. Physician-assisted suicide is simply incompatible with the physician's role as healer.... [P]hysicians must relieve suffering by providing adequate comfort care." Never to be tied to one decision in a matter this controversial, however, the letter goes on to state that, "[T]his obligation is paramount: it is ethical for physicians to provide effective pain medication even if the medication may have the side effect of suppressing respiration and hastening death." So obviously, the AMA has decided it is inherently wrong for a physician to end a life of suffering, unless of course the patient feels good before he dies.... The American Medical Association, while continuously regarded the "experts,"

The author uses flippancy to deride the AMA's position. Do you think this helps his case?

COMMENTARY: Alias Dr. Death

Public debate over the rights and wrongs of physician-assisted suicide grew especially heated during the 1990s, when Dr. Jack Kevorkian, a Michigan physician, enabled nearly 50 terminally sick people to end their lives. His actions divided the nation into those who defended his acts and those in whom he fostered revulsion and anger.

Born in 1928 in Pontiac, Michigan, Kevorkian trained at the University of Michigan Medical School, graduating in 1952. It was soon after this that he earned his soubriquet Dr. Death from his controversial proposals to perform medical experiments on death-row victims shortly before giving them their lethal injection. After serving as a staff pathologist in Michigan and southern California, Kevorkian turned during the 1980s to the practice for which he became infamous: that of offering a suicide clinic. He had two methods of helping people commit suicide. The first was to give them his so-called "Mercitron" or "suicide machine." The second was to administer carbon monoxide via a cylinder and mask. His first patient, 54-year-old Janet Adkins, was in the early stages of Alzheimer's disease when, on June 4, 1990, she took a lethal dose of drugs via the Mercitron. Kevorkian was charged with murder, but was aquitted when Michigan was found to have no law against physician-assisted suicide.

Several more assisted suicides followed, but Kevorkian escaped a long prison term through a series of legal loopholes, though his medical licence was finally withdrawn. In 1999, however, Kevorkian was convicted for his part in helping Thomas Youk to die. He was sentenced to 10–25 years in prison.

Jack Kevorkian was hailed as a hero by some for his dedication to ending the suffering of terminally ill patients. Others describe his actions as legalized murder and an affront to common medical ethics.

represents only a very small percentage of the doctors in the United States. Despite the legal hold on aid in dying, a 1996 study of over 800 American critical care nurses showed nearly one in five admitted to hastening their patients' death when requested: 16 percent by performing active euthanasia and 4 percent by performing passive euthanasia, or withholding treatment. A poll taken by the American Journal of Respiratory and Critical Care Medicine in February 1996 of over 850 physicians in that area of medicine revealed that an outstanding 96 percent had discontinued critical care treatments with the expectation that the patient would die.

Do you think there is a moral difference between active and passive euthanasia? The end result is the same.

Motives behind the law

The U.S. government and the "official" medical community, however, refuse to condone a practice that is both ethical and practical, regardless of the opinions of the professional community as a whole. This doubtless stems from two reasons. First of all, none can deny the existence of the overpowering Judeo-Christian code of ethics governing U.S. officialdom. For example, the Hippocratic oath, that which the American Medical Association recommends to all new doctors, is a religious oath and has nothing to do with medicine. As Dr. Kevorkian said, in a speech to the American Humanist Association after receiving the 1994 Humanist Hero Award, "If you meet a physician who says, 'Life is sacred,' be careful. We didn't study sanctity in medical school. You are talking to a theologian first, probably a businessperson second, and a physician third." The second, and more obvious reason is money, that which makes the wheels of U.S. society spin. During the [later period] of a terminally ill person's suffering, enough pain medication and treatments are prescribed to earn the pharmaceutical industry billions of dollars. Were the terminally ill patient to take his life, and death, into his own hands and end his suffering early, the medical "profession" would lose those billions.

The origin of the medical ethical code known as the Hippocratic oath is attributed to Hippocrates—a Greek physician who lived about 460–377 or 359 B.C.

The United States government, hand in hand with big business, has slowly been devouring rights inherent to humanity. Still we praise this nation as our very deaths fall out of our hands. The terminally ill have a right to die with a scrap of dignity left in them, and there is no more responsible way to die than with the full cooperation of the men in whose hands most of us place our complete faith. Yet their hands are tied on this issue by red tape. Who will wipe their tears as patients they have helped for years wither away and die in the most pitiful manners possible, and they have nothing to do but ignore their pleas or watch helplessly?

Do you think economics has a place in this debate? Or is it mainly a moral question?

The author concludes with an appeal to the reader's emotions.

WHOSE RIGHT TO DIE?
Ezekiel Emanuel

NO

In physician-assisted suicide a doctor supplies a death-causing means, such as barbiturates, but the patient performs the act that brings about death. In voluntary euthanasia the physician performs the death-causing act after determining that the patient indeed wishes to end his or her life. Neither term applies to a patient's refusal of life-support technology, such as a respirator or artificial nutrition, or a patient's request that it be withdrawn; these have had ethical and constitutional sanction nationwide for years. And neither term applies to what is sometimes called indirect euthanasia, when the administration of drugs primarily for pain relief may have the secondary effect of causing death, as the physician is well aware. This practice, too, is ethically and legally sanctioned. [These] judgments are based on misreadings of history, misinterpretations of survey data, mistaken reasoning, and simple misinformation.

What is the legal position of physician-assisted suicide in your state? Has it been an issue in state politics?

Myth No. 1: It is primarily advances in biomedical technology—especially life-sustaining technology—that have created unprecedented public interest in physician-assisted suicide and voluntary euthanasia. Physician-assisted suicide and euthanasia have been profound ethical issues confronting doctors since the birth of Western medicine, more than 2,000 years ago. The ancient Hippocratic oath enjoins physicians to "neither give a deadly drug to anybody if asked for it, nor make a suggestion to this effect." The oath was written at a time when physicians commonly provided euthanasia and assisted suicide. Even in America legalized euthanasia, rather than being a new issue, has been publicly debated and rejected [notably in 1870 and 1906].

In its original form the Hippocratic oath also forbade physicians from taking money for consultations and from performing surgical procedures.

Thus, decades before the discovery of penicillin (1928) and the development of mechanical respirators (1929), dialysis (1945), and other life-sustaining technologies, serious public discussions of physician-assisted suicide and euthanasia took place in the United States.

Myth No. 2: Legalizing physician-assisted suicide and euthanasia is widely endorsed. Yes, polls show that a majority of Americans support physician-assisted suicide and euthanasia—indeed, have supported legalizing them for almost 25 years. But the support is neither strong nor deep. Careful analysis of the polling data suggests that there is a "rule of thirds": a third of Americans support legalization under a wide variety of circumstances; a third oppose it under any circumstances; and a third support it in a few cases but oppose it in most circumstances. [However,] the most accurate characterization of the survey data is that a significant majority of Americans oppose physician-assisted suicide and euthanasia except in the limited case of a terminally ill patient with uncontrollable pain.

Myth No. 3: It is terminally ill patients with uncontrollable pain who are most likely to be interested in physician-assisted suicide or euthanasia. The empirical studies of physician-assisted suicide and euthanasia in The Netherlands

> *"Everyone is responsible for his life before God who has given it to him. It is God Who remains the sovereign Master of life. We are obliged to accept life gratefully and preserve it for His honor and the salvation of our souls. We are stewards, not owners, of the life God has entrusted to us. It is not ours to dispose of."*
> —CATECHISM OF THE ROMAN CATHOLIC CHURCH

(where the practices have long been accepted), the United States, and elsewhere indicate that pain plays a minor role in motivating requests for the procedures. A 1996 update of the 1991 Remmelink Report on euthanasia practices in the Netherlands revealed that in only 32 percent of all cases did pain play any role in requests for euthanasia; indeed, pain was the sole reason for requesting euthanasia in no cases. What does motivate requests? According to studies, depression and general psychological distress. Many Americans say they

---

Should public opinion be a factor in this debate? Who gets to set society's morals, the public or the experts?

In 1990 the Dutch government installed the Commission on the Study of Medical Practice Concerning Euthanasia (the Remmelink Commission). Its report was issued in 1991.

Should mental distress be treated differently from physical pain?

A protester against euthanasia at The Hague in the Netherlands. Physician-assisted suicide has been tolerated by Dutch courts for more than 20 years, but the guidelines of the system are widely abused.

would support physician-assisted suicide or euthanasia for patients in pain; they oppose the practices for patients who worry about being a burden, about life's being meaningless, about hopelessness. But patients with depression and psychological distress are most likely to request death; patients in pain are less likely to request it.

Myth No. 4: The experience with euthanasia in the Netherlands shows that permitting physician-assisted suicide and euthanasia will not eventually get out of hand. The slippery slope feared by opponents and supporters alike is the route from physician-assisted suicide or euthanasia for terminally ill but competent adults to euthanasia for patients who cannot give consent: the unconscious, the demented, the mentally ill, and children.

What does the Dutch experience actually show? In 1981 [a case of euthanasia] resulted in an agreement between Dutch prosecutors and the Royal Dutch Medical Society, under the terms of which physicians who participated in physician-assisted suicide or euthanasia would not be prosecuted for

In an earlier case in 1973 a Dutch physician gave her elderly, deaf, and partially paralyzed mother a lethal injection. She was convicted of murder but received only a week's suspended jail sentence and a year's probation.

murder if they adhered to certain guidelines. The main guidelines are that 1) the patient must make an informed, free, and explicit request for physician-assisted suicide or euthanasia, and the request must be repeated over time; 2) the patient must be experiencing unbearable suffering—physical or psychological—that cannot be relieved by any intervention; 3) the attending physician must have a consultation with a second, independent physician to confirm that the case is appropriate for physician-assisted suicide or euthanasia; and 4) the physician must report the facts of the case to the coroner, as part of a notification procedure developed to permit investigation and to ensure that the guidelines have been followed.

Lessons from the Dutch example

The update of [the Remmelink] report found that beyond the roughly 3,600 cases of physician-assisted suicide and euthanasia reported in a given year, there are about 1,000 instances of nonvoluntary euthanasia. Most frequently, patients who were no longer competent were given euthanasia even though they could not have freely, explicitly, and repeatedly requested it. Before becoming unconscious or mentally incompetent about half these patients did discuss or express a wish for euthanasia; nevertheless, they were unable to reaffirm their wishes [before] euthanasia was performed. Second, euthanasia of newborns has been acknowledged. Cases have involved babies suffering from fatal or severely disabling defects, though the babies were not in fact dying.

According to David Thomasma in the Journal of Law, Medicine & Ethics (24: 1996), a Dutch physician may withhold treatment from a "defective" infant who would otherwise live a "senseless life."

Many in favor of legalization urge caution in applying the experience of the Netherlands to the United States, citing the many significant geographic, cultural, and political differences between the countries…. The kinds of departures from agreed-upon procedures that have occurred in the Netherlands are likely to be even more commonplace here.

The proper policy, in my view, should be to affirm the status of physician-assisted suicide and euthanasia as illegal. In so doing we would affirm that as a society we condemn ending a patient's life and do not consider that to have one's life ended by a doctor is a right. This does not mean we deny that in exceptional cases interventions are appropriate, as acts of desperation when all other elements of treatment—all medications, surgical procedures, psychotherapy, spiritual care, and so on—have been tried. Physician-assisted suicide and euthanasia should not be performed simply because a patient is depressed, tired of life, worried about being a burden, or worried about being dependent.

Does admitting that physician-assisted suicide is acceptable in some cases weaken the principle of the author's case against the practice?

Summary

In the first article Mike Hait stresses the wish of patients to reassert control over their failing lives. They do not want the last memories of themselves to be those of a weak, dying decrepit. Voluntary physician-assisted euthanasia allows people in great pain and indignity not to be forced to continue a life that they feel is not worth living, nor to end it in a sordid or lonely way. Hait believes that when an individual can choose the final moment of his or her life, the final memories taken away by family and loved ones will be those of a strong character dying with dignity.

In the second article Ezekiel Emanuel does not rule out physician-assisted suicide. He condones it under the most extreme circumstances but argues that all other avenues—medication, counseling, and so on—should be exhausted first. In support of this he cites a report on the situation in the Netherlands. There thousands of sick and terminally ill people opt for assisted suicide or euthanasia each year, and it is tolerated by the courts of justice. But many also die, it is claimed, from "nonvoluntary" euthanasia, and the guidelines for physicians are regularly abused. This situation, states Emanuel, would be as unacceptable in the United States as it is in the Netherlands.

FURTHER INFORMATION:

Books:

Battin, M., *The Least Worst Death*. New York, Oxford: Oxford University Press, 1994.

Beauchamp T., J. Childress, *Principles of Biomedical Ethics* (4th edition). Oxford: Oxford University Press, 1994.

Ogden, R., *Euthanasia, Assisted Suicide and AIDS*. British Columbia: Perreault Goedman Publishing, 1994.

Rachels, J., *The End of Life: Euthanasia and Morality*. Oxford: Oxford University Press, 1986.

Articles:

Alemayehu E., D. Mooloy, G. Guyatt, J. Singer, et al. "Variability in Physicians' Decisions on Caring for Chronically ill Elderly Patients: An International Study." *Canadian Medical Association Journal*, 1991, 144: 9.

Alpers A., L. Bernard, "Physician-assisted Suicide in Oregon." *Journal of American Medical Association*, 274: 6.

Wolf, Susan M., Philip Boyle, Daniel Callahan et al. "Sources of Concern about the Patient Self-determination Act." *New England Journal of Medicine*, 1991, 325: 23.

Young E., S. Jex, "The Patient Self-determination Act: Potential Ethical Quandaries and Benefits." *Cambridge Quarterly of Healthcare Ethics*, 1992, 2.

Useful websites:

www.religioustolerance.org/euthanas.htm
A look at the issues surrounding euthanasia with emphasis on religious viewpoints.

www.euthanasia.org/quotes.html
Comprehensive resource material collected from medical journals, primarily in support of physician-assisted suicide.

The following debates in the Pro/Con series may also be of interest:

In this volume:

Topic 7 Should organ replacement be a commercial enterprise?

Topic 11 Should religion affect parents' medical decisions?

SHOULD DOCTORS BE ABLE TO ASSIST IN EUTHANASIA?

YES: *For the terminally ill who opt for it, euthanasia saves them from a desperate, undignified, lonely, and painfully slow death*

YES: *Many American physicians already admit to practicing euthanasia, and legalization would only improve practice*

A GOOD DEATH
Does physician-assisted euthanasia promise a dignified death?

MALPRACTICE
If introduced, would strict euthanasia guidelines be followed?

NO: *New drugs and improved care make it possible to die with dignity without euthanasia*

NO: *The Netherlands' example shows that euthanasia is often administered after only a single request, and that infanticide is performed on deformed babies; why risk the same slippery slope in the United States?*

SHOULD DOCTORS BE ABLE TO ASSIST IN EUTHANASIA? KEY POINTS

YES: *In both cases the physician is complicit (Dutch physicians do not distinguish between active and passive euthanasia)*

YES: *A physician should provide adequate care for patients and, if called on to do so, end their suffering as they see fit*

DEFINING DEATH
Is euthanasia effectively identical to withholding life-saving treatment?

HIPPOCRATIC OATH
Is euthanasia in keeping with the spirit of the Hippocratic oath?

NO: *To allow a patient to refuse treatment is to recognize human rights, while to supply or administer lethal drugs is murder*

NO: *A physician's duty is to be a healer, not a destroyer, of life*

EUTHANASIA

Modern debate on euthanasia has been greatly fueled by the beliefs and actions of physician Jack Kevorkian. Since his first ads offering his services to terminally ill patients and their families in 1987, Kevorkian has assisted in over 100 deaths and is now serving a prison term for second-degree murder. Meanwhile, various laws and rulings on euthanasia have emerged but the international jury on it is still out.

1987 Jack Kevorkian, a Michigan physician, places small ads in local newspapers advertising "death counseling."

1988 Kevorkian publishes "The Last Fearsome Taboo: Medical Aspects of Planned Death" in German journal *Medicine and Law*.

1989 Using $30 worth of scrap parts Kevorkian develops a "suicide machine" that will allow sick people to kill themselves.

June 4, 1990 Kevorkian is present at the suicide of Alzheimer's-disease victim, 54-year-old Janet Adkins, who died using his suicide machine.

December 12, 1990 Murder charge against Kevorkian is dismissed.

1991 A physician-assisted suicide bill is rejected by the legislature in Maine.

October 23, 1991 Kevorkian attends the deaths of two women in Michigan.

November 21, 1991 Kevorkian's medical license is suspended in Michigan.

July 21, 1992 New murder charges against Kevorkian are dismissed.

November 1992–February 1993 Kevorkian attends 10 deaths brought about by carbon-monoxide poisoning.

December 3, 1992 The state of Michigan bans assisted suicide.

1993 A new law in the Netherlands prevents the prosecution of physicians for assisting the suicide of a terminally ill patient provided strict conditions are fulfilled.

April 27, 1993 Kevorkian's Californian medical license is suspended.

January 27, 1994 Kevorkian is cleared of the charges of two deaths.

May 2, 1994 Kevorkian is acquitted in a further death charge.

November 8, 1994 Oregon voters approve Ballot Measure 16, which legalizes physician-assisted euthanasia under limited conditions. The legislation becomes law in 1997.

March 28, 1995 A Japanese doctor found guilty of murdering a terminally ill patient receives a suspended sentence. The court rules that mercy killing in Japan would not be unlawful under certain conditions.

May 25, 1995 Australia's Northern Territory legalizes physician-assisted suicide under strict controls—the first legislature in the world to do so.

June 26, 1995 Kevorkian briefly opens a "suicide clinic" in Springfield, Michigan.

July 1, 1995 The Northern Territory assisted-suicide law comes into force with 81 percent of Australians supporting euthanasia.

March 7, 1996 The Ninth U.S. Circuit Court of Appeals rules unconstitutional a Washington State law criminalizing physician-assisted suicide for the terminally ill.

March 8, 1996 Kevorkian is acquitted of causing two deaths in 1991.

April 3, 1996 The Second U.S. Circuit Court of Appeals declares unconstitutional a New York State law that criminalized physician-assisted suicide for terminally ill patients.

May 14, 1996 Kevorkian is again acquitted of causing two other deaths.

September 22, 1996 A cancer patient by the name of Bob Dent becomes the first person to take advantage of the physician-assisted suicide law in Australia's Northern Territory.

March 25, 1997 The Australian Senate overturns the Northern Territory legislation under which four people have died.

May 20, 1997 The Constitutional Court of Colombia legalizes euthanasia for the terminally ill.

June 12, 1997 Kevorkian's fourth trial is declared a mistrial.

November 4, 1997 A euthanasia law comes into force in Oregon, Canada that allows lethal doses of barbituates to be given to terminally ill patients.

December 1997 A farmer in Saskatchewan appeals against a charge of second-degree murder for killing his severely disabled daughter and has his mandatory 10-year sentence reduced to two years.

March 14, 1998 Kevorkian's 100th assisted suicide is a 66-year-old Detroit man.

March 25, 1998 The Canadian government rejects the establishment of a committee to study physician-assisted suicide.

March 26, 1998 A woman in her mid-80s becomes the first to die by physician-assisted suicide under the Oregon law.

Mid–1998 U.S. attorney general Janet Reno states that "doctors who use the law to prescribe lethal drugs to terminally ill patients will not be prosecuted."

November 3, 1998 Voters in Michigan reject a proposed euthanasia law, which had been condemned by Kevorkian as restrictive. Voters in Maine also reject proposed legislation for physician-assisted suicide.

November 22, 1998 The CBS program "60 Minutes" airs a tape showing Kevorkian lethally injecting Thomas Youk, 52, who suffered from Lou Gehrig's disease.

November 24, 1998 Kevorkian is charged in Michigan with Youk's first-degree murder, violating assisted suicide law, and delivering a controlled substance without a license.

1998 In the first year of legal physician-assisted suicide in Oregon, 15 people in the state end their lives in this way.

April 13, 1999 Kevorkian, convicted of second-degree murder and delivery of a controlled substance in Youk's death, is sentenced to 10–25 years in prison.

November 23, 2000 The Dutch parliament begins moves to formally decriminalize physician-assisted suicide, even though physicians have not been liable to prosecution since 1993.

Topic 11
SHOULD RELIGION AFFECT PARENTS' MEDICAL DECISIONS?

YES
"SPIRITUAL HEALING ON TRIAL: A CHRISTIAN SCIENTIST REPORTS"
CHRISTIAN CENTURY, JUNE 22–29, 1988
STEPHEN GOTTSCHALK

NO
"SUFFERING CHILDREN AND THE CHRISTIAN SCIENCE CHURCH"
THE ATLANTIC MONTHLY, APRIL 1995
CAROLINE FRASER

INTRODUCTION

In recent years there have been some high-profile cases in which parents belonging to particular religious faiths have refused certain medical treatments for their children. Occasionally this has resulted in the death of a child, which is invariably met by a public outcry. While this is a very emotional debate, there are well-formed arguments on both sides. Some of them center around the First Amendment right to practice religious beliefs versus the state's duty to protect children's health. Other considerations can be better understood by exploring these peoples' beliefs.

For followers of two churches—the Church of Christ, Scientist (usually known as Christian Scientists) and the Jehovah's Witnesses—these issues are complex dilemmas that involve not only the natural love of a parent for a child but also their deep-seated beliefs.

Faith and healing are, to the secular mind, quite distinct, but in many religions they are closely linked. The Bible, for example, tells of miracles of healing—of the blind, the lame, the lepers, the mentally disturbed. The Catholic church recognizes places of pilgrimage to which the sick journey in search of cures. Attested cures that cannot be explained by medical science are a requirement on the Catholic Church's road to sainthood.

All religious groups use prayer to promote healing. In the Church of Christ, Scientist, however, healing, and attitudes toward it, has assumed greater prominence. Worshipers believe that faith is necessary in order for healing to take place. And in order to heal, an individual must pray and understand the scriptures: Sin and sickness are treated together. This belief dismisses the efficacy of conventional medicine. Prayer is the medium of healing: Adults pray for themselves and others, while parents pray for their children. It is this latter stance that has proved so controversial. Those outside the church claim that parents deny the possibility of medical treatment to their children; Christian Scientists claim that they do provide treatment for their children: healing through faith.

"The government must pursue a course of complete neutrality toward religion."
—JOHN PAUL STEVENS,

ASSOCIATE JUSTICE,

U.S. SUPREME COURT

Equally controversial is the practice of Jehovah's Witnesses, who refuse blood transfusions for religious reasons. They are known for their literal interpretation of the Bible and particularly its emphasis on Armageddon and the Second Coming. They are also known for their enthusiastic missionary activity and for their refusal to acknowledge many of the claims made on them by secular governments. But it is their refusal to accept blood transfusions, based on scripture, that has earned them much adverse publicity.

The Pro argument centers around Ginger and David Twitchell, Christian Scientists who lost their son because their religion prevented them treating him with conventional medicine. The author Stephen Gottschalk uses this tragic event to examine the issues the Twitchells—and others—struggle with. Gottschalk points out that Christian Scientists believe that prayer is an effective form of treatment, even if it is not recognized by conventional

medicine. For them prayer often produces better results than state health provision. Furthermore, Christian Scientists do not believe that they are above the law and its duty to protect children's' health; they simply ask that their form of treatment should not be rejected just because it is religious, especially when there is no clear evidence to show that it is ineffectual.

The Pro author concludes by saying that as tragic as the death of the Twitchell's son is, he is the only child to have died under Christian Science care during the last decade (this figure is estimated to be a lot higher by the Con author). He believes that with this low mortality rate, we should endeavor to find out more about Christian Science methods before we reject them.

Caroline Fraser—the Con author—focuses her argument on James Andrew Wantland, who died from diabetes because his Christian Scientist parents did not have his illness assessed by conventional doctors. She asserts that the survival of the children of Christian Scientists—such as James Andrew Wantland—into adulthood is just a matter of "dumb luck."

As a Christian Scientist, Fraser is well qualified to talk out about the conflict between an adult's right to practice his or her religion and a child's right to live. She argues against the "right" to deny children medical treatment and points out that Christian Scientists in other countries—notably Canada and the United Kingdom—have struck a balance between state law and their religious convictions. The author does not suggest that these people have been compromised in any way and concludes by stating that children deserve to be protected from their parent's religious beliefs.

SPIRITUAL HEALING ON TRIAL
Stephen Gottschalk

YES

Read more about the Twitchell court case at www.watchman. org/cults/cs guilty.htm.

✓ In May a young Christian Science couple pleaded Innocent in a Boston courtroom to charges of manslaughter in the death of their two-year-old son. Ginger and David Twitchell had sought to treat their son's bowel obstruction through spiritual means. The case may not go to trial, for the Twitchells' conduct appears to fall under a Massachusetts statute that, according to an attorney general for the Commonwealth, "expressly precludes imposition of criminal liability as a negligent parent for failure to provide medical care because of religious beliefs." The district attorney can prosecute the couple only by finding a way around this statute....

Punish the parents?

Do you agree with this policy? If your actions result in the death of a person, should you be charged in a court of law whatever the circumstances?

Even some of those who oppose laws accommodating Christian Science healing for children (in Massachusetts and most other states) hold that prosecutions of already grieving parents makes little sense. In a strongly worded statement condemning such laws, the American Academy of Pediatrics declared that it did not "advocate punishment of offending parents as a solution." Of the Twitchell case specifically, Kenneth Simmons, law professor at Boston University, said, "I think there is a very good argument that this is an illegal prosecution, and beyond that I also believe it's an unwise prosecution because Christian Scientists looking at that law would quite reasonably believe that they are protected."

Religious convictions and state duties

Gottschalk identifies the central question in the debate.

The issue in the case appears to revolve around a conflict between the parents' First Amendment rights to practice their religious beliefs and the state's duty to protect the health of children. Most commentators hold that while adults have the right to practice spiritual healing for themselves, they have no religious right to endanger their children's health. The most intriguing and least-noticed aspect of the debate is that Christian Scientists agree with this position. They do not emphasize their religious right as over against the state's interest, but accept parents obligation to maintain their children's health and the state's interest in seeing that this is done. A fair estimate of Christian Science healing, they maintain, would show it to be an effective form of treatment which responsibly fulfills this obligation, with a support system including nonmedical nursing and care facilities for the sick. As a church member put it to an interviewer: "The refusal of medical care is because we have found through experience and demonstration of healing that spiritual means—prayer and spiritual treatment—work more effectively for us" ("Christian Scientists Say Prayer is Best Medicine," Lawrence Eagle Tribune, May 9).

It is important to establish what is meant by "spiritual treatment." Christian Scientists hold that behind all diseases are mental factors rooted in the human mind's blindness to God's presence and our authentic relation to God, revealed in the life of Christ. They hold that treatment is a form of prayer or communion with God in which God's reality and power, admitted and witnessed to, become so real as to eclipse the temporal "reality" of disease and pain. Such treatment they see as actively and specifically ministering to human need. As one Christian Scientist explained it to a high-school group: "Healing happens when your sense of God becomes greater than your sense of the problem."

Find out more about spiritual treatment at http://religiousmovements.lib.virginia.edu/nrms/chrissci.html.

How might prayer ease disease and pain? Is it a form of self-hypnosis, for example? Conventional medicine also recognizes the importance of mental attitude in overcoming disease.

The right to religious convictions

Christian Scientists do not claim that their practice of spiritual healing should be accommodated in law simply because it is religious, but rather that it should not be proscribed by law simply because it is religious, and in the absence of clear evidence that it is ineffectual. In view of laws requiring medical care for children, they assert that not accommodating their form of healing in law would be to proscribe it. But would such accommodations violate the establishment clause of the First Amendment? No, say Christian Scientists. Pointing to other statutes and court decisions recognizing special practices of the Amish, Roman Catholics, Seventh-day Adventists, and Jews, among others, they argue that in their case also, such laws are necessary to implement the free exercise clause of the First Amendment. Remarked church spokesperson Nathan Talbot: "We abhor the idea that the Constitution gives anyone the right to martyr a child. But our approach to healing demands fair consideration. As with any form of treatment, Christian Science deserves to be judged on the basis of an overall assessment of its results, rather than on the a priori assumption that nothing but medical care should be acceptable by the state as a means of caring for the health of the young...."

The establishment clause prohibits the government from passing legislation to establish an official religion or preferring one religion over another. For a discussion of this clause see www.law.umkc.edu/faculty/projects/ftrials/conlaw/estabinto.htm.

The militantly secular views that dismiss spiritual healing are known quantities. In the current debate over Christian Science, it is almost commonplace for those holding these views to write off accounts of spiritual healing with the reductionistic if not pejorative term "anecdotal," since they refer to real-life events rather than ones that occur in a laboratory context. (Even so, what is surprising about Peel's book is how much medical corroboration there is for the healing accounts.)

Would you have liked Gottschalk to elaborate on this medical support for the results of Christian Science methods?

Assessing the evidence

From a Christian standpoint, the decision not to take seriously the evidence for spiritual healing has sobering implications. If one rejects out of hand the evidence for Christian healing, many would ask, is one not rejecting an aspect of Christian experience necessary to the realization of the gospel's promise today? As Gordon Dalbey noted six years ago: "The ministry of physical healing stands in the center of our Christian faith. And yet, though the Gospels are filled with stories of healing, and the Church itself is born through an act of healing (Acts 3), most church people seem anxious to disown these stories, as if they embarrassed us" ("Recovering Christian Healing," *The Christian Century*, June 9–16, 1982).

The rise of Christian healing

Probably fewer church people would be embarrassed by these stories today. During this decade, the recovery of Christian healing has accelerated to the point that it has become an undeniable part of the Christian landscape. As with most grass-roots movements, it has included differing and in some instances contradictory approaches. And both Christian Science and the form of Christian healing that has become part of mainstream church life should be clearly differentiated from the "faith healing" associated with TV evangelism, itinerant evangelists (portrayed, for example, in the recent CBS television film "Promised a Miracle"), and fundamentalist groups such as Faith Assembly. A recent article in a Christian Science periodical observed, "Many Christians who have ministries of healing reject the label 'faith healing.' It's becoming apparent that blind faith doesn't stand up to the scrutiny of an increasingly sophisticated and technological society" (David B. Andrews, "The Future of Christian Healing: Fresh Convictions and Spiritual Realism," *Christian Science Journal*, June 1988, p. 33)…

Find out more about Faith Assembly at www.fachurch.orgl.

The most questionable aspect of Christian Science for many is its view that medical and spiritual treatment cannot be beneficially combined. For Christian Scientists, this approach follows from a belief that spiritual treatment rests on a basis wholly different from that of medicine. It does not mean that one cannot pray as any Christian would that another experience more of God's healing love. But it is motivated by a concern that patients not rely for healing on contradictory forms of treatment—and also by deference to the efforts of medical professionals if their care has been elected. The church strongly emphasizes that choice of treatment remains wholly individual and voluntary. However, those engaged in the ministry of Christian Science healing for the public must usually withdraw their names from listings in church periodicals for a stipulated period of time if they decide to make use of medical care for themselves....

The success rates of conventional medicine

Yet for Christian Scientists, as for those in the medical community, failures in practice often cause genuine soul-searching. A brief interview with David Twitchell on ABC's "20/20" gave a public glimpse of a private struggle. "Maybe a doctor could have saved Robyn," he said. But then he added, "Have you ever asked a doctor for a guarantee?"—a pointed comment, considering the consent forms typically required for those undergoing medical treatment listing multiple risks for which hospitals disclaim responsibility. Yet for Twitchell the honest regret remained: "If we were closer to God we could have stopped this from happening. In that way I blame myself."

Losses are not high

...The death of a child under any circumstances or method of care is jarring. It is difficult to determine the number of Christian Scientists relying upon spiritual means for the healing of children, but the handful of losses among their children does not seem dramatically high for a small but widespread denomination. In Massachusetts, where Christian Science is relatively strong. Robyn Twitchell is the only child to have died under Christian Science care during [the last] decade.

It is the successes of a healing system, not just its failures, that its opponents must reckon with. Future decades may see that reluctance to take the evidence for spiritual healing seriously as one last form of resistance to the drastic deconstruction of the mechanistic concept of reality.

Does the fact that there has only been a "handful of losses" make any difference to the underlying principles of the debate? Do numbers matter?

SUFFERING CHILDREN AND THE CHRISTIAN SCIENCE CHURCH
Caroline Fraser

By telling the story of an individual, Fraser makes it clear that this is not an abstract debate about morality: It is a matter of life and death that affects real children.

"Beloved in Thee I Am Well Pleased" is the epitaph on the gravestone of James Andrew Wantland. According to the Gospel of Saint Luke, God spoke these words to his son, Jesus, at Jesus' baptism. Given that James Andrew Wantland—Andrew, he was called—was 12 years old when he died, the choice of epitaph is striking. It does not express the sentiments one usually associates with the untimely death of a child. It suggests satisfaction, rather than regret or loss or sorrow. On the grave of a mature person it would presumably pay tribute to a life of accomplishment and fulfillment; on that of a child it seems almost too much to bear. But Andrew was the child of Christian Scientists, and the children of Christian Scientists have much to bear.

I know. I am one. Most people who have heard of Christian Science know one thing about it: Christian Scientists do not "believe" in doctors. More accurately, Christian Scientists do not believe in medical science, or what they call "materia medica." They generally do not accept medical care for themselves, and many do not permit it for their children. They believe they can heal through prayer. Had my brother or sister or I contracted a serious illness or met with a life-threatening accident while we were growing up, we would have been expected to heal ourselves, just as we were expected to heal ourselves of colds, flu, allergies, and bad behavior. That we survived to adulthood was a matter of luck. Andrew Wantland was not so lucky.

Christian Science healing largely follows Science and Health with Key to the Scriptures, *written by Mary Baker Eddy in 1875.*

Young life cut short

In 1992, the year he turned 12, Andrew had the slightly gawky look of a boy who is growing fast. He had braces on his teeth (Christian Scientists often accept dental care), and his hair was cut short. His ears stuck out a little. He was big for his age and, his mother says, weighed about 140 pounds.

Andrew lived with his [Christian Scientist] father, James Wantland.... His grandmother, Ruth Wantland, ... lived nearby. Andrew's parents had divorced in 1984, and he and his sister had lived with their mother, Gayle, who had been granted primary custody, until 1989. That year Gayle remarried. She wanted to move with her children and her new husband to Pennsylvania, but James Wantland wanted his children to stay with him. A judge agreed that the move might prove disruptive, and decided that Andrew and his sister should live with their father during the school year. Gayle Quigley, who had been raised as a Christian Scientist but had left the faith after her remarriage, told the judge that she wanted her children to be provided with mainstream medical care and not just Christian Science treatment. James Wantland indicated … that he would comply.

"When it comes to fractions of any of the primary components [of blood], each Christian, after careful and prayerful meditation, must conscientiously decide for himself."
—*THE WATCHTOWER*, JUNE 15, 2000

Gayle alleges that sometime in the fall of 1992 Andrew, who had started the seventh grade … began to lose weight and complained of feeling weak. His friends noticed that he had developed a constant cough and that he drank a lot of water. On Sunday, December 20, after Andrew had missed a week of school with what his family called "the flu," Andrew's father called an ambulance. Andrew was pronounced dead on arrival at St. Jude Medical Center in La Habra....

Andrew weighed only about 105 pounds at his death and was severely emaciated. The Orange County coroner's report listed three causes of death and their duration:

- Multiple system failure/days;
- diabetic ketoacidosis/months;
- diabetes mellitus/months.

In other words, Andrew Wantland died of diabetes after months of illness.

A call for common sense
Prayer is a resource for millions of people, and medical studies have shown that it can benefit the seriously and even the terminally ill. No one would argue with the

Sufferers from insulin-dependent diabetes need regular injections of insulin to regulate their blood glucose.

COMMENTARY: The death of Robyn Twitchell

In recent years several cases have come to trial in which parents have faced criminal charges for denying their children medical treatment on religious grounds. One such was the Boston, Massachusetts, trial of Ginger and David Twitchell in 1990. In 1986 their two-year-old son Robyn had fallen sick, screaming and vomiting. The next day the Twitchells, who were Christian Scientists, asked the church for its advice. For four days a practitioner treated Robyn with prayer alone. On the fifth day Robyn died while still at home. An autopsy revealed the cause of death to be acute peritonitis resulting from a medically treatable bowel obstruction.

Giving evidence, David Twitchell said that Robyn had seemed merely to have had a bad case of influenza, and that at one point the practitioner's prayers appeared to be working: Robyn's condition seemed to improve shortly before he died. (Experts confirmed that the symptoms could have ebbed on occasions.) The jury convicted the Twitchells of manslaughter, though the Massachusetts Supreme Court later commuted the conviction to 10 years' probation, with the additional proviso that the Twitchells give their three remaining sons periodic medical checkups.

The wider Christian Science church resented the case as a challenge to its freedom. David Twitchell expressed his personal sentiments at the trial: "If medicine could have saved him, I wish I had turned to it."

Ginger and David Twitchell pictured during their trial in 1990. The Twitchells, a Christian Scientist couple, were indicted for involuntary manslaughter of their son.

Christian Scientist's right to religious freedom, but the unnecessary deaths of Christian Science children raise pressing questions about the conflict between an adult's right to practice his or her religion and a child's right to live.

The dogmatic reaction of the Church in many of these cases is particularly puzzling in light of the reality that most Christian Scientists strike a balance between their faith and their children's welfare. Christian Scientists willingly obey this country's laws requiring the presence of a physician or a licensed midwife during childbirth; some have cesarean sections (including the Christian Science mother in Florida who was tried for the death of her daughter). My own recollections and interviews with those currently practicing suggest that some Christian Scientists are willing to have their children vaccinated. Moderate Christian Scientists say, "C.S. stands for Common Sense," and a number of those I interviewed insisted that the individual parent must decide which children's illnesses or injuries can or cannot be "handled in Science." Most Church members support the religious exemptions to the laws but privately question the judgment of those parents who have been compelled to make use of them.

Fraser points out illogicalities and inconsistencies in the Christian Scientist attitude toward medicine.

International differences

In Great Britain and Canada, countries with no ambiguous religious-exemption laws, Christian Scientists are required, along with everyone else, to provide their children with medical care. But although Christian Scientists in those countries seem to have adapted to that arrangement, it is difficult to find any Christian Scientists in this country who agree that the British system is preferable. I interviewed several eminent American Christian Scientists, distinguished in their respective fields, who calmly and thoughtfully discussed with me the troubling issues raised by the child cases and the conduct of the Church in handling them, but when I later attempted to obtain permission to quote them by name on this subject, they became defensive and declined to be quoted.

Using an international perspective helps imply that American Christian Scientists are somehow more extreme than those in other countries.

Why might interviewees not want to be quoted in Fraser's article?

Some of these same eminent Christian Scientists have publicly criticized the Church's broadcasting and publishing plans. Why voices like theirs have not been raised within their Church in protest against the agonizing, drawn-out suffering and death endured by Andrew Wantland, Ashley King, and Ian Lundman, among many others, is inexplicable. As it is, if 7,000 children attend Christian Science Sunday schools in this country, then 7,000 children may have nothing standing between themselves and death but [Mary Baker Eddy's book] *Science and Health* and dumb luck.

Summary

The Pro author, Stephen Gottschalk, suggests that the spiritual treatment performed by Christian Scientists is beneficial to some people, but the problem is that its methods are not recognized by mainstream secular society. He claims that people in general know very little about Christian Science practices, but that most reject its form of treatment out of hand. This ignores some of its achievements and successes.

In this argument Christian Scientists are not preventing medical treatment for their children, they are simply using a different kind of treatment. Gottschalk acknowledges that the death of a child is always a tragic event, but death rates in Christian Science families are extremely low (one in the last decade, according to the author) and therefore warrant attention.

Caroline Fraser, writing in the second piece (which comprises several extracts from a longer article), draws on the personal experiences of her own childhood spent growing up in a Christian Science home. She describes how she and her siblings were expected to help bring about their own healing through prayer. She also gives the example of a young boy who died because his father apparently denied him medical treatment. There are many such children, she claims, who die because of their parents' beliefs. That she herself survived such a fate amounts, she claims, to nothing but luck.

FURTHER INFORMATION:

Books:

Penton, M. James, *Apocalypse Delayed: The Story of Jehovah's Witnesses*. Toronto: University of Toronto Press, 1985.

Keyston, David Lawson (editor), *The Healer: The Healing Work of Mary Baker Eddy*. Claremont, CA: Aequus Publications, 1998.

Eddy, Mary, *Science and Health with Key to the Scriptures*. Claremont, CA: Aequus Publications, 1998.

Peel, Robert, *Mary Baker Eddy: The Years of Discovery*. Austin, TX: Holt, Rinehart and Winston, 1966.

Useful websites:

www.watchtower.org/library/hb/article_00.htm
The official Watchtower stance on blood transfusions in relation to the scriptures.
www.aap.org/policy/00118.html
A policy statement by the American Academy of Pediatrics on the issues involved in forgoing life-saving medical treatment.
www.religioustolerance.org/medical.htm
A general religious site, with reference to groups that reject medical treatment in favor of prayer.
www.tfccs.com/GV/CSPS/SENT/Sentinel032_00.html
A Christian Science stance on medicine.
www.theatlantic.com/unbound/flashbks/xsci/suffer.htm
The full text of Caroline Fraser's article, "Suffering Children and the Christian Science Church."
www.tfccs.com/
Site of the Church of Christ, Scientist.

The following debates in the Pro/Con series may also be of interest:

In this volume:

Topic 7 Should organ replacement be a commercial enterprise?

Topic 10 Should doctors be able to assist in euthanasia?

SHOULD RELIGION AFFECT PARENTS' MEDICAL DECISIONS?

YES: A minor's medical care rests by law in the hands of a parent or guardian

YES: It is enshrined in the Constitution that Americans can freely practice their religion— and thus all that entails

CHILDREN'S RIGHTS
Do parents have ultimate legal control over their children?

RELIGIOUS FREEDOM
Do parents have a right to fully practice their religion of choice?

NO: Every child has a right to life and, therefore, to receive life-preserving medical treatment

NO: The state has ultimate jurisdiction over the individual; after all, it is the state that is empowered by the Constitution and bestows responsibilities on parents

SHOULD RELIGION AFFECT PARENTS' MEDICAL DECISIONS? KEY POINTS

YES: Spiritual treatment is effective for most Christian Scientists and has a better success rate than conventional medicine. It is a valid, if different, type of treatment.

YES: Christian Scientists believe that God alone has the power to heal; that power is timeless

MEDICAL BENEFITS
Does CS offer an effective but different type of treatment to conventional medicine?

GOD'S WORD
Does the word of the Bible still have relevance thousands of years later?

NO: Sick children should not rely on prayer to cure them; survival becomes a lottery

NO: Modern medicine uses techniques unknown in biblical times; they should be embraced when lives are at stake

Topic 12
SHOULD MEDICAL RESEARCH ON ANIMALS BE ALLOWED?

YES
"THE ILLOGIC OF ANIMAL RIGHTS"
WWW.PULPLESS.COM/JNEIL/ANIRIGHT.HTML
J. NEIL SCHULMAN

NO
"ANIMAL EXPERIMENTATION: A FAILED TECHNOLOGY"
WWW.ANTIVIVISEZIONE.IT/ENGL.%20SHARPE.HTML
ROBERT SHARPE

INTRODUCTION

Animal rights are not a new issue. Many people have long protested about the ill treatment of animals. But animal rights today are more controversial and high profile. Protesters break into laboratories that keep animals for medical experiments and set them free. Most cosmetics companies have bowed to public pressure and no longer test their products on animals.

Scientists, however, argue that medical research is a different matter. In order to establish the safety of new drugs, they have to be tested. Animal testing, no matter how undesirable it might be, is the only option. Opponents argue that such tests are still morally indefensible and that they do not work.

Since Claude Bernard, the famous French physiologist, began a program of animal experiments in the 1860s, medical, and clinical tests have been carried out in great numbers on rats, mice, primates, cats, dogs, rabbits, frogs, and guinea pigs. Much has been

discovered from their physiology, and drugs are tested on animals before they are approved for human use.

By law, drugs must undergo clinical trials before they can be considered safe for general use. If they cannot be tested on suitable animals, on whom can they be tested? But animal tests have their limits because of differences between animals and human beings. Even primates, including the chimpanzee and the bonobo, with which humans share most of their DNA, are different in such significant ways that testing drugs on these species does not always warn about side effects in humans.

Experiments involving animals have become such a charged issue that few researchers undertake public debate. They are sometimes represented in the popular press as unfeeling. Attention is focused on the often painful tests performed on animals in the cause of medical research, while reports of the moral dilemmas that researchers experience are seldom printed.

Many scientists claim that the public does not really understand the issues, and they feel hurt by the presumption that they do not care about animals. Laboratory animals are well cared for and experience no suffering until the actual experimentation begins. They usually have a better diet, for example, than most pets.

"We have enslaved the rest of the animal creation, and have treated our distant cousins in fur and feathers so badly that beyond doubt, if they were able to formulate a religion, they would depict the devil in human form."

—WILLIAM RALPH INGE,

(1860–1954), CHRISTIAN PLATONIST

Some researchers believe that the public is guilty of double standards: Most people still eat meat, but they close their minds to the cruelty of a factory farm or an abattoir. In the same way, nearly everyone uses medicines, but many people are equally prepared to close their minds to the animal testing that formed part of the development of those drugs.

The debate is not about whether any testing should be carried out, but how tests are conducted, particularly if those tests should be made on animals. Most scientists agree that the use of animal models is important. An example frequently quoted is AIDS research. The former U.S. surgeon general C. Everett Koop says, "We would be in absolute, utter darkness about AIDS if we hadn't done decades of basic research in animal retroviruses." The effects of AIDS treatments under development are studied in primates. Almost every medication used for HIV-related conditions has been tested on animals.

Possible vaccines cannot be tested on non-HIV positive people, who might become infected. Instead, treatments are tested on chimpanzees. Yet these experiments do not give chimpanzees AIDS: They can become infected with HIV, but they do not subsequently suffer from AIDS or its symptoms.

Serious questions concerning the morality of animal testing remain. Some people take animal rights so seriously that they take the law into their own hands and resort to violence against animal researchers and their property.

This emotional issue is discussed below in two very different articles. In the first article J. Neil Schulman forcefully denies that animals have rights. He does not focus on the issue of animal experimentation but states that, as a rational corollary of the inferiority of animals to human beings, animal experimentation is not unacceptable.

The title of the second article by Robert Sharpe's tells the story: "Animal Experimentation: A Failed Technology." Sharpe does not focus on cruelty, but on the efficacy of testing on animals. His conclusion is that animal testing is largely a waste of time and is now conducted out of habit rather than for valid scientific reasons.

THE ILLOGIC OF ANIMAL RIGHTS
J. Neil Schulman

✓ The so-called "animal rights" movement is relying upon a logical fallacy based on mutually exclusive premises.

Starting a debate by picking holes in your opponent's logic gives you an instant advantage.

"Animal rights" premise #1: Human beings are no different from other animals, with no divine or elevated nature which makes us distinct;

"Animal rights" premise #2: Human beings are ethically bound not to use other animals for their own selfish purposes.

If a "natural law" exists, says Schulman, then we fulfill it by using animals, not by abstaining from using them.

If human beings are no different from other animals, then like all other animals it is our nature to kill any other animal which serves the purposes of our survival and well-being, for that is the way of all nature. Therefore, aside from economic concerns such as making sure we don't kill so quickly that we destroy a species and deprive our descendants of prey, human animals can kill members of other animal species for their usefulness to us.

> "With animals we may have a cure for AIDS in ten years. Without animals we will never cure AIDS in our lifetime."
> —ROBERT GALLO,
> AIDS RESEARCH PIONEER

It is only if we are not just another animal—if our nature is distinctly superior to other animals—that we become subject to ethics at all; and then those ethics must take into account our nature as masters of the lower animals. We may seek a balance of nature; but "balance" is a concept that only a species as intelligent as humankind could even contemplate.

We may choose to temper the purposes to which we put lower animals with empathy and wisdom; but by virtue of our superior nature, we decide … and if those decisions include the consumption of animals for human utilitarian or recreational purposes, then the limits on the uses we put the lower beasts to are ones we set according to our individual human consciences. "Animal rights" do not exist in either case. Even though I personally believe we were created by God, unlike advocates of the Judeo-Christian tradition I do not rely upon the question of whether humans have a "soul" to distinguish humans from animals. Like secular rationalists, I'm content to resolve the issue of the nature of human beings, and … of animals, by scientific means: Observation, experiment, and the debate of paradigms. Each of these criteria is simply a proof of intelligence and self-consciousness:

> Schulman sets out to establish, by observable criteria, that humans are distinguishable from animals.

1) Being observed as producing or having produced technological artifacts unique to that species;
2) Being observed as able to communicate from one generation to the next by a recorded language unique to that species;
3) Being observed as basing action on abstract reasoning;
4) Being observed as engaging in inductive and deductive reasoning processes;
5) Being observed as engaging in nonutilitarian artistic activity unique to that species.

I'm sure there are other criteria we could use, but these are obvious ones…. None speculates about the unobservable functioning of a neural network; all of them are based on observable effects of intelligence and self-consciousness.

Conclusively, we are of a different nature than other animals we know. Neither cetaceans nor other higher mammals, including the higher apes, qualify as "human" under these criteria. We do not observe these significations of intelligence and self-consciousness in any other species we know, such criteria being neither necessarily anthropocentric nor even terracentric.

> "Anthropocentric" means human-centered. "Terracentric" means centered on the land.

The right to withhold rights

By the "survival of the fittest" no animal has rights: only the tools to survive as best it can. The chicken has no right not to be eaten by the fox…. If we are merely animals, no other animal has any ethical standing to complain against the human animal for eating them or wearing their skins.

Rabbits in the lab. Researchers say such testing is essential for the development of new drugs, while opponents say it is futile and that funds should be poured into humane alternatives.

But, if we are superior to other animals—if our nature is of a different kind than other animals—then why should we grant rights to species who cannot talk, or compose symphonies, or induce mathematical equations, or build satellites which send back television pictures of other planets? Why shouldn't we humans simply regard lower animals as things which may become our property? We may be kind to animals if it is pleasing to us to do so, but we should not grant animals an equal stature that nature has not given them. Respect for nature requires a respect for the nature of what things are … and we are better, stronger, smarter, than the animals we hunt, ranch, farm, fish, trap, butcher, skin, bone, and eat. They certainly have no ethics about us, for they are just animals. Nor are any "animal rights" activists themselves merely animals. There is no organization called Porpoises for the Ethical Treatment of Animals. It is People who make those demands of other People.

Schulman challenges humans to treat animals as they like simply because they can. Is this reasonable?

Can we judge ourselves superior to animals in the way Schulman claims? How might such thinking affect our views of other weaker or poorer people?

Abusing or using?

Those who argue for animal rights argue that since animals are living and feel pain, that therefore nature gives them a right not to be treated cruelly. This argument could only work on a being capable of empathy—and that requires an elevated consciousness. It is true that animals can feel pain, and that … requires that we not be cruel in our treatment of them. But what is cruelty? Beating a horse that won't pull a wagon? Making animals fight each other for sport?

There are degrees of cruelty to animals, Schulman notes. Should they all be judged the same way?

That's no longer the issue….The issue is ranching minks to skin them for fur; castrating and slaughtering steers to eat them; hunting and shooting deer, ducks, and elks; testing cosmetics on animals; doing medical experiments on animals to advance medical knowledge. Do we have a moral obligation not to use animals for human … purposes, which is another way of asking whether animals have the right not to be treated as objects to be exploited for their usefulness?

The idea of a right means that which has rights may not be treated as a utilitarian object for the fulfillment of the purposes of others. Animal rights would mean animals would be immune from being used to fulfill any human purpose.

Schulman concludes by taking the case of those who support animal rights to its logical extreme. This is often an effective way to make a point.

ANIMAL EXPERIMENTATION: A FAILED TECHNOLOGY
Robert Sharpe

NO

In 1865 the famous French physiologist Claude Bernard published his *Introduction to the Study of Experimental Medicine*, a work specially intended to give physicians rules and principles to guide their study of experimental medicine. Bernard regarded the laboratory as the "true sanctuary of medical science," and considered it far more important than the clinical investigation of patients. Furthermore, this influential figure created the impression that animal experiments are directly applicable to humans.

Bernard's *Introduction* was to prove the charter for 20th-century medicine, but he was not alone in establishing the vivisection method. Another key figure was Louis Pasteur, whose apparently successful attempts to develop a vaccine against rabies had further glamorized the role of laboratory research and animal experiments. The current reliance on animal models of human disease was further popularized by the German doctor Robert Koch, who was Pasteur's rival in developing the germ theory of disease.

The growing influence of laboratory scientists like Bernard, Koch, and Pasteur turned animal tests into an everyday practice: medical research came to rely on artificially induced animal models of human disease. And since the direct study of human patients requires so much more skill and patience so that unnecessary risks to volunteers are avoided, it was perhaps not surprising that researchers preferred the greater convenience offered by "disposable species." But with animals now being used not only to assess, to develop surgical techniques, and to acquire physiological knowledge, what are the implications for patients? In view of the complex and often subtle nature of human disease, it is not surprising that, for the great majority of disease entities, the animal models are considered either very poor or nonexistent.

> In 1885 Pasteur used the rabies virus in vaccine form to save the life of a nine-year-old boy, Joseph Meister, bitten by a rabid dog.

> What does the use of words like "convenience" and "disposable" convey about Sharpe's view of researchers?

> Of about 30,000 known human diseases only 350, or 1.16 percent, are shared by animals.

Animals and humans are different

Huge resources have been expended on animal-based cancer research, yet artificially induced cancers in animals have often proved quite different to the spontaneous tumors which arise in patients. Indeed, [the British medical journal] *The Lancet* warned that, since no animal tumor is closely related to a cancer in human beings, an agent which is active in the laboratory may well prove useless clinically. This was certainly the case with the U.S. National Cancer Institute's 25-year screening program in which 40,000 plant species were tested for antitumor activity. As a result of the program several materials proved sufficiently safe and effective on the basis of animal tests to be considered for clinical trials. Unfortunately, all of these were either ineffective in treating human cancer or too exotic for general use. Thus in 25 years of this extensive program not a single antitumor agent safe and effective enough for use in patients has yet emerged, despite promising results in animal experiments.

Even in primates, presumably the animals closest to us in evolutionary terms, a disease can take quite a different form. The use of monkeys to investigate cerebral malaria led to the suggestion that coma in human patients is due to an increased concentration of protein in the cerebrospinal fluid, and that this leakage from the serum could be corrected with steroids. However, monkeys do not lapse into coma, nor do they have sequestered red cells infected with parasites, as typically seen in the human disease. In fact, steroids do not help patients, and subsequent clinical investigation of the human condition showed that the monkey model may simply not be relevant.

Chimpanzees share 98.5 percent of their genome with humans. The figure for gorillas is about 2.3 percent and orangutans a little under 4 percent.

Effective alternatives

The generally poor quality of animal models has been advanced as a strong argument for testing new drugs in volunteers and patients as early as possible to reduce the possibility of misleading predictions. Indeed, it has been stated that most pharmacologists are happy if 30 percent of the usual actions of drugs, as determined by experiments on animals, are reproduced in humans. So it is not surprising that many of the therapeutic actions of drugs are discovered through their clinical evaluation on patients or by astute analysis of accidental or deliberate poisoning rather than by experiments on animals. This is particularly the case with many psychotropic medicines because adequate animal models of serious mental illnesses such as schizophrenia, mania, dementia, and personality and behavior disorders simply do not exist.

Some people advocate testing drugs solely on humans. Would you volunteer to be a "guinea pig"?

"Psychotropic medicines" are those that alter a patient's mental state or mood.

Clinical work has also proved the cornerstone of advances in surgery. With the rapid developments in surgical techniques following the discovery of anesthetics in the

19th century, a number of surgeons argued strongly that advances must come from clinical practice rather than from animal experiments.

The same principles apply today when transplants and other surgical feats are being attempted. The crucial point is the underlying biological differences which make the animal experiments hazardous. It is therefore revealing that, despite thousands of experiments on animals, the first human transplants were almost always disastrous. Only after considerable clinical experience did techniques improve. At California's Stanford University, 400 heart transplants were carried out on dogs, yet the first human patients both died because of complications which had not arisen during the preliminary experiments.

The danger of relying on animal experiments is most vividly illustrated by the growing list of animal-tested drugs which are withdrawn or restricted because of unexpected, often fatal, side-effects in people. Examples include Eraldin, Opren, chloramphenicol, clioquinol, Flosint, Ibufenac and Zelmid. Reliance on animal tests can therefore be dangerously misleading. In fact, what protection there is comes mainly from clinical trials where 95 percent of the drugs passed safe and effective on the basis of animal tests are rejected.

Inefficacy leads to tragedy

One of the most common animals used in toxicity tests is the rat, yet comparisons with humans reveal major differences in skin characteristics, respiratory parameters, the location of gut flora … allergenic hypersensitivity, and teratogenicity. Differences in respiratory parameters are particularly important in inhalation studies, where rats are used extensively. Another study investigated whether rodent carcinogenicity tests successfully predicted the 26 substances presently thought to cause cancer in humans. An analysis of the scientific literature revealed that only 12 of these have been shown to cause cancer in rats or mice. The implications for humans are obvious.

As a result of the thalidomide disaster, which left 10,000 children crippled and deformed, teratogenicity tests became a legal requirement for new medicines. While it is true that thalidomide had not yet been tested specifically for birth defects prior to marketing, a close analysis of the tragedy suggests that animal testing could actually have delayed warnings of thalidomide's effect on the fetus. By June 1961, Dr W. G. McBride, an obstetrician practicing in Sydney, had seen three babies with unusual malformations and had

The heart drug digitalis raises blood pressure in dogs but lowers it in humans. The body chemical acetylcholine dilates a dog's coronary arteries, but constricts human coronary arteries.

"Teratogenicity" is the capacity to produce birth defects.

In 1959–1962 thousands of children were born with poorly developed limbs. Their mothers had taken thalidomide, a drug prescribed as a sedative, during their pregnancy.

strongly suspected thalidomide. To test his suspicions, McBride commenced experiments with guinea-pigs and mice, but when no deformities were found, he began to have doubts that were to nag him for months.

"No animal experiment with a medicament, even if it is carried out on several animal species, including primates under all conceivable conditions, can give any guarantee that the medicament tested in this way will behave the same in humans."

—SIR ERNST BORIS CHAIN,

CODEVELOPER OF PENICILLIN,

FEBRUARY 1970

Further experiments revealed that even if thalidomide had been tested in pregnant rats, the animals so often used to look for fetal damage, no malformations would have been found. The drug does not cause birth defects in rats or in many other species, so the human tragedy would have occurred just the same. It is examples like this which suggest that much animal testing is more in the nature of a public relations exercise than a serious contribution to drug safety.

Us or them

Those who defend experiments on animals often present us with a simple choice: which life is more important, they ask, that of a child or that of a dog? Indeed the basic rationale behind animal experimentation, as spelled out by Claude Bernard, is that lives can be saved only by sacrificing others. But since animal-based research is unable to combat our major health problems and, more dangerously, often diverts attention from the study of humans, the real choice is not between animals and people; rather it is between good science and bad science, because they all tell us about animals ... when we really need to know about people. Only a human-based approach can accurately identify the principal causes of human disease, so that a sound basis for treatment is available and preventive action can be taken.

Do you think that Sharpe has made an effective case that the issue is not about animals versus humans?

Summary

In support of animal testing J. Neil Schulman defends an unpopular view with vigor. He attacks the premise, used by animal rights activists, that humans are mere animals and therefore have no right to exploit other animals. Quoting measurable criteria, he sets out that humans are in many ways superior to animals and may therefore exploit the usefulness of animals. That said, he adds that if humans were mere animals, then they would be equally at liberty to exploit animals—just as animals themselves do. And if humans may not exploit animals for experimentation, then how can they justify the cruelty involved in the meat industry? Neatly inverting the scenario, he points out that animals exhibit no ethical sensibilities toward humans. Nevertheless, Schulman draws a line at cruelty to animals.

Robert Sharpe does not dwell in depth on the emotional issue of cruelty. His theme is efficacy. He presents a selection of failed programs in which animal testing has not prevented severe side effects in patients, has not warned of the dangers of disability as a result of taking medication (for example, the thalidomide case), and has not prevented basic mistakes occurring because subtle differences in animal and human physiology have not been fully appreciated. Animal experimentation, he claims, is futile.

FURTHER INFORMATION:

Books:

Croce, Pietro, *Vivisection or Science? An Investigation into Testing Drugs and Safeguarding Health*. New York: Zed Books/Palgrave, 2000.

Fox, Michael Allen, *The Case for Animal Experimentation*. Los Angeles: University of California Press, 1986.

Garattini, S., and D. W. van Bekkum (editors), *The Importance of Animal Experimentation for Safety and Biomedical Research*. Boston: Kluwer, 1990.

Page, Dr. Tony, *Vivisection Unveiled: An Exposé of the Medical Futility of Animal Experimentation*. Charlbury, England: Jon Carpenter Publishing, 1997.

Smith, Jane A., and Kenneth M. Boyd, *Lives in the Balance: The Ethics of Using Animals in Biomedical Research*. New York: Oxford University Press, 1991.

U.S. Dept. of Health and Human Services, *Guide for the Care and Use of Laboratory Animals*. Bethesda, MD: National Institutes of Health, 1985.

Useful websites:

www.home.earthlink.net/~supress/faq.html
Questions of Nature of Wellness, California.

www.actupgg.org/BAR/art0042.html
Essay by Matthew Sharp of Act Up on the reasons why "America Supports Animal Testing."

www.navs.org/index.cfm
Site of the National Anti-Vivisection Society. Has links to other related sites.

www.curedisease.com/
Americans for Medical Advancement present arguments for alternatives to animal experimentation.

The following debates in the Pro/Con series may also be of interest:

In *Environment*:

Topic 13 Are zoos morally wrong?

Topic 14 Should endangered species be cloned?

SHOULD MEDICAL RESEARCH ON ANIMALS BE ALLOWED?

YES: Animal research has led to breakthroughs in drugs for AIDS, polio, and many other diseases

SPECIES BARRIER
Does animal testing actually work?

NO: In many instances drugs tested on animals have proved ineffective or dangerous when taken by humans

YES: Without animal testing vital drugs would be decades, rather than years, in the making

ALTERNATIVES
Should we use animal testing when there are alternatives?

NO: We should use cruelty-free alternatives, many of which are ignored simply because they are more costly than animal tests

**SHOULD MEDICAL RESEARCH ON ANIMALS BE ALLOWED?
KEY POINTS**

YES: Humans are superior to other animals and have a nontransferable code of ethics

ANIMAL RIGHTS
Do humans have the right to exploit animals as they see fit?

NO: The technological superiority of humans gives them no right to exploit animals; it is all the more their duty to care for animals

PART 3

SCIENCE AND THE FUTURE

INTRODUCTION

At the beginning of the 21st century humankind faced many dilemmas and choices about its future. There were many problems to be solved. The global population had for the first time reached 6 billion. If it continues growing at the current rate, it will reach 7.8 billion by 2025 and 9 billion by 2050—an increase of 50 percent in only 50 years. Such growth will put unprecedented pressure on humans' relation with the planet and with each other. All those people will have to have somewhere to live; they will need food and energy. The impact of the human species on the Earth will be greater than ever. Does science have the ability to solve any of the problems the future will bring? Or will the application of human technology cause as many new problems as it solves?

Since the massive breakthroughs in scientific methods in the 19th century, people have imagined a future radically transformed by technology. Some of the creations of early science-fiction writers have become fact: Invisible waves carry TV pictures around the world; laser beams are used for microsurgery to transplant organs or reattach limbs; humans have walked on the Moon and seen photographs taken on the surface of Mars; submariners have spent months in the depths of the ocean.

But the enthusiastic embrace of scientific advance has always been paralleled by a deep suspicion and fear.

The evil genius who uses science to threaten the rest of humankind is a well-know stereotype of books and movies. Frankenstein's monster is a familiar symbol of human tampering with the natural world. Critics envisage a future in which computers do not serve their users but take over the world.

One of the reasons people do not trust science is often because they do not understand it. Different scientific disciplines have become so increasingly specialized that in some cases experts studying closely related subjects do not understand each other's work. Ironically, however, the same lack of understanding can lead people to be too optimistic about science and its possible achievements.

Responsible science

Humankind has affected the planet for millennia. Now, however, industry and modern life styles create increased pollution; the need for productive farmland, timber, and energy is dramatically decreasing Earth's wilderness regions and natural resources. Selective breeding of strains of domesticated plants and animals is leaving wildlife facing increasing pressure for survival. Scientists estimate that species are becoming extinct at the rate of roughly three a day. Topic 13 asks *Does Humankind Maintain the Diversity of Species on Earth?* and considers the moral and practical implications of this human impact. Humankind relies on other species for food, medicines, and clothing, but it also has a duty to ensure the survival of its own species. There are more discussions of similar subjects in *Pro/Con* volume 3, *Environment*.

Who takes the blame?

Topic 14 Should Scientists Be Responsible for the Effects of their Inventions? considers another aspect of responsibility, this time not of the species as a whole but of individuals. Many people are worried that scientists can be irresponsible, giving little consideration to the potential hazards of their research and the effects of their inventions. Other people believe that

pure science. The reason the United States landed astronauts on the Moon in 1969 was in many ways simply to prove that it could. Today, however, space travel is seen as yielding more practical results. First, the rapid development of space technology produces many spin-offs that benefit daily life. Second, the growth in the human population and the deteriorating quality of the planet, the oceans, and the atmosphere are leading some people to envisage a future in which humans colonize new worlds in space.

Space travel is highly controversial, however. Not the least criticism of it lies in its huge costs. The practical benefits it brings, critics say, cannot make up to the vast sums spent on it by governments that would be better

---

"Science knows no country because knowledge belongs to humanity and is the torch which illuminates the world."
—LOUIS PASTEUR, FRENCH CHEMIST

---

scientists are not responsible if others use their inventions in harmful ways. They point out that often the same invention can have both beneficial or harmful uses.

Funding space exploration

Long before space travel became even a faint possibility, people envisioned traveling to other planets. When the United States and the Soviet Union engaged in the so-called Space Race of the 1960s, each trying to outdo the other with technological achievements, the goal of putting people into space was still largely seen as a triumph of

off spending money on solving problems on Earth. *Topic 15 Should Governments Continue to Fund Space Exploration?* examines whether governments still have a role in space or whether private businesses should now take over. One possible cheaper and more realistic alternative to colonizing space is to make better use of our own planet.

Topic 16 Should Humans Colonize the Oceans before Other Planets? considers a real proposal put forward by one organization to create new "countries" on huge artificial islands tethered in the sea.

YES

"WHY WE PRESERVE THE DIVERSITY OF LIFE"
FROM *THE PLACES WE SAVE: A GUIDE TO THE NATURE CONSERVANCY'S PRESERVE IN WISCONSIN*
THE NATURE CONSERVANCY

NO

"CLONING IS NO EXTINCTION PANACEA"
WWW.WIRED.COM/NEWS/TECHNOLOGY/0,1282,41704,00.HTML
AMY HEMBREE

INTRODUCTION

Extinction is part of life on Earth. According to the laws of evolution proposed by Charles Darwin in the mid-19th century, successful species adapt to their environment; less successful species die out. There have been hundreds of thousands of extinctions throughout and even before recorded history. Among celebrated examples of ancient extinctions are the dinosaurs; more recent extinctions include the flightless dodo bird from the Indian Ocean island of Mauritius and the U.S. passenger pigeon.

Yet the Earth remains vastly diverse in its plants and animals. In some biomes—the Amazonian rain forest, for example—biodiversity, the range of lifeforms maintained by a particular environment, is immense. Scientists are still discovering new species of insects, plants, and fish. Yet the rate of extinctions has grown rapidly. In the past few decades people have become ever more aware of just how fragile Earth's ecosystems are. But do people have a moral duty to try to maintain the diversity of life on Earth?

Those people who answer "yes" to this question believe that humans, as the dominant species, have a responsibility to act as the custodians of the planet. They also believe that because the accelerating pace of extinction is the result of human activity, people have a moral duty to try to reduce the harm caused by such activity. They point out that few regions of Earth remain as wildernesses untouched by humans—only certain stretches of tropical rain forest in Central Africa and the Amazon, and the frozen wastes of Antarctica, northern Canada, and Siberia.

Elsewhere, humans destroy habitat and pollute the earth, the atmosphere, and the oceans. There are other, less direct forms of human impact on the balance of nature. The greenhouse effect, caused by gases released by human activity that trap the sun's heat in the atmosphere, is causing global temperatures to gradually rise. Such a rise will eventually alter the ecological balance of the planet, potentially leading to further extinctions.

"We cannot hope either to understand or to manage the carbon in the atmosphere unless we understand and manage the trees and the soil too."
—FREEMAN DYSON, U.S. PHYSICIST

People who argue that humans have no duty to maintain biodiversity do not argue that it is not a desirable aim. The greater the variety of life on Earth, for example, the more likelihood of those life forms proving useful. Undiscovered plants might have medical properties to counter fatal diseases, for example. But opponents of efforts to maintain biodiversity argue that such efforts fly in the face of inevitable change.

Every animal and plant occupies a niche in its particular biocommunity. All organisms in a biocommunity depend on one another in a complex network of food webs, so disruption to any part of the community can have potentially wide-ranging effects. But such communities are not fixed. They constantly change, and human activity is only one of the factors that can influence them. Natural changes—the gradual cycle of colder and warmer epochs, geological activity, drought and storms, bushfires, floods—also have an

effect on life on Earth. There is little that can be done to mitigate their effects. Human activity, some people argue, is simply another factor. While the extreme effects of our behavior can be reduced, much of our impact on Earth is inevitable. Humanity should not feel guilty about its part in the rise and fall of species, a process that would continue without any human presence, albeit at a slower rate.

The two articles that follow take opposing views on the question of maintaining biodiversity. The Nature Conservancy of Wisconsin argues that there are compelling scientific, esthetic, and ethical reasons in its favor. Perhaps the most powerful plea is that as the dominant species on Earth, we have the power to preserve or destroy other living things and the habitat we depend on for survival.

The second article looks at an aspect of the scientific community's response to the need for conservation: the cloning of endangered species. Amy Hembree describes a split that has developed among conservationists. One group believes in "frozen zoos," whereby cells and tissue of endangered or extinct animals are collected and stored so that clones can be created at a later date.

The opposing group sees the protection of natural habitats as the best hope of saving nature's biodiversity from extinction. Some cloning experiments are described and the results examined. The author concludes that, although preserving habitat offers the best hope for ensuring biodiversity, cloning has an important part to play in conservation.

WHY WE PRESERVE THE DIVERSITY OF LIFE
The Nature Conservancy

For more than 45 years, The Nature Conservancy has focused on its mission—preserving the plants, animals, and natural communities that represent the diversity of life on Earth by protecting the lands and waters they need to survive. The Conservancy has committed itself to what Aldo Leopold called the "first precaution of intelligent tinkering." We have committed ourselves to "keeping every cog and wheel" for the benefit and enjoyment of future generations.

What are those cogs and wheels? They are natural communities such as tallgrass prairies, oak savannas, calcareous fens, boreal forests, and mixed hardwood forests. They are plant and animal species, such as the Blanding's turtle, the regal fritillary butterfly, and the prairie white-fringed orchid. They include all of the individual variation within these living organisms and the many interactions between them.

Is self-interest the main motivation?

While there are many reasons for saving species and their habitat, self-interest seems to be the most compelling for many people. The natural world provides us with many of the medical, agricultural, and commercial products we use today. For example, 41 percent of the prescription medications dispensed in the United States contain chemicals derived from plants and animals. An extract from the rosy periwinkle, which grows in the tropics, is used to treat childhood leukemia. Millions of Americans with high blood pressure depend on regular doses of digoxin, which is obtained from a European species of foxglove. Taxol, a substance derived from Pacific yew, is being used in the treatment of certain types of cancer. It was a fungus that gave us penicillin.

Norman Myers, a consultant on environmental issues and resource economics at Oxford University, has estimated that societies around the world use about 7,000 kinds of plants for food and have come to depend on only about 15 highly domesticated forms. The productivity of these 15 major crops cannot be maintained, let alone expanded, without a constant

Can you think of any other examples in which plants or animals are used in medicines?

infusion of fresh genetic variability. Much of this genetic material comes from wild plants, the relatives of modern crops. Wild plants also serve as sources of new crops that can eventually be cultivated and used by people.

Industry depends just as heavily on wild plants for raw materials as do agriculture and medicine. Take the humble seaweeds, for example. These marine plants serve as a source of vitamin C, poultry meal, and meat and fish preservatives. They are used to grow bacteria, to keep toothpaste in the tube, to make ice cream smooth, to make puddings thick, and to help candy bars last longer. Many other plants are gathered by industry for their oils and fibers.

These are just a few examples of the many economic benefits that humans derive from the natural world. Many species of plants and animals have not even been discovered and named by scientists, let alone tapped for their economic potential.

The beauty of nature

While the economic benefits of conservation are important, there are also aesthetic reasons for saving species and natural communities. The beauty of nature lifts our hearts and inspires our minds. Who hasn't been inspired at least once by the beauty of a flower, a bird, or a lake to take the lens cap off a camera or dip a brush into paint and try to capture the moment forever? Nature has had a dominant influence on the arts since the first cave paintings. Nature is also our favorite place to recreate, be it hiking up a mountain, canoeing a rapid river, or strolling through a forest with binoculars ready for a fleeting glimpse of a brightly colored songbird.

Do you think people are more likely to be convinced of the need to support biodiversity by economic or esthetic arguments? Which case do you find is more impressive?

"Over increasingly large areas of the United States, spring now comes unheralded by the return of birds, and the early mornings are strangely silent...."
—RACHEL CARSON, *THE SILENT SPRING*

We learn from the natural world. The forests, wetlands, and grasslands; the plants and animals that dwell therein; and all the many interactions between them are natural laboratories. Scientists conduct research there; teachers use them to train the scientists of tomorrow. There are numerous examples of

COMMENTARY: Rachel Carson

The environmentalist writer Rachel Carson pictured seated at her typewriter in 1963.

The U.S. writer, scientist, and ecologist Rachel Carson (1907–1964) grew up in the rural town of Springdale, Pennsylvania. From an early age she had a great love of nature, which she later expressed in many scientific articles and books. She graduated from the Pennsylvania College for Women (now Chatham College) and received her MA in zoology from Johns Hopkins University in 1932. In 1936 she became an aquatic biologist with the U.S. Bureau of Fisheries (later the U.S. Fish and Wildlife Service) and eventually editor-in-chief for that organization.

Carson wrote articles on conservation and natural resources. Her first article, "Undersea," was published in 1937 in the *Atlantic Monthly*. It formed the basis for her first book, *Under the Sea-Wind* (1941), which was highly praised for its combination of scientific accuracy and elegant prose. Her second book, *The Sea around Us* (1951), became a national bestseller and was translated into 30 languages. *The Edge of the Sea*, her third book, was published in 1955.

Rachel Carson is best remembered, though, for her book *The Silent Spring* (1962). In it she warned of the dangers of environmental pollution from pesticides at a time when there was little worldwide awareness of the problem. She called for humanity to change the way it viewed the world and challenged the agricultural practices of scientists and the government.

The common quality that shaped all of Carson's writings was the view that humanity is only one part of nature, which is a vast, interconnected, and interdependent ecosystem. Humans, she argued, are, however, distinguished from the rest of nature by their ability to change the natural world. Sometimes that ability causes irreversible damage. Carson pointed out that although we are the only species with the power to effect change, we remain as vulnerable to the results of the harm we inflict as the rest of the ecosystem. Carson testified before Congress in 1963, when she called for new policies to protect human health and the environment. Her arguments were an important part of the campaign that culminated in the late 1960s and 1970s in bans on such pesticides as DDT.

Rachel Carson continues to inspire people today with her love of nature and her commitment to preserve the living world and all its creatures.

how we learn from nature. Probably one of the best known is the invention of the airplane. Orville and Wilbur Wright ... studied the wing structure and flight of birds to craft the first flying machine. A more recent example is the successful germination of a 1,288-year-old lotus seed ... by scientists at UCLA. They are hoping that their research will yield clues to the aging process in other organisms, including humans.

Can you think of any other examples in which plants or animals have been found to be useful in research?

As the number of human inhabitants of our planet continues to grow and to require more space and resources, our forests, wetlands, and prairies are increasingly being damaged or destroyed. These ecosystems and the species that comprise them provide many essential services such as pollination, soil production, breakdown of pollutants, and stabilization of hydrologic cycles; without these services our planet would cease to exist as we know it. Without intact, fully functioning ecosystems to use as models and as the source of living components, there is little chance that scientists will be able to rebuild or restore these damaged ecosystems.

The responsibility of humankind

Finally, there are ethical reasons for habitat conservation. Because humans are the dominant species ... we have the power to preserve or destroy other living things and the habitat we all depend on for survival. With this power comes responsibility. Aldo Leopold may have put it best ... when he said that "each individual is a member of a community of interdependent parts ... The land ethic simply enlarges the boundaries of the community to include soils, waters, plants, and animals, or collectively: the land." He goes on to say that this doesn't mean we shouldn't use these natural resources. But we should respect their right to continue to exist and ... continue to exist in their natural state.

What similarities are there, if any, between Aldo Leopold's land ethic and traditional Native American views about how we should treat the land?

For all of these reasons and many more, the Nature Conservancy has committed itself to the protection of ecosystems and the rich diversity of life that thrives therein. This is an ambitious goal and one that cannot be accomplished without the help of concerned citizens who are willing to take action to make habitat conservation a reality.

"One of the most exciting aspects of the Nature Conservancy's direct conservation approach is that one person can truly make a difference," said Mary Jean Huston, director of the Wisconsin Chapter of the Conservancy. "One person with a dream of saving a special piece of land can often make it happen. And that's what this organization is about: Caring people doing something very tangible to make the Earth a better place for future generations."

Do you agree that "one person can truly make a difference"? Is there a particular site in your neighborhood that should be "saved"? In what ways is it under threat?

CLONING IS NO EXTINCTION PANACEA
Amy Hembree

NO

In the tooth-and-nail fight to stay on the planet, wild animals are losing, with experts estimating that species are becoming extinct at a rate of 10,000 to 30,000 a year. But what if cloning could slow those numbers?

The recent announcement [by] scientists at the University of Oxford in England that they had mapped the first-ever complete mitochondrial sequences from an extinct species is a reminder that, while the *Jurassic Park* scenario of bringing back the dinosaurs remains a fantasy, the notion of cloning endangered animals is entirely possible. But a split has developed among conservationists.

"Mitochondrial sequences" are part of the cell structure of every species.

The preservation of tissue samples

In one camp are the "frozen zoos," organizations that collect the sperm, cells, and other tissues of endangered and extinct animals. In the other are those who believe that such work distracts from the real issue of habitat destruction, one of the primary reasons animals are endangered in the first place.

The Audubon Nature Institute conducts scientific research into species conservation, including the storage of genetic materials for use in the future. Visit the Audubon Nature Institute website on www. auduboninstitute. org/html/.

"There is no one solution to saving endangered species," [said] Dr. Betsy Dresser, senior vice president and director of the Audubon Nature Institute's Center for Research of Endangered Species (AICRES). "It's truly a multifaceted kind of problem. Simply saving habitat, which is not simple and is incredibly complex, is not going to save endangered species."

Scientists agree that making more woolly mammoths, T. Rexes or anything from ancient DNA, is not possible. Forays to clone their DNA—and the Oxford researchers' mapping of the sequences of a Madagascan elephant-bird and two giant moas, a flightless bird from New Zealand that disappeared about 400 years ago—were not an effort to bring the animals back, but to study their evolution. Critics of endangered species cloning say that's just where the genetic efforts should stop.

Cloning for conservation

Of the moa study, Dr. Alan Cooper, Director of Oxford's Ancient Biomolecules Center, said in a statement, "It is critical that we do not become complacent in our conservation efforts and start assuming that we will be able to bring things back to life if they do become extinct." Which isn't to say no one is working on it. In January [2001], Advanced Cell Technology (ACT) successfully cloned a gaur named Noah, an endangered wild ox native to Southeast Asia, only to see it die of a bacterial infection two days later.

Undaunted, ACT's vice president of medical and scientific development, Dr. Robert P. Lanza, says the company now has government permission to clone a bucardo, an extinct Spanish mountain goat, using cells taken from the last member of its species.

While conservation isn't ACT's main line of work— the company has patented a method of cloning mammals for human transplantation and the production of biopharmaceuticals—Lanza said the work with the gaur and the bucardo utilizes the same technology. "This is more of a demonstration than an experiment," he said.

Biodiversity and technology

However, Glenn McGee, professor of bioethics at the University of Pennsylvania School of Medicine and former member of ACT's ethics board, said cloning is a waste of time and [that it is] a danger to the real work of conserving biodiversity.

"It's cute science run amok," McGee said.

Like many conservationists, he worries the public will consider animal cloning not only as a panacea, but as a good excuse to let slip the more difficult remedies of controlling pollution and overpopulation, and protecting land from development.

McGee says using expensive technology to save animals while destroying their habitat is pointless, and that while "frozen zoos" can produce a few animals, not enough can be cloned to foster true biodiversity.

"You can't repopulate with a couple of genomes," he said. Right now, cloning "doesn't produce a large group of animals. It only produces one. And you can't have Noah's ark from only one or two animals."

But the idea isn't to "mass produce" animals, AICRES Dresser said. Located in New Orleans, AICRES holds thousands of tissue samples from hundreds of species. AICRES has produced test-tube caracals, a species of African cat, as well as an African wildcat by implanting an embryo into a domestic housecat.

"We're using these technologies as management tools," she said, adding that cloning and assisted reproduction is in

Is cloning an effective method of conservation? What problems can you foresee in this approach?

Do you agree that only by adopting an integrated system of conservation can true biodiversity be preserved?

the early stages of development, and that DNA frozen today could be invaluable to future scientists working to save an endangered species.

An exact copy or a rough approximation?

However, another criticism is that cloned animals won't be at all like their extinct and endangered forebears. "Cloning itself is an abnormal procedure," said Dr. Stuart Newman, professor of cell biology and anatomy at New York Medical College and a board member of the Council for Responsible Genetics.

One of the problems boils down to eggs. While many tissues can be kept frozen for years, eggs "don't freeze well at all," Dresser said. The current technique is to use cells from the extinct animal with the egg of a closely related animal that's still alive. In the case of Noah the gaur, the mother was not a female gaur, but a common Angus-Hereford cow. "They're hoping to come out with something that looks fairly normal," Newman said. "I don't think they'll be getting the exact animal back."

Dresser disagrees. "The genetics are the same from a cloned animal." Which is to say that although Noah was born from a cow egg, it was still all gaur. Dresser said that some questions remain about the mitochondrial DNA, the structures inside cells that produce energy. "We don't think those are transferred, but nobody really knows that for sure," she said.

Is a cloned animal as genuine as the original? What, if anything, might be lost in the cloning process?

Even if cloning does save some species, the issue of saving biodiversity remains. With countless species going extinct, replacing every creature in an ecosystem probably would be impossible. To fully reconstruct a habitat would mean not only recreating monkeys, wolves, and birds, but also beetles, flies, and frogs. "I doubt it's possible to get them all," said AICRES spokeswoman Sarah Burnette. Both ACT's Lanza and the staff at AICRES agree that habitat preservation is crucial, but maintain that cloning and assisted reproduction are indispensable aspects of conservation. As Burnette put it, "What if 100 years from now people finally figure out how to save the habitats, but there are no animals? [Cloning] is part of the answer."

COMMENTARY: The Quagga Project

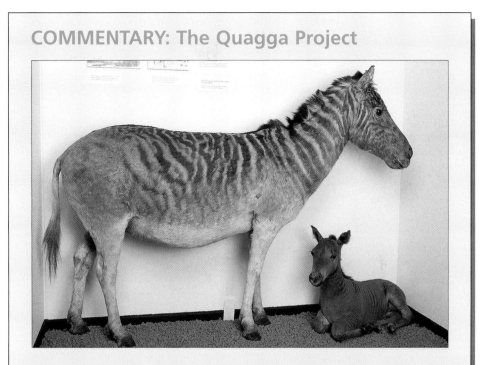

The quagga was a horselike mammal closely related to the zebra. It was native to the desert areas of the African continent until it became extinct in the wild in the 1870s. The last captive quaggas died in Europe in the 1880s. In appearance it was yellowish-brown with stripes on its head, neck, and forebody only. The extinct quagga was not a zebra species of its own but a subspecies of the plains zebra, and therein lies the key to the Quagga Project. In theory it may be possible, by means of a complex breeding program, to reverse the quagga's extinction. Selecting a population of plains zebras, the Quagga Project aims to breed a mammal that in its external appearance, and possibly in its genetic makeup, will be close, if not identical, to the original quagga.

In museums around the world a total of 23 quagga skins survive intact, together with a number of skeletal remains. From these it is possible to get an indication of the appearance and genetic characteristics of the quagga. It shared many characteristics with present day zebras of the African plains, including its distinctive coloring and the arrangement of its stripes (see the reconstucted quagga model from a museum above). Scientists believe that some of the quagga genes may be present in living zebras. By bringing together carefully selected live individuals and so concentrating the quagga genes, a population should emerge that will be closer to the original quagga than anything existing today.

The Quagga Project began in April 1987 at a Nature Conservation farm in South Africa, and the first foal was born in December 1988.

Summary

The two articles reproduced here agree on the need to maintain biodiversity but examine different approaches to this end.

The Nature Conservancy of Wisconsin argues that there are compelling scientific, esthetic, and ethical reasons in its favor. One practical example is given: 41 percent of all the prescription medications dispensed in the United States contain chemicals derived from plants and animals. As the dominant species on Earth, we have the power to preserve or destroy other living things and the habitat we depend on for survival. By destroying natural habitats, we are narrowing our chances of finding other and even more useful sources of medicines in the future. Enlightened self-interest demands that we preserve our natural heritage for future generations.

The second article by Amy Hembree looks at the cloning of endangered species. Amy Hembree describes two approaches by conservationists. One group believes in the preservation of cells and tissue from endangered or extinct animals so that clones can be created by future scientists. The opposing group sees the protection of nature's biodiversity from extinction as the main hope for mankind's survival. The author concludes that although the preservation of habitat can promise continuing biodiversity into the future, the potential of cloning to assist in this is indispensable.

FURTHER INFORMATION:

Books:

Burgess, Bonnie B., *Fate of the Wild: The Endangered Species Act and the Future of Biodiversity*. Athens, GA: University of Georgia Press, 2001.

Cracraft, Joel, and Grifo, Francesca T., *The Living Planet in Crisis*. New York: Columbia University Press, 1999.

Darwin, Charles, *The Origin of Species*, edited by Greg Suriano. New York: Grammercy, 1998.

Wilson, Edward Osborne, *The Diversity of Life*. Cambridge, MA: Belknap Press, 1992.

Useful websites:

www.unep.ch/bio/conv-e.html
Convention on Biological Diversity (1992).
www.earthcharter.org/draft/charter.htm
The Earth Charter Initiative.
darwin.bio.uci.edu/~sustain/bio65/Titlpage.htm
Peter J. Bryant, "Biodiversity and Conservation."
www.nhm.ac.uk/science/projects/worldmap/
Natural History Museum, Biodiversity World Map.
www.defenders.org/bio-cont.html
The Biodiversity Center site.
www.sciencematters.com/cloned/
Information and articles on cloning.
sciencebulletins.amnh.org/biobulletin/biobulletin/story893.html
"Maintaining Genetic Diversity Is the Key" article.
www.epa.gov/fedrgstr/EPA-IMPACT/2001/January/Day-16/i950.htm
Department of the Interior Policy on Maintaining the Biological Integrity, Diversity, and Environmental Health of the National Wildlife Refuge System.

The following debates in the Pro/Con series may also be of interest:

In this volume:

Topic 14 Should scientists be responsible for the effects of their inventions?

DOES HUMANKIND MAINTAIN THE DIVERSITY OF SPECIES ON EARTH?

YES: The natural world supplies many of the agricultural, medical, and commercial products we use today

YES: We can learn from the natural world

YES: The beauty of nature lifts our hearts and inspires our minds

YES: Ecosystems and species provide essential services, such as pollination, without which we could not survive

SCIENCE AND ECONOMICS
Does biodiversity have scientific and economic value?

ESTHETICS
Is the esthetic value of the natural world important?

NO: Maintaining biodiversity means preserving all species, not just those we find useful. It's impossible and illogical to preserve the whole diversity of life on Earth

NO: Preserving nature means preserving all species, even those that are a nuisance or spread disease, and not just those we find beautiful

DOES HUMANKIND MAINTAIN THE DIVERSITY OF SPECIES ON EARTH?
KEY POINTS

YES: We are the most powerful species on Earth and are responsible for preserving other living things and the habitat we all depend on for survival

YES: We have a responsibility to maintain biodiversity for the benefit and enjoyment of future generations

ETHICS
Are humans ethically bound to preserve biodiversity?

NO: Extinctions are an inevitable part of life, and we shouldn't "play God" by trying to preserve all species

NO: Trying to preserve unsuccessful species prevents the natural process of evolution and the survival of the fittest

INTRODUCTION

Who destroyed the city of Hiroshima? The answer seems very simple. On August 6, 1945, shortly after eight o'clock in the morning, a U.S. B-29 bomber, *Enola Gay*, dropped the world's first atomic bomb on the Japanese city. The blast obliterated 62,000 of the 90,000 buildings and killed instantly—and later through radiation sickness—up to 200,000 people. The plane's crew, commanded by Lieutenant Colonel Paul Tibbets, actually destroyed the city. But what about the superiors who ordered their mission? Or the politicians who approved the dropping of the new weapon, led by the new U.S. president Harry S. Truman? How much responsibility do they bear?

However, that the bomb even existed to be dropped at all depended on three years' effort by a team of research scientists of the U.S. Manhattan Project, put together to create a weapon that would ensure the defeat of Germany and Japan and bring an end to World War II. They surely took ultimate responsibility for creating the bomb. The team included some of the world's leading theoretical physicists, who drew on the theoretical research of a generation of earlier scientists, including Albert Einstein and Ernest Rutherford. And the same research that underlay the development of the world's most destructive weapon also created a new generation of nuclear power plants, which supporters claim are cleaner, safer, and cheaper ways to generate electricity than any others.

The story of the atom bomb is a clear demonstration of how difficult it is to attribute responsibility for a scientific development. Yet many people argue increasingly that science should be held to account for its negative consequences. Genetic engineering and plans to clone human beings feed a public perception of scientists as amoral, or even immoral, geniuses who want to play God with no regard for the harm they might do.

But in what ways are scientists directly responsible for the use to which their inventions are put, sometimes years after their deaths? Some analysts argue that the most important criterion is the use to which an invention is put. An invention can be seen as good or bad according to how it is used; a knife, for example, is beneficial as a cooking utensil, but harmful if it is used to stab someone. Another criterion is intention: Did a scientist intend a particular discovery or invention to achieve a particular harmful end?

"Science by itself has no moral dimension. But it does seek to establish truth. And upon this truth morality can be built."

—WILLIAM H. MASTERS,

U.S. GYNECOLOGIST

An instructive case study in assessing scientific intentions is that of the German chemist Fritz Haber (1868-1934). Haber is best known for synthesizing ammonia, but during World War I he worked for the German army to manufacture large quantities of nitric acid, used to make high explosives.

He also developed chlorine gas, used for the first time in warfare by the Germans in 1915 in gas attacks on the Western Front during World War I. Since the gas was developed solely for this purpose, Haber can have had no illusions about what he was doing. If he hadn't developed the gas, critics have argued, chlorine gas would not have been available for use in the trenches in 1915.

When Haber was awarded the Nobel Prize in 1918 for the synthesis of ammonia, he was publicly slighted by chemists from Allied nations because of his role in the development of chlorine gas. They clearly felt that he should bear some responsibility for his actions.

Haber's story becomes more complicated, however. His chlorine gas research was the basis for the development of the gas used to kill the Jews and other victims in Nazi Germany's concentration camps in World War II, yet Haber himself was a Jew who fled Germany when the Nazis came to power in 1933, and he died the following year, long before the concentration camps were built. So should he be considered responsible for the use of the gas chambers simply because, without his earlier work, they might not have been possible?

The following articles discuss different sides of this complex question. "The Franck Report" outlines the observations of scientists working on the Manhattan Project (the U.S. nuclear bomb program) in 1945. It was written two months before the first atomic bomb was dropped on Japan and describes the grave implications nuclear war would have for the United States and the world. The report accepts that the scientists involved must take responsibility for creating a weapon of unparalleled destructive power.

In the second article the authors argue that the development of the atomic bomb came as a result of the pressing needs of war and, consequently, was entirely justified. In this case, they say, the scientists were not at fault.

THE FRANCK REPORT
Committee on Political and Social Problems, Manhattan Project

The only reason to treat nuclear power differently from all the other developments in the field of physics is its staggering possibilities as a means of political pressure in peace, and sudden destruction in war. All present plans for the organization of research, scientific and industrial development, and publication in the field of nucleonics are conditioned by the political and military climate in which one expects those plans to be carried out. Therefore, in making suggestions for the postwar organization of nucleonics, a discussion of political problems cannot be avoided. The scientists on this Project do not presume to speak authoritatively on problems of national and international policy. However, we found ourselves, by the force of events...[in] the last five years, in the position of a small group of citizens cognizant of a grave danger for the safety of this country, as well as for the future of all the other nations, of which the rest of mankind is unaware.

Do you agree with the author's contention that the development of nuclear technology has an inescapable political dimension?

The political implications of atomic power

We therefore felt it our duty to urge that the political problems, arising from the mastering of atomic power, be recognized in all their gravity, and that appropriate steps be taken for their study and the preparation of necessary decisions. We hope that the creation of the Committee by the Secretary of War to deal with all aspects of nucleonics indicates that these implications have been recognized by the government. We feel that our acquaintance with the scientific elements of the situation, and prolonged preoccupation with its world-wide political implications, imposes on us the obligation to offer to the Committee some suggestions as to the possible solution of these grave problems.

Scientists have often before been accused of providing new weapons for the mutual destruction of nations, instead of improving their well-being. It is undoubtedly true that the discovery of flying, for example, has so far brought much more misery than enjoyment or profit to humanity. However, in the past, scientists could disclaim direct responsibility for the use to which mankind had put their disinterested discoveries. We cannot take the same attitude now because the success which we have achieved in the development of nuclear power is fraught with infinitely greater dangers than were all the inventions of the past. All of us, familiar with the present state of nucleonics, live with the vision before our eyes of sudden destruction visited on our own country, of Pearl Harbor disaster repeated in thousandfold magnification, in every one of our major cities.

Pearl Harbor in Hawaii is a major base for the U.S. Navy in the Pacific Ocean. On December 7, 1941, Pearl Harbor was attacked by Japanese forces, causing massive destruction and heralding the entry of the United States into World War II.

Protection against new weapons

In the past, science has often been able to provide adequate protection against new weapons it has given into the hands of an aggressor, but it cannot promise such efficient protection against the destructive use of nuclear power. This protection can only come from the political organization of the world. Among all arguments calling for an efficient international organization for peace, the existence of nuclear weapons is the most compelling one. In the absence of an international authority which would make all resort to force in international conflicts impossible, nations could still be diverted from a path which must lead to total mutual destruction, by a specific international agreement barring a nuclear armaments race.

Prospects for an armaments race

It could be suggested that the danger of destruction by nuclear weapons can be prevented—at least as far as this country is concerned—by keeping our discoveries secret for an indefinite time, or by developing our nucleonic armaments at such a pace that no other nations would think of attacking us from fear of overwhelming retaliation.

The answer to the first suggestion is that although we undoubtedly are at present ahead of the rest of the world in this field, the fundamental facts of nuclear power are a subject of common knowledge. British scientists know as much as we do about the basic wartime progress of nucleonics—with the exception of specific processes used in our engineering developments—and the background of French nuclear physicists plus their occasional contact with our Projects, will enable them to catch up rapidly, at least as far as basic scientific facts are concerned. German scientists, in whose discoveries the whole development of this field has originated, apparently did not develop it during the war to the same extent to which this has been done in America; but to the last day of the European war, we have been living in

For background information on the Franck Report and the Manhattan Project visit www. nuclearfiles. org/bios/f_j/franck james.htm.

constant apprehension as to their possible achievements. The knowledge that German scientists were working on this weapon and that their government certainly had no scruples against using it when available, was the main motivation of the initiative which American scientists have taken in developing nuclear power on such a large scale for military use in this country. In Russia, too, the basic facts and implications of nuclear power were well understood in 1940, and the experiences of Russian scientists in nuclear research is entirely sufficient to enable them to retrace our steps within a few years, even if we would make all attempts to conceal them. Furthermore, we should not expect too much success from attempts to keep basic information secret in peacetime, when scientists acquainted with the work on this and associated Projects will be scattered to many colleges and research institutions, and many of them will continue to work on problems closely related to those on which our developments are based. In other words, even if we can retain our leadership in basic knowledge of nucleonics for a certain time by maintaining the secrecy of all results achieved on this and associated Projects, it would be foolish to hope that this can protect us for more than a few years....

Surviving a future nuclear war

[I]f the race of nuclear armaments is allowed to develop, the only apparent way in which our country could be protected from the paralyzing effects of a sudden attack is by dispersal of industries which are essential for our war effort, and dispersal of the population of our major metropolitan cities. As long as nuclear bombs remain scarce (this will be the case until uranium and thorium cease to be the only basic materials for their fabrication) efficient dispersal of our industry and the scattering of our metropolitan population will considerably decrease the temptation of attacking us by nuclear weapons.

Ten years hence, an atomic bomb containing perhaps 20 kg (44 lb) of active material, may be detonated at 6 percent efficiency, and thus have an effect equal to that of 20,000 tons of TNT. One of these may be used to destroy something like 3 square miles of an urban area. Atomic bombs containing a larger quantity of active material but still weighing less than one ton may be expected to be obtainable within 10 years which could destroy over 10 square miles of a city. A nation which is able to assign 10 tons of atomic explosives for the preparation of a sneak attack on this country, can then hope to achieve the destruction of all

Plutonium is now a more common constituent of nuclear warheads. A manmade element, plutonium was originally made in military reactors first developed by the United States during World War II. It was used in the atomic bomb dropped on the city of Nagasaki, Japan, on August 9, 1945.

industry and most of the population in an area from 500 square miles upwards. If no choice of targets, in any area of 500 square miles of American territory, will contain a large enough fraction of the nation's industry and population to make their destruction a crippling blow to the nation's war potential and its ability to defend itself, then the attack will not pay, and will probably not be undertaken. At present, one could easily select in this country 100 blocks of 5 square miles each whose simultaneous destruction would be a staggering blow to the nation. (A possible total destruction of all the nation's naval forces would be only a small detail of such a catastrophe.) Since the area of the United States is about 6 million square miles, it should be possible to scatter its industrial and human resources in such a way as to leave no 500 square miles important enough to serve as a target for nuclear attack.

The truth of this statement was proved on September 11, 2001, when terrorists struck the World Trade Center in New York City with two hijacked passenger planes, killing thousands of people and paralyzing the U.S. financial market.

The need for international agreement

We are fully aware of the staggering difficulties of such a radical change in the social and economic structure of our nation. We felt, however, that the dilemma had to be stated, to show what kind of alternative methods of protection will have to be considered if no successful international agreement is reached. It must be pointed out that in this field we are in a less favorable position than nations which are either now more diffusely populated and whose industries are more scattered, or whose governments have unlimited power over the movement of population and the location of industrial plants.

If no efficient international agreement is achieved, the race of nuclear armaments will be on in earnest not later than the morning after our first demonstration of the existence of nuclear weapons. After this, it might take other nations 3 or 4 years to overcome our present head start, and 8 or 10 years to draw even with us if we continue to do intensive work in this field. This might be all the time we have to bring about the re-groupment of our population and industry. Obviously, no time should be lost in inaugurating a study of this problem by experts.

IS SCIENCE TO BLAME FOR THE BOMB?
John Gillott and Manjit Kumar

Atomic research in the United States. was instigated by President Franklin D. Roosevelt in 1939. He had received a warning from Albert Einstein of the possibility of Nazi Germany developing nuclear weapons. The Manhattan Project began in 1943 with the objective of building the first atomic bomb.

X When Robert Oppenheimer, the scientist in charge of the Manhattan Project to build the atomic bomb, witnessed the awesome power of the test explosion on July 16, 1945, at Alamogordo in the New Mexico desert, a black thought flashed through his mind. He recalled a line from the *Bhagavad Gita*, the sacred text of the Hindus: "I am become death, the shatterer of worlds."

By the 1950s, Oppenheimer's moment of self-doubt had become a widespread loss of confidence within the scientific community. Richard Feynman, the great American physicist, spoke of scientists' fear of their "God-like" power....

Motives for building the atomic bomb

The bombing of Hiroshima and Nagasaki quite rightly arouses strong feelings of revulsion and fear. [But] consider first the scientists. What was the motivation of the scientists who built the atomic bomb? It was anti-Nazi feeling. And what motivated the leading players in the subsequent H-bomb effort: Edward Teller, John von Neumann, and Stanislaw Ulam? Anticommunism. In neither the A-bomb nor the H-bomb project was the prime motivation of scientists an abstract urge to expand the powers of human reason. Their motivations had much more to do with politics and war. Of course, they were fascinated by the science—but that did not lead to Hiroshima.

For more information on the atomic bombing of Japan visit the Hiroshima Archive website at www.lclark. edu/~history/ HIROSHIMA/.

The motivations of the American government [arose] from economic and strategic conflicts with the other major powers, and racial conflict in Asia. Atomic science was just a means, if a very effective one, to an end.

[S]cientists did not carry on making the bomb as a result of some purely scientific impulse. They carried on for the same reasons American soldiers continued to fight—a mixture of patriotism, anti-Japanese feeling, and the simple momentum of being caught-up in war. Of course there was an element of scientific curiosity about whether they could make a bomb, but that was satisfied by the test-fire on July 16 at Alamogordo. Moreover, even if scientists like Feynman were too carried away with success to think, Oppenheimer, the military, and the American government were not. Not only did they have clear, and nonscientific motivations, they also planned everything painstakingly. There was no unstoppable 'slide' from science to destruction. Rather, there was a very precise mobilization of science for military purposes....

The uses of science

Atomic science, like all science, can be used peacefully or for military purposes. As the French physicist and Communist Party member Frédéric Joliot-Curie quite rightly argued, atomic forces are "forces liberated by Man, and Man has complete power to direct their use exclusively for peaceful ends. The situation would be quite different if we had to deal with a brutal threat from natural forces such as that offered by the forecast of an imminent collision between our planet and an immense meteorite." Even the construction and testing of an explosive device is something that could be used for peaceful purposes—such as deep underground mining. From this point of view Emilio Segrè hit the mark when he described the test detonation at Alamogordo as "one of the greatest physics experiments of all time."

To reinforce this point, consider a historical comparison. Just as the Second World War has been called "the physicists' war," so the [F]irst is often called "the chemists' war." In that war, chemistry was used by all sides to make poison gases— used to terrible effect on the Western Front. But chemistry has also given us countless drugs and compounds which have improved our well-being. Chemistry, like physics, is neither good nor bad in itself—it all depends on what you do with it.

The authors draw a distinction between "science for science's sake" and science directed toward a specific and pressing goal. Is there a moral element in this distinction?

The misuses of knowledge

Of course, atomic science was developed in order to make a bomb. But that is neither here nor there. Radar was developed for military purposes in the same war—but it is also a great tool for safety in civilian aviation today. All in all, it is only in the perceptions of commentators, not in reality, that atomic science and destruction are forever directly linked.

One result of drawing science and humanity into the frame in accounting for Hiroshima over the past 50 years has been to encourage public suspicion of science, and a low opinion of humanity. By equating scientific knowledge with the misuse of that knowledge in the service of militarism, the reactions to Hiroshima cast a long shadow over science.

In 1905, Nobel Prize-winner Pierre Curie, co-discoverer of radium, noted that "in criminal hands radium might prove very dangerous, and the question arises whether it would be to the advantage of humanity to know the secrets of nature."

Can you think of other inventions, discoveries, or technological developments that were intended for military use but were later utilized for civilian purposes?

However, reflecting the relative optimism of the period, he declared that he was of the opinion that "humanity will obtain more good than evil from future discoveries." Writing 40 years later, Curie's son-in-law, Frédéric Joliot-Curie, also saw science in a positive light. Just days after the bombing of Hiroshima and Nagasaki, he argued: "I am personally convinced that, despite the feelings aroused by the application of atomic energy to destructive ends, it will be of inestimable service to mankind in peacetime." Joliot-Curie was clearly taking the long view. What is depressing is that his reaction to Hiroshima was exceptional, where his father-in-law's optimistic opinion had been mainstream in his day.

Do the benefits of nuclear technology (e.g., abundant and cheap electricity) outweigh the disadvantages (e.g., the potential for global destruction)?

Perceptions of science since 1945

After 1945, scientific achievement was never simply celebrated as it should have been. In 1992, the Bulletin of the Atomic Scientists felt unable to celebrate the 50th anniversary of Enrico Fermi's achievement of the first controlled, selfsustaining nuclear chain reaction—because of the application to which this was put. That Fermi's work was explicitly part of war work ought to be irrelevant to scientific judgement. It was a great achievement, and should have been marked as such. But it was not—to the detriment of science.

This point is at the heart of the debate. Should science be ashamed of its achievements?

Furthermore, pushing back the bounds of knowledge was frowned upon after the war because people did not trust in humanity's ability to use knowledge for good. At root, this attitude was antiscientific in that it encouraged limits to scientific inquiry....[Oppenheimer] argued in November 1945, "it is not possible to be a scientist unless you believe that the knowledge of the world, and the power which this gives, is a thing which is of intrinsic value to humanity, and that you are using it to help in the spread of knowledge, and are willing to take the consequences."

...[W]e might not agree with Pierre Curie's notion of good and evil, nor with Oppenheimer's idea of what to do about "the consequences." But at least they believed humanity could make rational choices about how to apply its knowledge. That makes it possible to argue about the legitimate uses of science. By contrast, the contemporary conflation of knowledge with use and misuse leaves little room for a discussion—the only option is a fatalistic rejection of scientific inquiry, accompanied by curbs and regulations on the work that is done.

What are the limits to scientific research and experiment? If something can technically be done, does that necessarily mean that it should be done?

The argument that science and human ambition ... are responsible for Hiroshima falsely denigrates humanity and its scientific achievements. Worse still, it also serves to shield militarism from exposure.

The lessons of Hiroshima and Nagasaki

However offensive traditional conservatives might find scrutiny of the Allies' motives in dropping the bomb on Japan, they are prepared to feign horror at Hiroshima. They understand the apologetic potential of conflating scientific knowledge and its misuse by the military. For if science and humanity in general are to blame for the bomb, then militaristic governments and generals cannot be held responsible for the slaughter. Appleyard's claim that "the atom bombs dropped on Hiroshima and Nagasaki suddenly revealed science itself as an uncontrollable extension of the human will to destruction," sums up his anti-humanism. It also serves to let militarism off the hook by spreading the blame about. Hiroshima ceases to be the result of a struggle for global domination among capitalist powers in a specific historical context, and becomes instead a general indictment of human nature and scientific knowledge.

The idea that science is responsible for Hiroshima serves both to denigrate human advance and knowledge, and to whitewash the true causes of war. Combating the militarism that gave rise to the bomb then becomes impossible. After all, if militarism is a manifestation of "the human will to destruction," the responsibility of all and therefore nobody in particular, then what can we hope to do about it?

"Militarism" means the belief in military efficiency as the supreme ideal of the state and the subordination of all other interests to those of the military. In the 1930s and 1940s Japan was a militarist state.

Physicists and militarists

After the Second World War, some scientists sought to redress the misuse of science in the cause of war.... In the postwar period, the enterprise of physics came more and more to be linked to military research. As Daniel Kevles relates, during this period, "all roads" seemed to "lead to the Pentagon." Those physicists opposed to militarism came to despair of preventing the misuse of their discipline. As a result, a generation of the more radical physicists abandoned the field for chemistry and biology—or left science altogether. In desperation, Einstein himself came to regret the role he had played in the development of atomic science, and, despite being a great humanist, he declared at one point that if a more extensive nuclear conflict was to erupt, "in the end men will get what they deserve."

...[O]ne thing is clear: blaming science or humanity for the problems caused by militarism neither helps humanity nor assists the fight against war—indeed it has the opposite effect. The moral of the story is that a concerted fight against militarism should go alongside a promotion of scientific inquiry without limitations.

Having originally urged President Roosevelt to develop the atom bomb, the great physicist Albert Einstein later regretted his decision, saying, "I made one great mistake in my life—when I signed that letter...."

185

Summary

In the first article scientists working on the Manhattan Project in the final stages of World War II warn of the implications of unleashing the power of nuclear bombs on the world. The scientists outline the grave and irrevocable consequences of launching humanity into a nuclear age and accept their responsibility in creating nuclear devices that are designed solely for destructive purposes. The entire article is an attempt to alert their political masters to the far-reaching nature of nuclear warfare, and they warn that the nuclear secrets that they have unlocked will not remain secret for long. Once the world has access to them, the fate of the United States will become infinitely more unsure.

In the second piece John Gillott and Manjit Kumar remove the responsibility from the scientist. Because technologies can be employed for more than one purpose, it is in the act of using the invention or discovery that responsibility lies. They contend that the atomic bomb was developed as a specific response to the evils of Nazism and war, and not simply as an academic exercise to expand human knowledge and power. Further, they plead for a break in the connection between scientific inquiry and the militarism that manipulates that science. They argue that it is not the will for discovery that blights humanity but the will for war.

FURTHER INFORMATION:

Books:

Rhodes, Richard, *The Making of the Atomic Bomb*. New York: Simon and Schuster, 1986.

Smith, A. K., and C. Weinder (editors), *Robert Oppenheimer, Letters and Recollections*. California: Stanford University Press, 1980.

Szanton, A., *The Recollections of Eugene P. Wigner*. New York: Plenum Press, 1992.

Useful websites:

www.dannen.com/decision/franck.html
Text of the Franck Report.

www.pugwash.org/award/Rotblatnobel.htm
Text of Josef Rotblat's acceptance speech for the Nobel Peace Prize.

www.vilmi.net/hut/Spring97/automatic/responsibility
Ianinis Hanen, "Scientists and Responsibility."

www.ntb.ch/SEFI/TWI/Responsibility.html
Juergen Mittelstrass, "Technology and Responsibility."

www.mfn-consulting.com/html/science.html
Marcel Neuts, "Science: An Engine of Social Change."

www.heffter.org/essay.html
David E. Nichols, "A Scientist Reflects on the Discovery and Future of LSD."

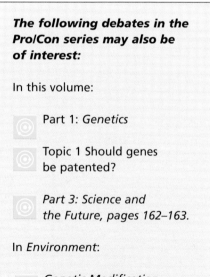

The following debates in the Pro/Con series may also be of interest:

In this volume:

Part 1: *Genetics*

Topic 1 Should genes be patented?

Part 3: Science and the Future, pages 162–163.

In *Environment*:

Genetic Modification, pages 160–161

SHOULD SCIENTISTS BE RESPONSIBLE FOR THE EFFECTS OF THEIR INVENTIONS?

YES: Weapons, for example, are designed to kill people

YES: Scientists can usually foresee the consequences of their inventions and discoveries

MORAL JUDGMENT
Do technology and inventions have moral value?

FORESIGHT
Should scientists be able to predict the results of their research?

NO: Scientific and technological achievements are neutral and have no moral value in themselves—only the way they are used can be morally judged

NO: Scientists cannot be responsible for the actions of others

SHOULD SCIENTISTS BE RESPONSIBLE FOR THE EFFECTS OF THEIR INVENTIONS?

KEY POINTS

YES: Scientists have a responsibility to inform humanity of the potential impact of their discoveries and inventions

YES: If a scientist develops a new weapon, he or she is accountable for the deaths that weapon causes

INTENTION
Should the inventor be judged for the results of his or her research?

NO: The intention of the user should be judged, not the inventor

NO: It is illogical to judge a scientist because of the uses to which his or her research has been put

Topic 15
SHOULD GOVERNMENTS CONTINUE TO FUND SPACE EXPLORATION?

YES
"PROS AND CONS OF SPACE TRAVEL"
WWW.GEOCITIES.COM/FAHDSHARIFF/SPACE.HTML
FAHD SHARIFF

NO
"THEY'RE GOING SPACE CRAZY"
BUSINESS WEEK, JULY 28, 1997
JOHN CAREY AND NEIL GROSS

INTRODUCTION

The debate over whether governments should fund space exploration is a relatively recent one. Space travel was pioneered under government auspices; the rocketry it uses was developed by state-funded arms programs; the race to put a human on the Moon was an essential expression of the conflict between the American and Soviet governments during the Cold War in the 1960s.

The U.S. government has drawn criticism ever since it started spending large amounts of money on space travel in the 1960s. With the end of the Cold War, however, and the explosion of the space shuttle Challenger in 1986, that criticism grew ever louder. At the same time, the U.S. government was perceived as continuing to fund the National Aeronautics and Space Administration (NASA) while trying to cut the costs of education and welfare. For many critics this seemed an inappropriate order of priority.

There are two main bases for criticizing government funding for space exploration. The first is that the vast sums involved—$14.5 billion for NASA in 2002—would be better off spent on dealing with problems on Earth. Such an amount would make a great difference in dealing with global poverty, war, genocide, famine, and many important environmental problems. Or it could be usefully spent on schools or hospitals. In this view space travel brings few benefits to humankind. To spend public money on it is not only wasteful; given the problems here on Earth, it is positively immoral.

Defenders of space travel counter firstly that while its cost sounds vast—and, indeed, is, by any personal standards—in the context of government spending in general it is relatively small. Although it seems that it would make a huge difference to government programs on Earth, it would be rapidly swallowed up and have little benefit. Second, they argue that space travel is useful to humankind. Space technology has produced many spin-offs that benefit our everyday lives; increasing our knowledge of space is a benefit in itself; and space offers opportunities for exploitation, such as by mining minerals on asteroids.

> *"[Space travel] will free man from the remaining chains, the chains of gravity which still tie him to this planet."*
>
> —DR. WERNHER VON BRAUN,
> ROCKET PIONEER

The prospect of exploiting space provides the second basis for critics of government funding for space programs. These critics do not argue that space exploration should be abandoned, simply that governments are not the sources to fund it. They argue that government-funded agencies are inefficient and expensive. Space exploration should be left to private firms competing in a marketplace. They are more imaginative, more likely to be innovative, and above all, cheaper. This view echoes arguments about whether private firms or public bodies are the best way to organize services such as education and welfare.

Supporters of continued government funding for space travel argue that the vast costs of initiating space programs in the 1960s were prohibitive for private firms. Such programs had to be funded by governments—originally in the Soviet Union and the United States, but today also in China and Europe, where a number of countries have joined together in the European Space Agency (ESA). It is not right that private firms should now be able to benefit from this expensive pioneering work. Because the development of space technology has been publicly funded, the rewards that now seem possible from space exploration should go to the people, via their governments.

There is also a principle, defenders of government funding argue, that such an important project as space exploration is rightly the province of governments. They are more reliable guardians of scientific advance and knowledge than private firms.

Should governments continue to fund space exploration? The first article, by Fahd Shariff, argues that the U.S. space budget is small compared to those of other departments, such as defense. John Carey and Neil Gross examine the current commercial space industry and conclude that commercial enterprises can build and operate hardware such as space probes cheaper than NASA can.

PROS AND CONS OF SPACE TRAVEL
Fahd Shariff

Of course space exploration is expensive. That's because it's very, very hard. It requires very complex and reliable technology and a big support infrastructure to be at all successful. It is true that the money could be spent directly on helping to fix the problems of the human species. For example, the price tag for a manned mission to Mars weighs in at $50 billion. Think what could be done with that money if spent on the education system, for example. Spending money on space exploration must be justified when there are still problems on Earth.

The author begins by acknowledging that space exploration is expensive and that the money could be usefully spent on Earth. This point then leads him to his main argument—justifying why space exploration should continue.

But whether space exploration is a waste of money is, I think, open to debate. To what do we compare the asking price of the Universe? Don't forget the successes of the space program. The *Voyager* probes, for example, have cost the average American taxpayer roughly 10 cents per year since their launch in 1977. The probes were designed to last three years, enough to explore the planets Jupiter and Saturn. *Voyager 2* went on to encounter the planets Uranus and Neptune, with an accuracy in navigation similar to throwing a pin through the eye of a needle 50 miles [80 km] away. The *Voyager* probes returned the equivalent of 100,000 encyclopedia volumes of new information and visions of the solar system, operating for some six times their projected design lifetimes. The *Voyagers* were spectacular successes.

Cost–benefit analysis

And are we really talking about huge amounts of money here? The $200 million spent on the Mars Pathfinder mission, for example, is a large amount of money. But compare this with the $2.4 billion spent in one year—1982—on the development of the MX cruise missile program. And this was $2.4 billion fifteen years before Pathfinder was launched, meaning this is an underestimate of the cost of the missile in today's money. I think it is hard to argue that the MX missile has brought more benefit to humanity than the Mars Pathfinder mission, yet it cost a lot more.

Is this a fair point? Many opponents of space exploration also oppose missile development.

It is true that space travel requires lots of money, a fact its opponents are always quick to point out to the public. What is often forgotten is the scale of other expenditures. Let's look at the U.S.A., which spends more than any other country on space exploration. In 1999 the U.S. plans to spend about $270 billion on defense, $200 billion on Medicare, and about $400 billion on social security. By comparison, the science budget is about $70 billion, from nonindustrial sources, of which $14 billion is to be spent on NASA…. [So] the U.S. space budget is about one-twentieth the amount spent on defense, and about one-twenty-ninth that spent on social security.

Look at www.whitehouse.gov/news/usbudget/blueprint/bud33.html for proposed 2002 government spending. How do the figures quoted here compare to the 1999 figures?

Making cuts from the wrong areas

I assume the reason [people] would cut the space budget would be to allow the money currently spent on space exploration to be spent on solving more down-to-Earth problems. Such as eliminating cancer, or providing better education. This is a very laudable goal. But I think [they] have the wrong target. Don't forget, the space program in America grew originally out of the military ballistics program. Were the space budget to be cut, I find it much more likely that the majority of the money would get redirected back to the military, resulting in a larger gap between defense spending and domestic spending. In other words, cutting the space program would do more harm than good to the American people. We should be able to fund both space exploration and domestic programs, such as education and health. If you're looking for a few billion dollars to spend on education, why take a quarter off the space budget, when you can take 1 percent of the defense budget?

If funds were reallocated to defense, would that cause more harm than good to the American people?

Don't forget that the manned space flight program is only one part of the space program, though it does take over a third of the space budget. Manned space flight is a far harder challenge than unmanned flight—humans require much more onboard support than computers! This means that manned space flight is much more expensive than unmanned. This is true for all space programs, not just the American space program we have been using as an example.

The cost of manned flights

I have a much harder time justifying the expense of manned space flight on financial grounds than advocating the space program in general. I don't have a problem advocating one attack helicopter's worth of money to fully fund a SETI program, or asking for the same amount to build a robot that will peel a little more away from the mystery of the solar system. But asking for a hundred million dollars to do a manned mission that could be done better and more cheaply by an unmanned rocket—such as the 1986 *Challenger*

"SETI" stands for Search for Extra-Terrestrial Intelligence. Astronomers use radio telescopes to search the sky for signs of intelligent life elsewhere in our galaxy.

mission—is harder to justify, in my opinion. It is true that there are some missions that could only be performed by human operators—such as the Hubble repair mission. But whether the majority of the manned missions are worth risking lives over is I think more debatable. Of course, the manned space flight program represents the first small steps in a much longer-term process. I do not think it is clear that we're ready to take those steps yet. But the unmanned space program is one of the finest achievements of the last 2,000 years of technology, representing value for money that is the envy of most other human endeavors.

What other technological achievements could claim this description?

> *"For one priceless moment in the whole history of man, all of the people on this Earth are truly one."*
>
> —RICHARD M. NIXON, RADIO TRANSMISSION TO THE FIRST MEN ON THE MOON, JULY 20, 1969

Manned missions serve public demand

If … the unnecessary manned missions are axed, it will make it harder for the necessary manned missions to be carried out successfully. The infrastructure and experience won't be there. The second factor is that the manned space flight program is the financial—and to a large extent political—reason for the existence of the space program in the first place. Though by far the greatest scientific returns come from unmanned missions, those in office and the public see the manned program as the face of space exploration. NASA is a servant of the public, as it must be, and is legislated on by those in power—not by scientists. Were the manned program to be axed, NASA would no longer be serving the public demand and would actually have more trouble surviving. So I think that it would be a nice idea to trim off the budget associated with unnecessary manned missions, but I also think it is an impossible idea to carry out. NASA's fortunes rise and fall with those of the manned space program.

Do you agree that the U.S. public demands manned space travel as a condition of support for NASA? See www.nasa.gov.

The author claims that $14 billion has bought the universe. Why do opponents argue that it has bought nothing?

But I really don't think the space program is a waste of money. In fact, I think that $14 billion a year is a very reasonable price for the Universe! And it doesn't have to be paid at the cost of education or health.

*Astronaut Alan Shepard plants the U.S. flag on the surface of the Moon in 1971. He was the
second person to go into space and the fifth man to walk on the Moon.*

THEY'RE GOING SPACE CRAZY
John Carey and Neil Gross

On the spectacular rock-strewn surface of the Red Planet, the Mars rover creeps along at a snail's pace. On Earth, however, the star of humanity's latest trip to the planets is flying—off store shelves, that is—as people snap up thousands of Mattel-made models of the *Sojourner* for $5 each.

On July 4, 1997, NASA's Pathfinder mission landed an unmanned robotic explorer on the surface of Mars. The robot carried out a range of scientific experiments.

Yes, there's money to be made exploiting the final frontier. But it's not just the predictable toys and B-movies. As the Mars *Pathfinder* mission reawakens Americans' romance with space exploration, companies are boldly dreaming of going where none has gone before. Theme-park rides on the Moon? Mines on asteroids? Trips into orbit, colonies on Mars? They're all in the business plans of a handful of companies and entrepreneurs with stardust in their eyes. Many of these dreams may never come true. But don't underestimate the power of free enterprise to jump-start humanity's push to the planets, says Robert Zubrin, founder of startup Pioneer Astronautics in Lakewood, Colo., and author of *The Case for Mars* (The Free Press). "We're at the dawn of a new era in space," he proclaims.

The costs of space travel may be large, but so are the rewards.

Of course, space is already a huge business. Satellites for TV, telecommunications, global positioning, weather, and other functions, along with rockets to launch them and earthbound controllers and processors, added up to a $77 billion industry last year, according to a new report from KPMG Peat Marwick LLP and three collaborators. For the first time, commercial revenues actually surpassed government expenditures. NASA, meanwhile, is taking steps to privatize operations. Last year it handed prime responsibility for the Space Shuttle to a joint venture between Boeing Co. and Lockheed Martin Corp. And with constellations of new satellites planned for personal phone services and remote imaging, analysts estimate growth of commercial space businesses at 20 percent per year. "After a lot of hype in the mid-1980s about commercial space, we're finally at a point where people are plowing their own money into it," says Peter M. Stahl, an analyst in Marwick's commercial space and high-technology group. A few brave souls are looking beyond mundane orbiting satellites. Casting about for a way to make money in space, former software magnate Jim Benson created SpaceDev LLC to explore asteroids. He points out that there are more than 400 known bodies zipping near Earth, some laden with resources such as steel, gold, platinum, and water. Benson doubts it's worth hauling this booty back to Earth. But when it costs thousands to supply a few glasses of water to the space station, water and building materials on nearby asteroids become attractive.

Mining asteroids

In addition to prospecting and perhaps mining asteroids, Benson figures that SpaceDev can build and operate space probes more cheaply than NASA and thus win contracts from governments and research bodies anxious to do more science in space. For less than $50 million, SpaceDev plans to shoot a spacecraft to an asteroid, land an instrument to prospect the body's wealth, and lay claim to its resources. The target hasn't yet been picked, but the mission could come as early as 1999. "We're trying to get the franchise on private space exploration," Benson says.

What are some of the implications of space exploration being put into private hands? How, for example, would it affect public access to new information?

NASA is surprisingly comfortable with schemes such as Benson's. This fall, the agency's own Lunar Prospector mission will send a probe to orbit the Moon and scope out resources, including water. The entire mission, including a spacecraft built by Lockheed Martin, is budgeted at just $63 million.

Making unearthly profits, however, is no easy task. Just ask LunaCorp, which has been trying to mount a private mission to the Moon for four years. The Arlington (Va.) company wants to send up a robot vehicle bristling with cameras and corporate logos. TV networks, in theory, would then buy exclusive footage, and visitors to amusement parks or space museums could experience the thrill of driving the rover across the lunar surface. Trouble is, LunaCorp can't find buyers for the $150 million mission. "There's an imagination barrier," laments LunaCorp exec Victoria Beckner. "Companies still think of space exploration as being the government domain." Similarly, Pioneer's Robert Zubrin dreams of commercial colonies on Mars. But he admits that "it's hard to sell a business plan that says, 'We'll go to Mars, Mr. Gates, on your money.'"

Cheaper rockets

The towering hurdle for all of these space ventures is cost. The price tag for a launch is still typically $50 million or more for a big communications satellite, or $8,000 to $25,000 per pound. That's why the busiest outpost on the commercial space frontier is the rocket business. A large cost reduction, explains Michael S. Kelly, president of Kelly Space &

Technology Inc. in San Bernardino, Calif., "will all of a sudden make a whole bunch of potential space businesses financially viable."

The conservative strategy is to find ways to shoot off traditional, expendable rockets more cheaply. Boeing, for instance, has a large stake in Sea Launch Co., which is converting an oil rig to a floating launchpad that can be hauled by boat to the optimal ocean launch spot. Boeing is also pumping millions into rocket research. "Things will take off as we get smarter," says space transportation program manager Dana G. Andrews.

Advantages over aerospace giants

The startups say they have one big advantage over aerospace giants: no cumbersome bureaucracy. Rick Fleeter, president of tiny satellite and rocket maker AeroAstro LLC in Herndon, Va., is building a demonstration rocket for the Air Force powered by an engine he made for a mere $100,000—compared with the $2 million to $4 million it would cost to buy one.

Other companies believe the key is reusable rockets. Kelly wants to enlist a Boeing 747 to tow his delta-winged spacecraft, the *Eclipse E-100*, into the air. Kistler Aerospace Corp. in Kirkland, Wash., is using old Soviet rocket engines to create a two-stage reusable vehicle. And Pioneer Rocketplane, co-founded by Zubrin in Colorado, is building a piloted spacecraft that takes off like a jet plane. Such a ship could also function as a hypersonic delivery truck, argues Pioneer executive vice-president Mitchell Burnside Clapp. "I'd like to make the claim that I can deliver a package to San Francisco the day before it was sent from Japan," he says.

None of these Buck Rogers schemes is guaranteed to open up the space frontier. Indeed, some competitors may be reaching too high. "If everyone wasn't so busy trying to cut launch costs by a factor of 10 or 100, we could easily cut them by two or four," frets AeroAstro's Fleeter. What's more, the claim that the private sector must take over space exploration could be counterproductive, prodding Congress to cut funding for future missions. That worries Louis Friedman, executive director of The Planetary Society, who likens space exploration today to the great era of government-funded voyages of discovery in the 1400s and 1500s. It was only after explorers such as Vasco da Gama and Christopher Columbus finished their voyages that the Dutch East India and Hudson Bay companies rushed in. In the same way, today's *Pathfinder* may be a small first step toward business in space.

U.S. President George W. Bush announced that NASA would receive around $14.5 billion in government funding for 2002. The figure represented a 2 and 7 percent increase over 2001 and 2000 respectively.

COMMENTARY: The International Space Station

Sixteen nations, including the United States, Canada, and Japan, have come together to build and maintain the ISS, or International Space Station. It will include six laboratories and provide more room for scientific research than any spacecraft ever built.

More than 40 space flights over five years and three space vehicles—the space shuttle, the Russian Soyuz rocket, and the Russian Proton rocket—will deliver the more than 100 major

The ISS, on March 18, 2001, separated from the Space Shuttle Discovery.

components. The parts will be assembled using a combination of human space walks and robot technologies. The ISS is scheduled to be completed in 2005, when it will become home to an international crew of seven for periods ranging from three to six months. The Human Research Facility provides a laboratory in which scientists will be able to study the effects of space travel on humans.

Recently there have been some criticisms of the costs incurred by NASA in developing the station. A NASA inspector general's audit revealed that NASA spent almost $100 million and wasted 19 months on a propulsion module for the station before discovering that the design was unacceptable. A propulsion module would give flight control to the station and would also help lift the station to higher orbits around the Earth using small rockets.

Two other outside reports also gave a poor rating to NASA management. A *Florida Today* investigation found mismanagement and overoptimistic planning had led to the station running $4 billion over budget. Some commentators believe that the financial problems associated with the station may lead to NASA having to cut scientific research—the main objective of building the station in the first place.

Summary

In the first article Fahd Shariff compares the amount of public funds spent on space research in the U.S. with the budgets of various government departments. Although large, the cost of running NASA and sending probes into space compares very favorably with other items of public expenditure. Shariff does, however, identify uncrewed missions as being generally better value than the much more expensive manned space flights.

John Carey and Neil Gross, in the second article, examine the current state of the commercial space industry. They note that revenues from commercial enterprises already outweigh government expenditure. Commercial enterprises are able to cut costs and can build and operate space probes more cheaply than NASA can. Part of the reason for this is that startups do not have the cumbersome bureacracy that plagues government organizations such as NASA. The authors do voice some concern, however, that increasing the role of private enterprise in space exploration will lead to Congress making funding cuts for further missions. The main points made on both sides of this debate are summarized in the diagram opposite.

FURTHER INFORMATION:

Books:

Kluger, Jeffrey, *Moon Hunters: NASA's Remarkable Expeditions to the Ends of the Solar System.* New York: Touchstone Books, 2001.

Spangenburg, Ray, et al., *The History of NASA (Out of This World).* New York: Franklin Watts, 2001.

Walsh, Patrick J., *Echoes among the Stars: A Short History of the U.S. Space Program.* New York: M.E. Sharpe, 1999.

Useful websites:

www.nasa.gov/
Nasa homepage.
science.nasa.gov/default.htm
Science@NASA.
education.nasa.gov/
NASA Education Programs.
www.jpl.nasa.gov/basics/
Basics of space flight.
www.economist.com/printedition/displaystory.cfm?story_id=561469
Economist article "Martian Invasion? Not Yet."
www.mcs.net/~rusaerog/aosmsf/aosmsf.html
Almanac of Soviet Manned Space Flight.

www.nsbri.org/HumanPhysSpace/appendix/appendixa.html
Summary of Human Space Flight History.
www.spaceflight.nasa.gov/station
International Space Station site. Has all kinds of useful and interesting information on the ISS.
www.fyi.cnn.com/fyi/interactive/specials/space.tourist.html
"Make Room for Space Tourists." Article by Dennis Tito.
www.fyi.cnn.com/fyi/interactive/specials/space/stories/shuttle.html
"Space Shuttles Blaze Path into the Future."

The following debates in the Pro/Con series may also be of interest:

In this volume:

 Topic 16 Should humans colonize the oceans before other planets?

The Story of Space Exploration, pages 212–213

SHOULD GOVERNMENTS CONTINUE TO FUND SPACE EXPLORATION?

YES: The space program is one of the greatest technological achievements of the past 2,000 years

YES: The Voyager probes, for example, were a spectacular success, returning with vast amounts of new information

TECHNOLOGY
Has the space program used technology to its greatest advantage?

NO: Turning space over to the private sector would mean a more efficient use of resources

EFFICIENCY
Is government funding the most efficient way to run the space program?

NO: The free market can build and operate space hardware such as probes more cheaply than NASA can

NO: Mismanagement and bureaucracy mean that NASA is vastly expensive compared to private business

SHOULD GOVERNMENTS CONTINUE TO FUND SPACE EXPLORATION? KEY POINTS

YES: Only governments can perform space exploration well because of its gigantic expense

YES: Space programs will benefit all humankind and should not be left in the hands of private firms

COST
Should governments pay the bulk of the cost of space exploration?

NO: Exploration has always been motivated by profit, and space is no exception. Governments should pay the costs of the initial exploration, but after that commercial interests should take over.

NO: Private industry revenues from the space industry are already more than government expenditure

Topic 16
SHOULD HUMANS COLONIZE THE OCEANS BEFORE OTHER PLANETS?

YES

WHAT IS OCEANIA ABOUT?
WWW.OCEANIA.ORG/INFO.HTML
THE ATLANTIS PROJECT

NO

"OUR FUTURE IN THE COSMOS—SPACE"
HTTP://INFO.RUTGERS.EDU/LIBRARY/REFERENCE/ETEXT/IMPACT.OF.SCIENCE.ON.SOCIETY.HD
ISAAC ASIMOV

INTRODUCTION

Ever since a 19th-century Italian astronomer mistakenly identified "canals" on Mars, people have speculated about whether intelligent life exists or could exist on other planets. With millions of stars existing in millions of galaxies, some astronomers believe that simple laws of probability suggest Earth is not the only planet capable of supporting life as we know it. Such thinking lies behind the prominence in the popular imagination of UFOs, alien abduction, and extraterrestrial contact.

In recent decades, however, some people have begun to change the question from "Is there anybody out there?" to "Is there anywhere out there we could go?" Such questions remain largely academic—the technology does not yet exist for humans to visit even the majority of planets in our own solar system, let alone those of other stars. That such questions can even be posed, however, does reflect enormous

advances in space travel, such as orbiting space stations and the reusable space shuttle.

There are other factors behind the desire to colonize beyond simple technical ability. Astronomers have long dreamed of being able to mine heavenly bodies, including the moon and passing asteroids, for minerals that are scarce or unknown on Earth. One extreme scenario behind space colonization suggests that humanity has inflicted great damage on Earth and that, as the planet becomes less able to support its population, the human species will have to find another home in order to find the resources it needs to survive.

Opponents of space colonization argue against it partly on grounds of cost. Any exploration would be so expensive that it could only be funded if it showed a reasonable chance of yielding valuable or practicable results. The chances against this, they argue, are so great as to make it virtually impossible.

There is an alternative to space colonization: Some critics have pointed out that space is not the only place for humans to settle. There are options available here on Earth to help us overcome the problems of pollution and overcrowding, such as the development of artificial islands at sea. Unlike space travel, the technology for this type of construction is already available, and vast areas of unpopulated "sea space" are already waiting for settlers.

The advantages for this kind of colonization are multiple. No one need abandon their home planet, their family, and their friends; the construction can be almost infinitely expanded to accommodate new settlers; new types of government and social hierarchies can be created from the best of what has gone before; and free and open commerce with the rest of the world will keep these island states solvent.

> "Man, the cutting edge of terrestrial life, has no rational alternative but to expand the environmental and resource base beyond Earth."
>
> —KRAFFT A. EHRICKE, ASTROPHYSICIST

Obviously there are many technical, social, and political issues to be overcome with the construction and population of these artificial islands. But in the eyes of many this scenario still remains far more viable than sending thousands of people off to a far corner of the galaxy, where they would be totally cut off from Earth.

In the first extract The Atlantis Project outlines its plans for the creation of Oceania, an artificial island in the Caribbean, initially capable of settling 10,000 to 30,000 citizens. Considerable groundwork on the project has already been done: An architect has designed the interlocking structures that would form the island, a social and political constitution has been devised, and a business plan has been developed. The group has, however, to overcome considerable funding problems before it can progress.

The reason for constructing this settlement is not because of over-population or a desire to escape pollution: The group wants to create an alternative political and social system to the one seen in the U.S. today. The authors would like to see a return to the pioneering spirit that characterized the first American settlers, as opposed to the suffocating laws and regulations that they believe compromise and inhibit American citizens today.

The second article—by the distinguished U.S. science-fiction writer and biochemist Isaac Asimov—is the text of a speech delivered at Rutgers University, New Jersey. It is also an inspiring echo of the pioneering spirit that settled America and conquered the West. Asimov believes that humankind will flourish only as long it continues to extend its range. Asimov suggests that humankind will have to seek other worlds. He believes that the technology is available, but that humankind lacks the will to use it.

WHAT IS OCEANIA ABOUT?
The Atlantis Project

YES

History of Oceania

The Atlantis Project began in February 1993, conceived shortly after Tamara Clark was defeated by massive election fraud in her quest for the State Senate in Nevada. Its goal is to create a new country called Oceania, with this country being constructed on an artificial island in the Caribbean.

Eric Klien, Tamara Clark's treasurer, was greatly upset to uncover systemic, massive, nationwide election fraud throughout the U.S. and realized that the resources needed to combat it were way beyond his means. The death threats and intimidation by goons that the election fraud investigation encountered were just a hint of the size and power of the opposition. Being told by the state senate that they were "too tired" to review our five boxes of evidence was the final blow in our attempt to get this instance of election fraud reversed.

Having given up on the United States, Eric looked for other countries with a bright future and found none. So the concept of a country on the sea was born. The project rapidly picked up steam in 1993, getting nationwide publicity on The Art Bell Show, *Details* Magazine, *The Miami Herald*, *Boating* Magazine, and more. Worldwide publicity was received as well in Canada, New Zealand, Hong Kong, England, and Belgium. Unfortunately, as the publicity increased the funds began to run out, and eventually the project ran out of money. A focus on donations instead of investments was its biggest mistake.

Read more about Tamara Clark at www.boogieonline. com/revolution/ by_name/C/ TamaraClark.html.

Find out more about these floating structures at http://oceania. org/oracle/oracl 019.html#struct.

Recovering from debt

Slowly, after the project's collapse in April of 1994, the project is being brought back to life. At the moment the main goal of the project is to pay off past debts of the project [and] to keep its supporters aware of the incremental progress that is being made. Once the project's debts are paid off, the project will go into full gear again. Eric Klien is currently undergoing numerous financial ventures to rebuild the project's finances.

As the slogan of Oceania suggests, we're out to "Break the Chains" that bind us. A complete Constitution and system of Laws were created early on. This way anyone involved may know about what they are investing their time and money [in]. Since this is the first time in modern history a new country will be formed where there was none before, future Oceanians have the distinct opportunity of creating a governmental structure from the start rather than being required to revolt and overthrow a previously entrenched regime. The formation of Oceania is truly a peaceful way towards an ideal. Today, every society is hopelessly entangled in bureaucracy, corruption, and/or outright slavery, forever muddled in the free-lunch philosophy. The founders of Oceania have set a course for freedom.

Appropriately named Oceania, our new country will be a floating sea city. We plan to build it about 50 miles off the coast of Panama in the Caribbean Sea. Hired architect, Sten Sjostrand, has designed this revolutionary new idea for habitation so it may grow almost infinitely. Our structure will consist of hexagonal, modular units (each about 1.60 acres). Although we believe the initial layout will be a horseshoe shaped harbor, the form of Oceania will continually evolve. Its development should be as unique as those who become involved in its various enterprises.

At the outset, Oceania's amenities will include space for light industry, small parks, day-care centers, theaters, schools, libraries, resorts, shopping malls, sports facilities, and ports for STOL airplanes, helicopters, and ships. The government of Oceania will be restricted in scope, allowing you to exercise your right to attain and keep honestly acquired wealth, and to use it as only you see fit. Genuine free-enterprise (as envisioned by Adam Smith, Ludwig von Mises, F.A. Hayek and Ayn Rand) will be practiced. Thus, what the market will provide is limited only by the imagination.

Capitalist paradise

Come live in Oceania ... or just visit. Either way, there will be no better place on Earth to do business. By its very nature, a land which, by law, keeps the non-productive and their government agents off the backs of the industrious capitalists, and more important, keeps the established firms from legislating its competition out of business, will have a thriving economy. The Law of Oceania has its basis in the separation of economy and state.

The rest of the world dwells in statist dominance over its productive class. Ranging from the most vicious socialist wealth-redistribution schemes to the over-regulated, protectionist fascist economies, we are offered strangulation and enslavement at every turn.

Most constitutions and systems of laws evolved over time. Do you think it is really possible to invent an "ideal" state from scratch? Whose ideal should it be?

Most countries in the world accept that free enterprise alone creates great economic problems. See the Economics volume for further debates about this topic.

In Oceania the sharks and barnacles will be in the sea, not on your property!

You can read a comparison between the Oceania constitution and the U.S. constitution at http://csf.colorado. edu/forums/ casenet/current/ msg00151.html.

Upon habitation, a stock market, banking, import/export, manufacturing—the whole spectrum of completely free, private enterprise—will commence. Doing business is a right in Oceania; no government licensure will be tolerated. Earning and keeping your wealth is a right in Oceania; taxation is outlawed.

Take a minute to imagine what it would be like running your business (including raising capital) or making investments without the obnoxious interference of government bureaucrats and tax extortionists. Your lawyer will be hired to help you with contracts, not to keep you out of jail for breaking a "law". Your accountant can help you attain a better bottom line ... not jump through government tax hoops.

In Oceania, we celebrate unabashed free-market capitalism. If you own a business, prepare to thrive in the competition. If you seek employment, revel in the idea of industries bidding for your services with ever higher wages and benefits. If you are a speculative investor, get ready to watch the wonder of the unchained human spirit unfold at your feet as inventors, artists, researchers, scientists—unlimited creative thinkers— vie for your support....

A haven for free thought

Are you ready to begin living like an adult? Are you ready to take responsibility for your own moral choices? Are you ready to leave others to their own vices and habits? Are you ready to live in a nation where the government will not be your nanny? Or your neighbor's?

Can you imagine a city where people tolerate each others vices and habits? What if your Oceania neighbor had a drug habit or their vice was child pornography? Would they be tolerated? Who would set the limits?

Oceanians will be expected to make their own lifestyle choices. Government will be prohibited from "sin-taxing", "warning", "zoning", and censoring what you listen to, watch, read, or write! Oceanians are expected to be tolerant of others doing things they disapprove of. This is not so hard once they realize they need not tolerate any unwanted associations of any kind. Any regulations will be done privately; private property enables us to maintain privacy.

Your religion is yours to follow ... or not. No majority-rule "community standards" will dictate laws over the individual or a congregation; you may pray as you see fit in your own house of worship; you may exclude the antagonizer. ...

America began with the intent of seeing that criminals who violated the rights to property and privacy were dealt with swiftly and punished accordingly. A fair trial was promised for the accused. Something happened along the way: The laws became more complicated and intrusive because lawyers and legislators were able to tamper with your sanctity. Things will be different in Oceania. For a crime to be so in our new country, there must be a victim. For a conviction, jurors who understand their proper rights and duties will be in charge.

The authors imply that the U.S. system is irreparable. Do you agree? Would you leave the country if you could?

ANSWERS TO COMMON QUESTIONS
What will be the cost and size of Oceania?

The initial size that is planned for this project will be built to house approximately 10,000 to 30,000 people and the businesses and industry to support this population. Of course, with the innovative architecture and design, the sea city will have the ability to expand….We are roughly looking at one billion dollars to start construction. This will build approximately 80 hexagons and some additional property development. Most of actual construction should come from business or other land development companies.

You can see an artist's impression of Oceania at www.daily.umn. edu/ae/Print/1998/ 07/storys/ POP1.html.

Where will Oceania be located?

The site that has been chosen for Oceania is approximately fifty miles northeast off the coast of Panama.

The reason for this location is:

- There has never been a hurricane in this area of the Caribbean in recorded history.
- The temperature is always moderate so those who live there will have pleasant living conditions. This will also encourage tourism.
- The water is only 100 feet deep, so it wouldn't be difficult to build up the sea floor if necessary.
- This area is also near major trade routes.

How will construction of Oceania be financed?

The construction of Oceania will be financed through selling off the platforms of Oceania to private investors. A single company will … sell off these platforms, then the company will be dissolved once all the initial land has been sold.

OUR FUTURE IN THE COSMOS—SPACE
Isaac Asimov

NO

Throughout the history of humanity, we have been extending our range until it is now planet-wide, covering all parts of Earth's surface and reaching to the bottom of the Ocean, to the top of the atmosphere, and beyond it to the Moon. We will flourish only as long as we continue to extend that range, and although the potential range is not infinite, it is incredibly vast even by present standards. We will eventually extend our range to cover the whole of the solar system, and then we will head outward.

The opening paragraph sets up the author's central argument: that humanity will continue to flourish only if it extends its range into space.

A space-centered society

I want to discuss our future in the cosmos. One of the things I think will mean the most to us and will make the future different from the past is the coming of a "space-centered society." We are going to expand into space, and I think it is fitting and right that we should do so. All through the 50,000 years of *Homo sapiens*, to say nothing of their hominoid precursors, humanity has been expanding its range of habitation. We don't know exactly where the first *Homo sapiens* made their appearance, but they have been expanding until they now inhabit the entire face of the Earth. For the first time in human history, we are faced with a situation in which we literally have no place on Earth to expand. We have crossed all the mountains; we have penetrated all the oceans. We have plumbed the atmosphere to its height and the oceans to their depths. Unless we are willing to settle down into a world that is our prison, we must be ready to move beyond Earth, and I think we are ready. We have the technological capacity to do so; all that we need is the will. I think it is quite possible, starting now, to build settlements in space, to build worlds miniature in comparison to the Earth but large in comparison to anything we have done so far. These worlds, in orbit around the Earth, would be capable of holding tens of thousands of human beings.

Do you agree with the author's point that the world has become a prison?

This idea of space settlement seems odd to people; it doesn't seem inviting. When I suggested such an idea in an article I wrote a few years ago, I received a number of letters arguing against the possibility of space settlements. The arguments weren't based on economics; the main argument was that nobody would want to live in space. Nobody would want to leave his comfortable home on Earth. As nearly as I could tell from their addresses, all the people who wrote to me were Americans, and I presume that they knew American history. Americans should understand exactly what it means to leave their comfortable homes and to go to a completely strange world. This country was a wilderness at the beginning, and even after it was settled, it was a foreign land for most people. We in the United States are the descendants (unless any of you happen to be American Indians) of people who came here from other continents in search of something. Our forefathers, who came, at first, under harsh conditions, knew it would take them weeks to cross the ocean. They knew that if they met a serious storm, they would probably not survive. They also knew that when they landed, they would find a wilderness and possibly hostile natives. Yet, they still came. Between 1607 and 1617, 11,000 Englishmen came to the new colony of Virginia. In 1617, the population of Virginia was 1,000. How was it possible for 11,000 people to come and yet to have only a population of 1,000? The answer is easy: 10,000 died. Yet people continued to come. Why? They came because life in Europe, for many, was intolerable and because they wanted to come to a new land to start a new life. Whatever the risks, whatever the chances, if they succeeded it would be something new. It is this same desire that will drive people into space and cause them to populate as many space settlements as they can build. The chances of survival in space will probably be greater than those of the first immigrants to the colony of Virginia.

Asimov appeals to Americans' traditional pioneering spirit. Do you think such an appeal would be as effective to a people with no such tradition?

How about the oceans, as the previous article suggests, or the polar wildernesses? Is Asimov right to assume that the next frontier for humanity is space?

Who will emigrate to space?

I imagine that when the time comes to begin emigrating to the space settlements, it will be hard work to make sure that not only the wretched of the Earth but also the educated people with usable skills are included. It's going to be just the reverse of what people are afraid of. In fact, I have also been told in some letters that space colonization would be unfair because only those nations with a heritage of rocket travel, space flight, or of high technology would be able to take advantage of this new frontier, leaving the rest behind. Again, that idea flies in the face of historical fact. As an example, when my father decided to come to the United States, he hadn't the slightest idea of what the ocean looked like; he had never seen it. He had no heritage of ocean travel. I don't think he had any idea what a ship looked like unless

Why do you think the author fears that the "wretched of the Earth" will be most likely to emigrate to space?

COMMENTARY: Isaac Asimov

The American author and biochemist Isaac Asimov (1920–1992) was born in Petrovichi in Russia and emigrated to the United States when he was three years old. He became a highly successful science and science-fiction writer and published more than 500 volumes during his lifetime.

He grew up in Brooklyn, New York, and graduated from Columbia University in 1939. Nine years later he was awarded a PhD and then joined the faculty at Boston University, an institution that he remained associated with for the remainder of his life.

Asimov began contributing short stories to science-fiction magazines in 1939. His 1941 story "Nightfall" is thought by many to be the greatest science-fiction short story ever written. He published his first book, *Pebble in the Sky*, in 1950. Asimov's most famous work of science fiction is his trilogy of novels—*Foundation, Foundation and Empire*, and *Second Foundation*—which he published between 1951 and 1953. The trilogy tells of the collapse and rebirth of an enormous interstellar empire set in the universe of the future. In Asimov's short-story collection *I, Robot* (1950) he puts forward a system of ethics for robots and intelligent machines, which has had a huge influence on the way in which other writers have treated this subject. His prolific writings on science include *Inside the Atom* (1956), *The Human Brain* (1964), and *Our World in Space* (1974).

he had seen a picture of one, and even when he was on the ship, he didn't know what kept it afloat or how anyone on the ship could tell where they were going when they were in the middle of the ocean. I'm not sure I know, frankly. Yet he managed to get to the United States without any tradition or knowledge of seafaring because he had something else. I will tell you what people will need to get to a space settlement: It isn't a background in rocketry, it isn't technological know-how, it isn't any tradition of high technology. I'll tell you what it is if you will pay close attention because it's rather subtle. What they will need is a ticket, because someone else is going to take them.

The author argues that a lack of technical knowledge does not prevent people from using technology.

A global project

I have a feeling that if we really expanded into space with all our might and made it a global project, this would be the equivalent of the winning of the West. It's not just a matter of idealism or preaching brotherhood. If we can build power stations in space that will supply all the energy the world needs, then the rest of the world will want that energy too. The only way that each country will be able to get that energy will be to make sure these stations are maintained. It won't be easy to build and maintain them; it will be quite expensive and time-consuming. But if the whole world wants energy and if the price is world cooperation, then I think people are going to do it.

We already cooperate on things that the whole world needs. International organizations monitor the world's weather and pollution and deal with things like the oceans and with Antarctica. Perhaps if we see that it is to our advantage to cooperate, then only the real maniacs will avoid cooperating and they will be left out in the cold when the undoubted benefits come in. I think that, although we as nations will retain our suspicions and mutual hatreds, we will find it to our advantage to cooperate in developing space. In doing so, we will be able to adopt a "globalist" view of our situation. The internal strife between Earthlings, the little quarrels over this or that patch of the Earth, and the magnified memories of past injustices will diminish before the much greater task of developing a new, much larger world. I think that the development of space is the great positive project that will force cooperation, a new outlook that may bring peace to the Earth, and a kind of federalized world government. In such a government, each region will be concerned with those matters that concern itself alone, but the entire world would act as a unit on matters that affect the entire world. Only in such a way will we be able to survive and to avoid the kind of wars that will either gradually destroy our civilization or develop into a war that will suddenly destroy it. There are so many benefits to be derived from space exploration and exploitation; why not take what seems to me the only chance of escaping what is otherwise the sure destruction of all that humanity has struggled to achieve for 50,000 years?

Do you agree that global cooperation will be needed for people to expand into space successfully? Could or should any country undertake such a project alone?

The author puts forward the proposition that the development of space is likely to bring world peace. Do you agree?

Summary

The Atlantis Project, in the first article, do not entertain ideas of space travel and space colonization. They believe that settling on artificial islands here on Earth is key to creating new, egalitarian societies radically different from what they see as the oppressive U.S. society of today. The expandable nature of these settlements means that many hundreds of thousands of people could eventually relocate there, and that would go a long way in reducing the crowding that we see in so many towns and cities around the world. The technology to build these islands already exists, and so contruction work could begin immediately if the funding could be secured.

Isaac Asimov, in the second article, states in the extract from his speech at Rutgers University that humankind has nowhere left to go on Earth and will flourish only if it extends its range beyond the confines of this planet. He believes that society is ready and that it already has the technology to build settlements in space, which would be capable of holding tens of thousands of human beings. But that, he contends, is only the first step. Asimov asserts that our planet will eventually be uninhabitable and encourages humankind to become space pioneers in search of a new home. And in the cooperation that would have to exist between nations in this venture, Asimov sees the emergence of world government and peace.

FURTHER INFORMATION:

Books:

Mallove, Eugene F., and Gregory L. Matloff, *The Starflight Handbook: A Pioneer's Guide to Interstellar Travel*. New York: John Wiley & Sons, 1989.

O'Neill, Gerard, *High Frontier: Human Colonies in Space*. Berkeley, CA: Space Studies Institute Press, 1989.

Schmidt, Stanley, and Robert Zubrin (editors), *Islands in the Sky: Bold New Ideas for Colonizing Space*. New York: John Wiley & Sons, 1996.

Zubrin, Robert, and Richard Wagner, *The Case for Mars: The Plan to Settle the Red Planet and Why We Must*. New York: Simon & Schuster, 1997.

Useful websites:

fo.rutgers.edu/Library/Reference/Etext/ Impact.of.Science.On.Society.hd/3/4
Isaac Asimov, "Our Future in the Cosmos—Space."
ade.cs.uct.ac.za/~etian/space/
Space Colonies Now! site.
www.oceania.org/
Official home page for The Atlantis project.
isi9.mtwilson.edu/~david/planets.html
History of and frequently asked questions about Oceania and The Atlantis project.
www.geocities.com/ResearchTriangle/6544/ Oconst.html
The constitution of Oceania.

The following debates in the Pro/Con series may also be of interest:

In this volume:

Topic 15 Should governments continue to fund space exploration?

The Story of Space Exploration, pages 212–213

SHOULD HUMANS COLONIZE THE OCEANS BEFORE OTHER PLANETS?

YES: The world has become a prison—it is time to break free and explore other possibilities

YES: The price of space colonization is prohibitive—a cheaper alternative is colonization of the oceans

EVOLUTION
Is space colonization the next logical step in human evolution?

TECHNOLOGY
Are technological requirements a barrier to space colonization?

NO: Technology means that we can easily and comfortably colonize the sea—we don't need to leave the planet just yet

NO: The technology for space colonization exists; we just need to find the will to use it

SHOULD HUMANS COLONIZE THE OCEANS BEFORE OTHER PLANETS?

KEY POINTS

YES: Sea cities will have their own laws and regulations, completely independent from the rest of the world

SOCIETY
Will these proposed colonies have their own constitution?

NO: Space colonization will ultimately result in a world government—the world will act as a unit on matters that affect the entire world

THE STORY OF SPACE EXPLORATION

From the first launch of a liquid-fueled rocket in 1926 the space race really took off in the second half of the 20th century, when the Americans and Soviets sent the first spacecrafts, animals, and people into orbit, and astronauts landed on the Moon. Machines and computers now carry out the most dangerous missions, but America and Russia have joined hands in space to create the International Space Station.

March 16, 1926 Robert Goddard launches a liquid-fueled rocket to a height of 184 feet.

June 1942 Wernher von Braun's A-4 rocket, later the V-2, makes its first flight.

February 24, 1949 Von Braun, working with U.S. scientists, launches *Bumper WAC*. It reaches an altitude of 244 miles, becoming the first human-made object in space.

October 4, 1957 Soviet satellite *Sputnik 1* becomes the first human-made object to orbit the Earth.

November 3, 1957 The Soviet Union launches *Sputnik 2*, carrying the dog Laika.

January 31, 1958 The first U.S. satellite, *Explorer 1*, is launched from Cape Canaveral.

October 1, 1958 NASA is founded to manage the U.S. space program.

January 2, 1959 Soviet *Luna 1* becomes the first human-made object to orbit the Sun.

September 12, 1959 *Luna 2* crash-lands, the first human-made object on the Moon.

March 25, 1961 President John F. Kennedy directs America to land a human on the Moon before the end of the decade.

April 12, 1961 The Soviet Union launches *Vostok 1*, carrying cosmonaut Yuri Gagarin into orbit around the Earth.

May 5, 1961 America puts its first human into space when Allan Shepard completes a suborbital flight aboard *Mercury 3*.

February 20, 1962 John Glenn, on *Mercury Friendship 7*, makes the first U.S. orbital flight around the Earth.

December 14, 1962 The U.S. interplanetary probe *Mariner 2* flies past Venus.

June 16, 1963 Cosmonaut Valentina Tereshkova becomes the first woman to enter space.

March 18, 1965 Cosmonaut Alexei Leonov performs the first spacewalk.

July 14, 1965 *Mariner 4* returns closeup pictures of Mars.

January 27, 1967 U.S. *Apollo 1* crew is killed in a launch-pad fire.

July 20, 1969 Neil Armstrong and Buzz Aldrin make the first landing on the Moon.

April 11, 1970 *Apollo 13* suffers a near-catastrophic failure when an oxygen tank explodes. However, the crew manages to return safely to Earth.

April 19, 1971 The Soviets launch *Salyut 1*, the world's first space station. It remains in orbit for two years.

November 13, 1971 *Mariner 9* becomes the first human-made object to orbit another planet, Mars.

July 15, 1972 U.S. probe *Pioneer 10* becomes the first craft to fly through the asteroid belt between Mars and Jupiter.

December 7, 1972 *Apollo 17* is the last Moon mission that has human representation.

May 25, 1973 The first crew is launched to the U.S. *Skylab* space station.

July 15, 1975 *Apollo 18* and *Soyuz 19* dock in Earth orbit. It is the first joint American-Russian space mission.

July 20, 1976 Photos of the surface of Mars are beamed back from the U.S. lander *Viking 1*.

September 1, 1979 *Pioneer 11* flies by Saturn.

April 12, 1981 Astronauts John Young and Robert Crippen conduct the first orbital test flight of the U.S. space shuttle.

January 28, 1986 Space shuttle *Challenger* explodes 73 seconds after liftoff, killing all seven crew members.

February 20, 1986 The core unit of the Russian *Mir* space station is launched.

March 13, 1986 The *Giotto* spacecraft provides detailed images of Comet Halley.

April 24, 1990 The Hubble Space Telescope is launched by the space shuttle *Discovery*.

August 10, 1990 The *Magellan* spacecraft enters orbit around Venus.

March 22, 1995 Cosmonaut Valery Polyakov completes a marathon stay of almost 438 days aboard the *Mir* space station.

December 7, 1995 NASA's *Galileo* spacecraft arrives at the Jupiter system.

June 25, 1997 The *Mir* space station narrowly escapes disaster when it collides with a cargo vessel during a failed docking maneuver.

July 4, 1997 The Mars Pathfinder mission sets down on the Red Planet and releases its Sojourner robotic rover on the surface.

October 15, 1997 NASA's nuclear-powered *Cassini* spacecraft launches from Earth and begins its journey to the planet Saturn.

October 29, 1998 John Glenn returns to space aboard the space shuttle *Discovery* 36 years after becoming the first American to orbit the Earth.

November 20, 1998 The first module of the International Space Station (ISS) is launched.

November 19, 1999 China conducts a test of its Shenzhou rocket.

October 31, 2000 The first crew of the ISS is launched aboard a Russian Soyuz rocket.

February 14, 2001 NASA's Near Earth Asteroid Rendezvous (NEAR) mission lands on the asteroid Eros.

March 23, 2001 After 15 years the *Mir* space station is deorbited.

April 28, 2001 U.S. businessman Dennis Tito pays $20 million to visit the ISS, making him the world's first space tourist.

GLOSSARY

acupuncture an alternative medical technique of Chinese origin in which the body is punctured with small needles at specific points to alleviate pain or cure disease. *See also* alternative medicine.

AIDS acquired immunodeficiency syndrome; when a person's immune system becomes severely weakened by HIV, he or she is said to have AIDS. Someone with AIDS develops serious infections caused by organisms that are normally harmless to healthy people. *See also* HIV; SIV.

alternative medicine any one of numerous therapies, healing techniques, and medical systems that conventional western medicine does not commonly use. *See also* acupuncture; complementary medicine; homeopathy.

atomic bomb a type of nuclear weapon that releases enormous amounts of energy generated by a rapid chemical chain reaction. Also known as the atom bomb.

biodiversity the full range of life forms—including animals and plants—maintained by a particular environment.

CAM complementary and alternative medicine. *See also* alternative medicine; complementary medicine.

chemotherapy the use of a variety of drugs to control the development of cancer.

chlorine gas a highly toxic greenish-yellow gas with a strong smell, used as a weapon in World War I.

chromosome the site inside a cell where genes are located. Every cell in the human body, apart from eggs and sperm, contains 46 chromosomes arranged in 22 pairs plus the two sex chromosomes.

clone an individual animal or plant produced by genetic engineering that has exactly the same genetic code as its parent.

cloning a term for the production of clones. In the most advanced form of cloning scientists remove the nucleus of an adult cell taken from the animal or plant to be cloned and then substitute it with another nucleus from a different organism. Also known as genetic replication.

complementary medicine any alternative medical system that is used to treat patients in conjunction with or in addition to modern conventional western medicine. *See also* alternative medicine.

DNA deoxyribonucleic acid; the acid located in the cell nucleus of an organism that is the molecular basis of heredity. The double-helix structure of DNA was discovered by a team of scientists in 1953.

Down's Syndrome an inherited genetic disorder in which the symptoms include moderate to severe mental retardation and various physical characteristics; first described by the English physician J.L.H. Down (1826–1896).

ecosystem a community of animals and plants, and their interrelated physical and chemical environment.

euthanasia the practice of killing or permitting the death of a terminally sick or injured person in a relatively painless way. Physician-assisted euthanasia refers to when a doctor helps a person commit suicide; voluntary euthanasia involves the person's family, lawyers, and doctors, all of whom help the sufferer end his or her life.

Frankenstein the fictional scientist in Mary Shelley's novel *Frankenstein*, first published in 1818, who creates a monster that later kills him.

gene a linear section of a DNA molecule that passes on a particular inherited characteristic, for example, height or color, in a plant or animal.

generic drug a drug made by copying the ingredients and manufacturing processes of a prescription drug. Generic drugs are usually much cheaper than the patented versions developed and produced by pharmaceutical companies, and are often made in developing countries. *See also* prescription drug.

genetic engineering the manipulation of DNA to change hereditary factors or produce certain biological products, such as disease-resistant plants.

geneticist a scientist who specializes in the field of genetics.

genetics the scientific study of heredity, which is the transmission of characteristics from an ancestor to a descendant; more specifically, the study of genes.

genome the catalog of thousands of genes that determines every characteristic of a species. The human genome contains around 30,000 genes.

greenhouse effect the phenomenon in which the release of carbon dioxide and other gases caused by human activity traps the Sun's heat in the atmosphere, resulting in a rise in global temperatures.

Hippocratic oath an ethical code of practice for medical practitioners, named for Hippocrates (c.460–377 B.C.), an ancient Greek physician and medical teacher.

HIV human immunodeficiency virus; a virus that infects and gradually destroys cells in the immune system, weakening the response to infections and cancers. *See also* AIDS; SIV.

homeopathy a form of alternative medicine in which minute doses of natural substances are administered to stimulate the body's defenses against illness or disease. *See also* alternative medicine.

Human Genome Project an international research program that aimed to construct genetic maps of the human genome.

ISS the International Space Station; funded by 16 nations, including the U.S., and scheduled for completion in 2005, the ISS will be a permanently manned spacecraft.

Manhattan Project the name of a U.S. government program set up in 1943; it developed the world's first atomic bomb.

medical marijuana a term for the drug marijuana when used under medical supervision to help alleviate the symptoms of conditions such as arthritis, glaucoma, and multiple sclerosis.

NASA the National Aeronautics and Space Administration, founded in 1958 to manage the U.S. space program.

nuclear transfer an early cloning technique in which scientists removed the nucleus of an egg cell from the animal or plant to be cloned and then substituted it with another nucleus from a different organism. *See also* cloning.

poliomyelitis a rare and highly infectious disease that can affect the nervous system, occasionally leading to paralysis. Usually known simply as polio.

prescription drug any drug that can legally be obtained only by means of a physician's prescription.

quack someone who pretends to have certain medical skills or qualifications, or who wrongly claims to be able to cure particular diseases or ailments.

quackery a term for the practices of a quack. *See also* quack.

SIV simian immunodeficiency virus; a virus that affects some species of primates, and that is 40 percent identical to HIV. Many experts think that SIV-infected monkeys in Africa may have been in some way responsible for the outbreak of the first cases of HIV in humans. *See also* AIDS; HIV.

Space Race a term for the race between the U.S and Russia in the 1960s to develop and launch new spacecraft. The race was driven by rivalry between the superpowers during the so-called Cold War.

virus a tiny organism or complex molecule that causes an infectious disease.

WHO the World Health Organization; founded in 1948, WHO is a body of the United Nations (UN) and exists to promote the good health and social well-being of people around the world.

Acknowledgments

Topic 1 Should Genes Be Patented?

Yes: From "Summary" by James A. Severson, House Committee on the Judiciary, Subcommittee on Courts and Intellectual Property, July 13, 2000. Copyright © Cornell University. Used by permission.
No: From "Patenting Life—Stifling Healthcare" by Sue Mayer and Ricarda Steinbrecher. Copyright © Econexus and GeneWatch UK. Used by permission.

Topic 2 Should It Be Legal to Clone Human Beings?

Yes: From "Genetic Encores: The Ethics of Human Cloning" by Robert Wachbroit, originally published in the Report from the Institute for Philosophy and Public Policy, Vol. 7, No. 4 (Fall 1997). Copyright © 1997 by Institute for Philosophy and Public Policy. Used by permission.
No: From "The Wisdom of Repugnance" by Leon R. Kass, first published in *The New Republic*, June 2, 1997. Copyright © 1997 by Leon R. Kass M.D., the Addie Clark Harding Professor in the Committee on Social Thought at the University of Chicago and Chairman of the President's Council on Bioethics. Used by permission.

Topic 3 Is Gene Manipulation Wrong?

Yes: From "'Perfect Children' Will No Longer Be an Oxymoron" by Brad Evenson, *National Post*, March 14, 2000 (www.nationalpost.com/content/features/genome/ 0316001.html). Copyright © 2000 by The National Post Company. Used by permission.
No: From "Gene Hunters Extraordinaire" by Michael Legault and Margaret Munro, *National Post*, March 16, 2000 (www.nationalpost.com/content/features/genome/ 0316001.html). Copyright © 2000 by The National Post Company. Used by permission.

Topic 4 Should U.S. Privacy Laws Include Genetic Testing?

Yes: "New Genetic Testing Methods Require Stronger Privacy Laws" by George Lewis. Copyright © 2001 by Henry Russell. Used by permission.
No: From "Genetic Testing in Life Insurance: To Be, or Not to Be" by Kari Gregory, Lance Kayfish, and Norma Nielson, from Risk Management and Insurance 439, (www.ucalgary.ca/UofC/ faculties/MGMT/inrm/finplan/life/genetic.htm). Copyright © 1997 by Kari Gregory, Lance Kayfish, and Norma Nielson, University of Calgary. Used by permission.

Topic 5 Do Complementary and Alternative Medicine Work?

Yes: From "Alternative Medicine and the Truth about Being 'Scientific' and 'Proven'" by Burton Goldberg (www.alternativemedicine.com). Copyright © 1993, 1999 by Alternative Medicine.com, Inc. Used by permission.
No: From "Homeopathy: The Ultimate Fake" by Stephen Barrett, M.D. (http://www.quackwatch.com/01Quackery RelatedTopics/homeo.html). Condensed with permission from Quackwatch.com.

Topic 6 Should Governments Limit the Price of Drugs?

Yes: From "The Price Isn't Right" by Merrill Goozner. Reprinted with permission from *The American Prospect*, Vol. 11, No. 20: September 2000. Copyright © The American Prospect/Merrill Goozner 2000. All rights reserved. Used by permission.
No: From "Why Do Prescription Drugs Cost So Much More?" a report published by Pharmaceutical Research and Manufacturers of America (www.phrma.org/publications/publications/ brochure/questions/toc.phtml. Copyright © by Pharmaceutical Research and Manufacturers of America.

Topic 7 Should Organ Replacement Be a Commercial Enterprise?

Yes: From "Arguments in Favor of Organ Selling: An Examination of Organ Selling and Sperm and Egg Selling" by Lauren Goldstein and Vikas Khanna (www.princeton.edu/~ldg/wws320index). Copyright © 2001 by Lauren Goldstein and Vikas Khanna.
No: From "I'd Sell You My Kidney If I Could" by Brian Nottage, Economy.com, September 13, 1999. Copyright © 1999 by Economy.com. Used by permission of the Dismal Scientist, produced by Economy.com, an economics and consulting firm.

Topic 8 Can the Origins of HIV/AIDS Be Traced to the Polio Vaccine?

Yes: "AIDS: A Plague That Humankind Has Inflicted upon Itself?" by Floyd Mann. Copyright © 2001 by Tim Cooke. Used by permission.
No: "The Relationship between AIDS and the Polio Vaccine: Truth v. Myth" by Stan Hancock. Copyright © 2001 by Tim Cooke. Used by permission.

Topic 9 Should the Conduct of Doctors Be Monitored?

Yes: From "Doctors Often Not Practicing What Clinical Guidelines Preach" by Linda O. Prager, *American Medical News*, September 13, 1999 (www.ama-assn.org/sci- pubs/amnews/pick_99/prfa0913.htm). Copyright © 1999 by American Medical News.
No: From "Doctors, Patients, File Class Action Suit to Block Federal Punishment for Medical Marijuana" by American Civil Liberties Union. Press Release January 14, 1997. Copyright © 1997 by American Civil Liberties Union. Used by permission.

Topic 10 Should Doctors Be Able to Assist in Euthanasia?

Yes: From "Give Me Liberty, Give Me Death" by Mike Hait, published in Impact Press Archives, February/March 1997. Copyright © 1997 by Mike Hait.

No: From "Whose Right to Die?" by Ezekiel Emanuel, *The Atlantic Monthly*, No. 3, Vol. 279, March 1997. Copyright © 1997 by Ezekiel Emanuel. Used by permission.

Topic 11 Should Religion Affect Parents' Medical Decisions?

Yes: From "Spiritual Healing on Trial: A Christian Scientist Reports" by Stephen Gottschalk. Copyright © 1988 by *Christian Century*. Reprinted with permission from the June 22–29, 1988 issue of the *Christian Century*. Subscriptions: $49/yr. from P.O. Box 378, Mt. Morris, IL 61054.

No: "Suffering Children and the Christian Science Church" by Caroline Fraser, *The Atlantic Monthly*, April 1995. Copyright © 1995 by Caroline Fraser.

Topic 12 Should Medical Research on Animals Be Allowed?

Yes: From "The Illogic of Animal Rights" by J. Neil Schulman (www.pulpless.com/jneil/aniright.html). Copyright © by J. Neil Schulman. Used by permission.

No: From "Animal Experimentation: A Failed Technology" by Robert Sharpe for the Italian Anti-Vivisection Scientific Committee (www.antivivisezione.it/engl.%20Sharpe.html) in *Animal Experimentation: The Consensus Changes* edited by Gill Langley. Used by permission.

Topic 13 Does Humankind Maintain the Diversity of Species on Earth?

Yes: From "Why We Preserve the Diversity of Life" published in *The Places We Save: A Guide to the Nature Conservancy's Preserve in Wisconsin.* Copyright © 1997 by The Nature Conservancy (nature.org). Used by permission.

No: "Cloning Is No Extinction Panacea" by Amy Hembree, February 21, 2001 (www.wired.com/news/technology/0,1282,4174,00.htm). Copyright © 1994-2001 by Wired Digital Inc., a Lycos Network company.

Topic 14 Should Scientists Be Responsible for the Effects of their Inventions?

Yes: "The Franck Report," Committee on Political and Social Problems, the Manhattan Project, June 11, 1945. Courtesy of U.S. National Archives, Washington D.C., Record Group 77, Manhattan Engineer District Records, Harrison-Bundy File, folder #76.

No: "Is Science to Blame for the Bomb"? by John Gillott and Manjit Kumar, *Living Marxism*, July/August 1995.

Topic 15 Should Governments Continue to Fund Space Exploration?

Yes: "Pros and Cons of Space Travel" by Fahd Shariff (www.geocities.com/fahdshariff). Copyright © by Fahd Shariff. Used by permission.

No: "They're Going Space Crazy" by John Carey and Neil Gross, *Business Week*, July 28, 1997.

Topic 16 Should Humans Colonize the Oceans before Other Planets?

Yes: "What Is Oceania About"? by The Atlantis Project. Copyright © 1993, 1995, The Atlantis Project.

No: "Our Future in the Cosmos—Space" by Isaac Asimov, originally published by NASA. Courtesy of the U.S. Government Printing Office.

Picture credits

SET INDEX